Foster Barham Zincke

A Walk in the Grisons

Being a third month in Switzerland

Foster Barham Zincke

A Walk in the Grisons
Being a third month in Switzerland

ISBN/EAN: 9783337152086

Printed in Europe, USA, Canada, Australia, Japan

Cover: Foto ©Andreas Hilbeck / pixelio.de

More available books at **www.hansebooks.com**

A THIRD MONTH
IN
SWITZERLAND

BY THE SAME AUTHOR.

THE DUTY and DISCIPLINE of EXTEMPORARY PREACHING.

Second Edition.

New York: C. SCRIBNER & Co.

A WINTER in the UNITED STATES;

Being Table-Talk collected during a Tour through the Southern Confederation, the Far West, and the Rocky Mountains, &c.

'We have here a record of the travels of a sagacious and just-minded man, who saw everything thoroughly, describes it in a perfectly unprejudiced manner, and refrains from forcing upon us theories of his own.'
— PALL MALL GAZETTE.

London: JOHN MURRAY.

EGYPT of the PHARAOHS and of the KHEDIVE.

Second Edition.

'Mr. Zincke speaks like a man of rare powers of perception, with an intense love of nature in her various moods, and an intellectual sympathy, broad and deep as the truth itself.'—SATURDAY REVIEW.

A MONTH IN SWITZERLAND.

'There is quite enough in this little volume to arrest the attention of anybody who cares for an hour's intercourse with the mind of one who has carefully pondered some of the deepest problems which affect the physical well-being of his fellow-creatures.'—SPECTATOR.

SWISS ALLMENDS, and a WALK to SEE THEM;

Being a Second Month in Switzerland.

'Here is a magician who can actually make the beaten tracks of Switzer- and more interesting than Magdala and Coomassie.'—EXAMINER.

SMITH, ELDER, & CO.: 15 Waterloo Place, London.

A WALK
IN THE GRISONS

BEING A

THIRD MONTH IN SWITZERLAND

BY

F. BARHAM ZINCKE

VICAR OF WHERSTEAD
AND CHAPLAIN TO THE QUEEN

Rerum natura tota est nusquam magis quam in minimis

LONDON
SMITH, ELDER, & CO., 15 WATERLOO PLACE
1875

All rights reserved

PREFACE.

THE SKETCH contained in this third volume concludes the triptych of my 'Months in Switzerland.' The first volume was issued in '73, the second last spring. A separate volume has been assigned to each sketch. In the original forecast of the work it was anticipated that sufficient range could not be given to it in less than three such sketches. So far, then, as that goes its design is completed.

My object has been to present a continuous picture of the scene, endeavouring throughout to give to its human element such prominence as the occasion might admit. That has now been done for some thousand miles. Of this continuous picture about four hundred miles, these being chiefly in the Grisons, are contained in the following pages.

In concluding the work I will ask my readers to recall two conditions I propounded for their consideration at its commencement, as imposed upon me by the nature of its subject, for, of course, the method of treatment must always be that which the subject makes appropriate. Of these the first is that fulness and minuteness of detail are here, as in a *tableau de genre*, unavoidable and indispensable. The character of the scenes and objects to be described, our familiarity with them, and the nearness of our point of view are the grounds of this necessity. Fulness and minuteness of detail are, again, required for the sake of the constantly implied comparison with home scenes, and with home life, which underlies the whole narrative, and is one of the sources of whatever interest it may possess, just as it was at the time with the excursions themselves. To this I will beg permission to add what also I have said elsewhere, that in these volumes it is a part of my aim so to take the reader along with me as to enable him to reconstruct the excursions in his own mind, almost as completely as if he had himself been one of the party. I, therefore, give the narrative of all that was seen, and of all that what was seen brought into my mind, not only from day to day, but almost from hour to hour. I should have failed in this part of my aim, if the reader had come to think that more had been seen than really was seen, or that my opportunities were in any respect greater than they really were, or that anything was grander, or more enjoyable, or in any way better, than it really was. If I have succeeded by the method I have followed in presenting a true picture, and if some, whose judgment I am glad to find favourable, think the picture worth looking at, then this part of my purpose is answered. Truth in these matters has a relative as well as an absolute element: the latter, as it belongs to the objects themselves, must needs be an unvarying factor, the former, as it is coloured by the observing eye, cannot but be an ever-varying reflection of times and persons. There are many things we of this day do not see as those who were before us saw them; and those who are to come after us will not see them as we see them. Hence the necessity that each generation should have on all subjects, into which the varying element largely enters, its own books; and this brings me to the second condition of which I am desirous of reminding my readers, which is that this work belongs to the category of those in which the writer's own impressions, feelings, and opinions are really the main part of what he has, properly, to offer to his readers. He is not engaged in solving some impersonal problem of science, or in discussing some question of history, or of criticism, as impersonally as it may be possible to discuss such questions, but in narrating how the natural scene, about which all will have their own ideas, and how what he saw of everyday life, about which every one will feel differently, impressed himself.

In the following pages I have thought it worth while again to invite attention to the industry, thrift, helpfulness, and honesty of the Swiss peasant proprietors, who are the basis and main stock of the Swiss social system. Some study of them may be of use to us, because we can in them trace up these solid sterling elements of character to their source in the educative power of property, especially of property in land; and the perception of the effects in them of this cause may lead us to inquire whether the character of our own agricultural labourers would not be raised, if they, too, were brought under the educative influences of property. Probably nowhere in Europe, it may be in the world, is the class that cultivates the soil so destitute of property as in this country. He amongst our agricultural labourers must be in an exceptionally good position who owns, or ever will own, anything except his clothes, and a few pounds' worth of old furniture. To be in this way cut off from all hope of improving their condition in life, and from the civilizing influences of property, and of the pursuit of property, must, one cannot but think, have deteriorating effects on the class. Should what we see elsewhere confirm us in this supposition, then we may become disposed to inquire whether there are not in this country some hindrances, as one cannot but imagine there must be, to the acquisition of property in land by our agricultural labourers; and whether the removal of such hindrances, supposing them to have been discovered, would not have a tendency to engender in the minds of this long disinherited class the idea of acquiring, and the desire to acquire, some little property in land, and so to lead on to their recovering the long-lost mental qualities necessary for enabling them to live by the cultivation of small holdings. In the note at the end of this volume I have endeavoured to show how the loss of these mental qualities was brought about in them.

I said in the first volume of this work, when speaking of peasant properties, that in these days both the man and the land can be turned to better account. What I meant by this, as I there explained, was that an able and energetic man has now opened to him more promising careers than that of living by the cultivation of three or four acres, and that these same few acres also might possibly now be made to yield a greater amount of produce if cultivated scientifically, and with a liberal application of capital.

This may be quite true; still, if things had their free course, we might come to find that many of our agricultural labourers were capable of recovering the qualifications needed for this kind of life, which, if we may judge from what we see in other countries, is the natural desire and ambition of a peasantry; and, too, it may be good for a nation so largely commercial and manufacturing as ourselves to have so sturdy and stable a class among the ingredients of its population.

And we may, perhaps, some day come to not dissimilar conclusions with respect to the artizans of our towns. Property, and the pursuit of property, may be found to be a remedy for much that we regret to see in them, and it may be proved to be possible by moral and intellectual training—their wages being already in very many cases sufficient for this purpose —to qualify a fair proportion of them for attaining to the possession of some little capital in money for investments of one kind or another. This appears to be the natural, and, if so, then the readiest and most generally available means for calling forth, and strengthening in them, as in all men, some very valuable elements of character. To this extent, and it is an extent that is far from inconsiderable, property, and the efforts necessary for attaining it, may prove in their case great humanizers. But for the initial desire to acquire property the starting point of a certain moral and intellectual condition is necessary. Roughs and wife-beaters have no thoughts about property. And the vast sum that is year by year squandered by our working classes on intoxicating drinks demonstrates that, as the general rule, among them the idea of property is dim and feeble. This, indeed, may be regarded as almost the distinguishing characteristic of the working classes of this country. Reading, writing, and arithmetic will not of themselves supply what is wanted. They supply tools, and some materials; but tools and materials do not teach us how to build. Training—moral and intellectual training where what has to be built is a human life—will be requisite still. With this to inspire and to guide them their efforts to acquire and to retain property may contribute much towards making them good fathers of families, and useful citizens, by creating in them habits of industry, forethought, thrift, self-reliance, self-restraint, self-respect, and respect for law and order.

F. B. Z.

WHERSTEAD VICARAGE:
November 24, 1874.

CONTENTS.

CHAPTER I.
Innertkirchen—The Susten—Andermatt 1

CHAPTER II.
Dissentis—Coire 19

CHAPTER III.
The Schanfiggthal—Peist—The Strela—Davos am Platz . 37

CHAPTER IV.
Davosthal—Alveneu—The Schyn—Thusis—Hohen Rhätien . 56

CHAPTER V.
The Via Mala—Schamsthal—Andeer 81

CHAPTER VI.
Aversthal 97

CHAPTER VII.
Juf—The Forcellina—The Septimer—Casaccia . . . 126

A THIRD MONTH IN SWITZERLAND.

CHAPTER I.

INNERTKIRCHEN—THE SUSTEN—ANDERMATT.

To see wide plains, fair trees, and lawny slopes,
The morn, the eve, the light, the shade, the flowers,
Clear streams, smooth lakes, and overlooking towers.—KEATS.

July 29.—My destination was the Grisons. I wished to see something of the aspects of nature and of the conditions of human life in that elevated region of central Europe. I arrived at Interlaken in the evening. It had been raining heavily all the afternoon. I found people complaining that the weather had of late been unusually cold and wet.

July 30.—Went to Meiringen to find a guide; or rather, as the excursion I was contemplating would not require a guide, one who might act as a light porter, and at the same time be in some sort a companion. On the recommendation of the manager of the Reichenbach Hotel, an acquaintance of the two last summers, to whom I had written requesting him to secure for me a good and true man possessed of these qualifications, I engaged Henri Leuthold, at a salary of 7 francs a day, which was to be raised by whatever amount I might think fair, when we had reached Pontresina, where living is dear, and guides are not fed and lodged by the hotel keepers, which is the practice at Meiringen, and many other places. This is a bad system, for, of course, the wine and bread and cheese given to the guide on arrival, and the dinner afterwards, are ultimately given by the traveller. It would be better for all parties in all respects, as we are now discovering at home, that all payments should be direct, instead of roundabout, and that they should be made in money only. Both the payers and the paid will, then, be making their calculations in one and the same denomination, and there will be no room for misunderstandings. It rained more or less all day.

July 31.—At 12 A.M. the rain ceased, and I at once started for Innertkirchen. Though so much rain had fallen, no sooner had it cleared up than, thanks to the natural underdrainage of the land which obtains throughout the greater part of Switzerland, the surface became clean and dry. In passing I looked into the structure of the Kirchet, that I might ascertain to what extent it is composed of old *moraine* rubbish and of rock *in situ*. As seen from the Innertkirchen side, it is clear that whatever there may be of the former can be only on its summit, for just below that you see the undisturbed stratification of the latter. I also looked at the existing deep and almost perpendicular-sided channel of the Aare to the right of the Kirchet, to judge whether it was due to a fissure of the mountain, or to the cutting action of the stream. I came to the conclusion that, though so deep and perpendicular, there is no evidence of any action but that of the latter cause. It is quite clear that the channel in its lower part, and for some way above the water, is entirely due to the recent erosion of the stream. This being undoubtedly the case so far, we have only to suppose that the cutting action of the water, which is now going on before our eyes at the bottom of the ravine, formerly in remote times had the same effect. What is now being done at the bottom was once being done at the top; and so throughout from top to bottom. The stream did not acquire its rock-excavating power recently. It would be illogical to ask for some other agent, when we find one quite adequate for the work that has been done, now doing precisely similar work on the same spot. Work, too, of a more or less similar kind, together with the presence of the same agent, is seen in every ravine in Switzerland. We may, therefore, be sufficiently certain that the whole of this deep perpendicular-sided channel was cut out by the existing stream.

We need not postulate an earthquake, or rend the mountain by any other means. On the face of the ravine there are no ruggednesses and no projections, excepting where pieces of rock have been thrown off by the action of frost. You know that they have been thrown off because the face of the rock is in these places less weather-stained, or wholly unstained. Had the ravine been a rent, there would probably, in whatever way it had been caused, have been many projections, and much inequality of surface. On the other side, however, a question may be suggested at this spot. The face of the mountain on the west side of the bed of the old lake is cut down very precipitously. How was this done? It could hardly have been the work of running water, for it is continued from the top of the mountain down to considerably below what was the level of the old lake. This may be due somewhat to glacier action, somewhat to the action of frost, and somewhat to the wash of the lake as it was subsiding. But whatever might have been the way in which this was brought about, it does not affect the question of the channel.

In the afternoon made a call on an old acquaintance at Unter Urbach, one of the four villages in the old lake bed, which form the commune of Innertkirchen. I found him, though a porter, yet the proprietor of nearly four acres of good prairie. This land had been bought out of the savings of his earnings as porter. First one acre was purchased. That first acre was the great difficulty, for when it had been obtained, money could be raised upon it to buy another piece. When that been paid for partly by the good man's earnings and partly by the produce of the first piece, a third piece could be looked out for, and so on up to the whole of the four acres, every subsequent purchase being more quickly cleared than its predecessors. I heard the same story of another acquaintance I had at Wrickel, the village in the north-west corner of the old lake bed. Indeed this effort to acquire land is the mainspring of the life of the peasants hereabouts. It is what sets in motion their whole life. The better sort of men are all making this effort, are all living for this purpose. It is the root of their industry, of their painstaking, frugal, saving lives. The opportunities there are under the Swiss system to acquire land give the land to those who deserve to have it. The system acts as a winnowing process. It sifts out the idle and profligate through the natural consequences of their idleness and profligacy; and rewards the thoughtful, the self-denying, and the hard-working through the natural consequences of their thoughtfulness, self-denial, and hard work. It is a self-acting case of social, moral, and intellectual selection.

It was very pleasing to contemplate how in the scene before me every little scrap of ground had been turned to the best account. If a few square yards could have been anywhere made or gained, the requisite labour had not been grudged. For this purpose everything had been done which ingenuity could have suggested, or hard work effected. We in very many places are allowing the sea to gain from us all it can. They gain from their lakes, and streams, and mountains all they can. Here every man's heart is in the land; with us no man's: not the landlord's, who may never have seen it, except when he walked over it with his gun; not the tenant's, who regards it with the feelings of a passing occupier; not the labourer's, who thinks only of his wages, and regards the land merely as the scene of his daily toil. For the casual beholder, it has no suggestions but those of a food-factory. That it should be a food-factory is certainly the first and most necessary use of the land, and we should be glad to be assured that we were making the most of it in this respect. It would, however, be more interesting, and perhaps the better for us, if it had also some moral suggestions to make to us. Here you see that men are thinking of it when they are rising up, and when they are lying down, and while they are walking by the way, that it shapes their lives, that it makes them what they are. These facts and considerations are not a demonstration of the preferableness of peasant proprietorship, but they are, I think, a demonstration of one advantage, and that not an inconsiderable one, that is secured by making the land accessible to all, which it never can be while each generation is permitted so to settle and charge it as practically to take it out of the market of the generation that will follow.

Having got through my visits I went with Leuthold to see the valley of the Urbach. For this purpose we ascended the western mountain, and having reached what to us was the commencement, but in nature the end, of the valley, we had the upland village of Unterstock on the left. We advanced up the valley for about an hour with grand mountain scenery before us. Our object was not only to see the character of the valley, and of its mountain ranges, but also to look at its winter stabling for cows, that I might know how they are lodged and kept up here at that season. For this purpose we went into several. As the stalls are very low, and the cows closely packed, the temperature, whatever it may be outside, can never be very severe within. When the cows have been housed for the season, the men who have charge of them come up from below every evening to milk them. They sleep in the hayloft; and having again milked them in the morning, carry down the milk to the villages of Innertkirchen. Should the weather prove bad, these men remain in the high valley all day. To enable them to do this whenever requisite, fuel, potatoes, and cheese are stored in each byre. To the potatoes and cheese the cows add milk. As this is the arrangement adopted, it must, doubtless, be under existing circumstances the best, though one would have supposed that these daily journeys for and with the milk must require far more labour than would be necessary for bringing down the hay. What decides the question may be that labour is scarce and dear in summer, but abundant and cheap in winter. If, however, the existing mountain footpath could be made available for carts, the cows would then probably be made in the autumn to bring down themselves and their winter fodder.

I had had some reasons for looking forward to the little excursion upon which I am now about to enter, and so I dwell for a moment on these little incidents of my first afternoon, as one does on the first whiff of a cigar, or the first sip of a glass of wine. He wishes to taste to the full, and to assure himself of the good qualities of, what he had been for some time anticipating. It would be disappointing if he did not find, or imagine that he had found, the fruition equal to the anticipation.

August 1.—Off at 5 A.M. for Wasen by way of the Susten. The books make it $26\frac{1}{2}$ miles. This I think somewhat beyond the true distance, though two English ladies assured me—they were the only English people I found at the hotel at Hof—that on riding across it yesterday they had found it more than fifty miles. It was a delightful walk, and offered many elements of interest. As to the culture and vegetation; they began with much variety. As we ascended, the walnut trees were the first to disappear from the prairies and the roadside; then the plums and apples. They were succeeded by the region of conifers with its gradations; first the spruce, then the larch, last of all the cembra. They in turn had to make way for the treeless upland pastures. In a Swiss valley the kind of trees around you, or the absence of trees, indicate the height to which you have ascended. They are a kind of natural hypsometer. The thinning out of the villages, and *châlets*, and prairies keeps pace with the thinning out of the species of trees. The Gadmenbach was never far from the path. You often cross, or see on the opposite side of the valley some blustering torrent, or some mere thread of water, hastening to join it. Cliffs of naked rock appeared at all elevations: sometimes protruded in the valley bottom below you; sometimes higher up on its sides; at all events generally on the summits in sight. At times we had glimpses of distant snowfields. The soil, which the industry of many generations has accumulated and preserved on the surface, is good on this, the Gadmen side of the Pass, and so the predominant colour around us was green of varying tints, generally the lively green of the prairies; at this time at its liveliest, for the hay had lately been carried, and the second growth was again springing up, without bents and seed stalks. There was enough in all this pleasantly to feed the eye and the mind. With these objects before you, you cannot but be kindly disposed towards every peasant you meet, for you see how hard he must be toiling, as his fathers must have done before him, to extort the means of living from the scene which is giving you so much pleasure.

At the distance of an hour or two from Hof, a stream—I was told that its name is Schwazbach—comes tumbling down its rocky course from the mountain on your left, and, rushing under a bridge you cross, hurries on to join the Gadmenbach a little below the bridge. It is composed, in American phrase, of two forks, which unite themselves into a single stream half-a-dozen yards above the bridge. At the point of the rocky interposed peninsula grows a willow of many branches, and no main trunk. The branches form angles with the stream of all dimensions, some being erect, while some were on that day only just clear of the water. My attention was first attracted by the little tree itself, which had managed to establish itself in so conspicuous a situation, and one so likely to have been undermined from either side. You have done well, I thought, to hold on there so long. As I looked at it I found that its branches were peopled with a horde of some hundreds of large black caterpillars. Each was two or three inches long. If my boyish entomological recollections are not at fault, we have not in England a willow-feeding species of this kind. As I observed the colony, thinking that the perpetual din and spray had done them no harm, I noticed that all that were there were on the upper half of the tree. On the lower half the younger leaves of every branch had been eaten off, some completely, some partially, the oldest only being untouched, just as was the case with the leaves of the branches of the upper part of the tree; what, then, had become of those who had eaten them? Down to a certain level every twig had its residents; below that level not one. It was evident that the lower twigs, too, had lately been tenanted; but where were their late tenants? They had not emigrated to the branches immediately above the deserted ones, for those had no more occupants than the topmost branches. Nor would any enemy have cleared off in this regular manner those on the lower branches, and neglected those on the upper ones. There could, therefore, be but one explanation. There had lately been two or three days of continuous heavy rain. This must have swollen our impetuous stream to an additional height of three or four feet. Up to this height, then, the lower branches had been submerged, and all that dwelt upon them swept away; just as might have been the case with the exposed portion of some village of poor peasants, on which an avalanche had fallen. Whether those who had lived in this exposed quarter of the village had been better or worse Christians than others would have had no effect in turning aside, or in bringing down the avalanche, any more than analogous considerations had to do, as we are told, either with the fall, or with the effects of the fall, of the tower of Siloam. With our caterpillars, at all events, no theory of misdoings, or shortcomings, is available. What, then, we call chance, or accident, but which may be nothing of the kind—prevails among caterpillars as well as among Christians. The avalanche falls, and crushes half a village of Christians; the stream rises, and drowns half a colony of sociable caterpillars. There is, however, this difference between the conditions of the two; the caterpillar not having the power of anticipating and guarding against many of the contingencies of its lot, will not, probably, die of natural decay. Sooner or later, in the present, or in the succeeding, stage of its existence, it will fall a prey to some stronger insect, or to some bird or beast—these went to feed the fish, or aquatic insects; but the Christian has that faculty which made him a Christian, and which enables him to foresee and provide against most of the accidents and chances to which he is exposed; and so he has, or should have, a fair chance of dying of natural decay. The mischief is that he has not been taught to exercise this faculty as much as he might, and ought; and that, therefore, he is still liable to be carried off more frequently than need be by polluted water, polluted air, overwork of body, or of mind, overfeeding, and many other such, not accidents, but preventible causes, among which must be reckoned his having placed his dwelling on a site exposed to avalanches, or floods, or malarious exhalations. Perhaps the time will come when not to do all that we have been permitted to do in the way of providing against the action of such causes will be regarded as irreligious, as a tempting of Providence, as a sinful neglect of the laws of God.

And so I walked on and on, and up and up, pleasantly contemplating the objects of the scene around, pleasantly spinning and weaving thought, and, when tired of that, pleasantly talking to Leuthold. I had already taken a liking to him. He was a clean-built, well-featured man, with a gentle voice, and gentle thoughts. His wife had for some time been in feeble health, and this seemed to be making him still more gentle and thoughtful. I now recall one of his sayings; 'If a man has health and strength for his work, and is satisfied with his family, he has the best riches.' His trade was that of furniture-making, by which he supported himself and his family during the winter. Not much can be earned in this way at Innertkirchen; and, therefore, and, too, because like his neighbours he was investing in land all he could save, he had to live hard. His fare during the long winter was potatoes, milk, and coffee, with meat only on Sundays. Of land, however, he had enough for two cows. I was amused at his having brought with him his ice-axe, for this would lead some of those we met to credit me with the intention of essaying difficult ascents, though I was not contemplating anything of the kind. It, however, indicated that he was himself ready for such undertakings. He confided to me his intention of purchasing on his return home some English volume, and of endeavouring by its aid to acquire a knowledge of the language. The following question which, after a pause of some moments, he put to me this morning will show that he had already made a beginning in this study; 'How many clocks will you dine to-day?'

At last we reached the little inn of Stein, at the foot of the great Stein glacier. We were here 6,122 feet above the sea, and about 1,300 below the Pass. For some time all that was bright, and soft, and humanly pleasing in the scene had been dying out. On our left we had lost the lofty ridge of the Gadmen Fluh, now screened by the Wendenhorn, behind which, and so out of sight to us, it was rising into the Titlis, its culminating point. On our right were grand ravine-torn, and perpendicular-faced precipices. At the little inn we found ourselves close upon the glacier. As this mighty mass has been advancing for the last thirty years, you will think that in the arrangements of inexorable Nature the days of the little inn are numbered; and so as you sit outside, in the warm sunshine, a rock for your table and seat, and the green turf for your footstool, with your bread and cheese and wine before you, and with the herd of kine, some quietly grazing around you, and some lying down, and meditatively chewing the cud, you will feel as if the vast icefield beside and above you were some cold-blooded, remorseless, living monster, that is leisurely and irresistibly advancing in his own fashion to spread himself over, and obliterate all around you. The turf, however, and the little inn will not be unavenged, for the sun, whose warmth you are now feeling so delightful at this altitude, or a diminution of pressure from the snowfields above, will some day oblige the monster to recoil again to his own proper domain of eternal cold and barrenness.

Having finished your bread and cheese, and *chopine* of wine, and well sunned yourself, your muscles will have recovered their tone, and you will begin to make the last ascent along the side of the northern mountain. The mighty monster is here a little beneath you, on your right, as it were sleeping with one of his feet resting against the mountain you are passing along, the other being to the west of the rocky eminence before you. His vast body and shoulders are spread out for many an acre between this eminence and the heights of the Sustenhörner and Thierberg, on which reposes his snowy, shaggy head. His hugeness, form, and position, make him worthy of far more notice than he has as yet received. The reason why so few go to see him is, I believe, that the books overstate the walk that is required for going. Of this, if taken from the west, an hour may be struck off at its commencement by starting from Hof instead of from Meiringen, which reduces it to ten hours of not hard work even for a first walk, as I found it this day. Or, if this be considered too much, it may be divided into two easy stages, by sleeping at Stein; and who would not be glad to sleep more than 6,000 feet above his usual level, and at the foot of so grand a glacier?

Having reached the summit of the Pass, an entirely different scene presents itself to your view. The aspects and colouring, and whole character of the Meienthal are almost the reverse of those of the Gadmenthal. It is but thinly clad with turf, which, too, is of sombre tints. There is none of the lively green you have left behind you. The forest is a long time in reappearing, and nowhere throughout do the pines grow vigorously. Here on this side man has to struggle more hardly to maintain himself. The villages are fewer and further between. Wherever you turn bleakness and barrenness are the predominant suggestions. This gives you new effects, and by simplifying the mountain masses, makes them appear grander.

After three hours, or more, you see straight before you a somewhat steep, half pine-clad ridge. You advance towards it, and at somewhat over ten hours from Hof, including your halt at Stein, you find yourself at Wasen in the valley of Uri, on the road to the St. Gothard, and that the mountain which had lately been before you, and which is a fine termination to your walk, is the western range of the Valley of Uri.

August 2.—Walked to Andermatt for breakfast.

The building of the new hotels I noticed last year at Göschenen, the northern entrance of the St. Gothard tunnel, was going on as briskly as then. Of course, before the railway is completed, there will be a post-road across the Susten, and so that route will have become a feeder to these hotels; and this new road will itself be fed by another from the Valais over the Grimsel, and through the Haslithal; and so there will be a considerable stream of people who, from that direction, will take the rail at Göschenen. There will also be many who will for this purpose come to the same point from the Grisons by way of Andermatt. Possibly, therefore, they may not be building too many hotels. At all events the tide of travellers in Switzerland is still rising, and probably will continue to rise, for we cannot at present imagine any reason for its subsiding, or point to any instances in which hotel building appears to have been overdone.

At Andermatt a telegram from his wife was awaiting my good guide, to tell him that if he wished ever again to see her alive, he must immediately return home. As he showed it to me tears rose to his eyes. Within five minutes of our arrival at Andermatt he was on his way back to Hof. Poor fellow! In his solitary walk home he would have reason and opportunity enough for recalling what he had yesterday said to me of the place domestic happiness occupied, in his estimation, among the constituents of the true riches. Though he had been with me only two days, I had already come to regard him very favourably, and would have trusted him farther than I could have seen him.

CHAPTER II.

DISSENTIS—COIRE.

*He looks around,
And seeks for good, and finds the good he seeks.*
                                        WORDSWORTH.

My first business now was to look for some one to take Leuthold's place. Among the candidates who offered themselves I did not find one whose appearance and style of talk suggested the probability of his proving somewhat of a companion. I, therefore, despatched a telegram to my wife, who was at Portresina, to send me by to-morrow's post a Poschiavo man, of whom some weeks back I had heard that he was desirous of acting as my porter. I was not unwilling to try him, because he was one of the class—a large and characteristic one in the Grisons—which goes abroad to seek fortune. He had sought his for ten years, but not with complete success, at the antipodes; and now having returned, somewhat disappointed at the result of his quest, was for the present open to any engagement that required only unskilled labour. Their own country being too poor to find them employment, temporary emigration, as most of us are aware, is resorted to by a large proportion of the youth of the Grisons. This is the national tradition. In all the capitals of the old and new world these temporary emigrants are found engaged in the production and sale of pastry and confectionery, of loaf-sugar and sugar-plums, of liqueurs and lemonade. My acquaintance had endeavoured to amass the competency on which he might return home, and which would entitle him to a place among the aristocracy of Poschiavo, by the concoction of lemonade and ices at Sydney, and at several of the New South Wales diggings. But what with fires, bad debts, and bad building ventures at speculative diggings, which had soon been deserted, he had not met with the success which generally crowns Grison ambition; and so it had come about that he was now maintaining himself, as chance enabled him, till he might recover heart for a new effort. Having despatched the telegram for him to meet me to-morrow evening at Coire, I went on in the afternoon by diligence to Dissentis.

As we slowly ascended the zigzags which carry the road through the carefully kept prairies immediately above Andermatt, the picture presented to us was full of interest to an English eye. I went over this ground in my 'Month in Switzerland' of last year, and in my narrative of the scenes and incidents of that excursion I said something of the history of the Oberalp alpe which we are now entering on, and of the various ways in which it is at present turned to account. I now again read the scene with undiminished interest. It was thoroughly Swiss. The mountain side was so steep that skilful engineering had been required to construct the road. With the exception of two or three small patches of potatoes on the lower part, nothing but grass could be grown. But how carefully had the grass been cultivated! Though on the mountain flanks, which must originally have been strewn with stones and rocks, not a stone was to be seen, and only a few protruding rocks remained, which were so large as to defy removal. Nowhere was there a noxious weed, or a bush. The smooth emerald-green felt of turf was spread out everywhere, frowned upon by overhanging craggy summits, whose work of centuries had now been all undone; or rather what was obstructive in that work had been undone, and what might be made serviceable had been turned to account. The showers of stones they had been sending down through all those long ages to bury the little soil they had helped to form, had by the labour of successive generations of peasant proprietors been all removed. There was nothing now that could obstruct the stroke of the scythe, or the possible growth of a blade of grass. Some of the summits were still streaked and patched with snow, which suggested that the frost, which rends the rocks, was up there seldom idle. Along the grassy slopes were no walls or hedges. Only where a boundary mark might be required, a stake had been driven into the ground. These rose but a few inches above the surface. Here and there might be seen a hay grange; but not many of them, for in the winter the people hereabouts are all collected into the little town. This, from the first rise, shows as a cluster of sombre gray houses, amongst which two churches stand pre-eminent. The season was late this year, and so on the grassy slopes, some of them very steep, were to be seen busily employed in spreading, or in collecting the hay several women. They were unshod, for here people are too chary of whatever costs money, to wear shoes when they can do without them. On their heads they had orange kerchiefs. The men at this season are most of them dispersed far and wide in their different summer employments, by which they will earn a great part of what will support their families in the long winter; and so the haymaking devolves in some places almost entirely on the women. To-day as they stirred it about they made the air fragrant with its scent, that air, which around us was so purely translucent, but which above our heads seemed to solidify into a firmament of indigo.

The effect of the scene upon you is enhanced by the sense of your being so many thousand feet above your ordinary level. You are, however, still going up, and the mown sward is shrinking into Alpine pasture. The haymakers now at a distance below show like pigmies. The little town is now no longer sombre gray, but has in the sunlight, and by the distance, become gleaming white.

As we approached the lake on the summit of the Pass we saw that much turf had lately been cut for the long cold winter. Up here nature gives no wood for fuel. Fortunately, however, the climate is not unfavourable to the growth of plants that in suitable situations produce peat; though there is considerable difficulty in drying the peat sufficiently to render it combustible. To effect this we found it set up on rocks, or, where these could not be found, on inclined banks from which the rain would quickly run off. I was sorry to see that there was much soil and sand in this peat, and that, therefore, it was not of the best kind for producing heat. Still it is the only fuel the locality supplies; and without it, such even as it is, fewer people could live at Andermatt, because in that case the cost of a prime necessary of life would be much increased.

At the head of the lake you are on the top of the Pass, and enter the Grisons. At first, for some distance, you descend rapidly; and may think, as you often have occasion to think on Alpine roads, and, too, with far more reason than here, that the traveller has some need of faith in the skill of the driver, in the excellence of the materials of the carriage and harness, and in the training and sure-footedness of the horses. For some time the road is down rather poor Alpine pastures, meagre, steep, and rocky: but as we are not looking at the scene with the eye of a Lincolnshire grazier, we are glad to think that these meagre-looking steep and rocky pastures will supply many a family with good milk and cheese, a part of the latter being convertible into such of the necessaries of their humble lives as they cannot produce themselves. And are there not grand mountain summits around you? And is not the valley before you the cradle of the famous Rhine? And are not all these mountains sending down affluents to the already vigorous infant? These are the thoughts with which you begin the descent.

You continue the descent, and in due time come to the first village. You then understand more fully than before the value of the meagre-looking, steep, and rocky pastures. In the way of cultivated human food nothing even here can be attempted but potatoes. For anything else it is still too high, cold, and wet; and the few potatoes will at the best be very poor, small, watery, immature; and a frost may at any time prevent their reaching even these degrees of all but worthlessness. There must, however, be a beginning, and these industrious people are not slow in making it. A little lower down you come upon attempts at cultivating in sheltered places with good aspects rye and barley. It is now August, but here the rye and barley are not yet in bloom. They are still green and growing; the ear, however, has just got out of the stem: that is as yet all. If these crops should ever get so far as to be worth harvesting, you see lofty frames, like monster clothes-horses, with many bars, upon which the sheaves will be fastened to improve the poor peasants' chances of drying and hardening the grain sufficiently for grinding. You will see, too, that these growers of rye and barley under difficulties are now busy in attempting to make hay under similar difficulties, and in a similar fashion. The mown grass is not spread out on the ground to dry; that would be too wet for such a purpose; but it also is arranged on frames, only of a different construction. Each is formed of a post rising about five feet above the ground, through which are passed two or three bars at right angles to each other. Each bar has two arms, and each arm projects from the post about three feet. On these arms the hay is loaded into a kind of cock, which has this arrangement of the post and bars for an internal skeleton. It is thus lifted off the damp ground, and is so held up throughout by the bars, or arms, as to be completely pervious to the air. In this way it is made in a ventilated cock; and when a fine day comes, the women come, and carry it home in large hempen sheets, and with joyful and thankful hearts: for are they not carrying home what will give their little ones milk in the long winter? And up here their little ones could not live without that milk.

As you approach Dissentis you see not only that the breadth of cultivable land has much increased, but also that you have descended into a more genial stratum of climate. Wheat, and even millet, have put in an appearance on the scene. Here, in favoured situations, I found the former so advanced that it seemed to be beginning to show symptoms of a disposition to change colour.

As two or three hours of daylight still remained I walked down the banks of the stream that descends from the Acletta valley, that I might see its junction with the Rhine, for here the Rhine, of course, occupies a prominent place in one's thoughts, for has it not a prominent place in the history of the Roman, the French, and the German Empires, and in the history, too, of the greatest captain of each—the great Julius, the great Napoleon, and the great Moltke? Behind it, as a natural and national bulwark, and on its banks, the German people from the beginning of their known national existence, were growing to maturity, and organizing themselves. If the history of the white race be regarded as a whole, this Rhine stands out as the most historic of all its rivers. Much has directly resulted from its being what it is, and where it is. Its absence would have so modified the history of the race as to have brought about a state of things widely different from that of to-day. The stream I was now tracking down to it—one of the first threads from which, as it were from so many roving machines, its first strand is spun—has below the town cut out for about a mile or less a deep ravine bed, along the rocky channel of which it tumbles, and twists itself, in its haste to incorporate itself with the nascent trunk of the famous river. It seemed by its bluster and haste to be emphasizing its desire to become a part of it, and a participant in its renown. The actual junction was achieved a little beyond the ravine, in a more quiet style. The impetuous affluent is now no longer in a hurry, but will taste to the full the contentment of the consummation of the hitherto so eagerly sought union. At this point were several trout-fishers. Up then almost to its source this famous stream is rich in fish. Its banks will soon be rich with vineyards.

As I had loitered for some time on the banks of the young Rhine, and of its affluent, the evening was closing in when I returned to Dissentis. As I passed up the main street I overtook the female swineherd of the place bringing home for the night the pigs of Dissentis. There were four or five score of them. She herself brought up the procession that none might loiter behind. She had been tending them all day in the ravine just mentioned, which was incapable of cultivation, and on some stony irreclaimable waste land on the Rhine bank. Each porker knew his own home in the town. Some ran on in advance of the herd to get as soon as possible to the supper they knew would be ready for them. Some did not separate themselves from the herd till they had arrived at the familiar door. These more quiet-minded members of the herd probably had no expectation of a supper prepared for them, and were, therefore, still thinking of the grassy pasture from which they had just been driven off. The swine were followed, at no great interval, by the goats with stiffly distended udders. They, too, dispersed themselves in the same fashion, from the desire to be promptly relieved of their burden. After the goats, last of all, came the deliberately stepping, sober-minded cows. The tinkling of their bells was heard over the whole of the little town. In a few minutes the streets were cleared: every man, woman, and child appeared to have followed the animals into the houses to give them their supper, or to draw the milk from them, as the case might be; or at all events to bed them for the night. Thus do these hard-pressed peasants from their earliest years learn to treat their dumb associates kindly, almost as if they were members of the family, to the support of which they so largely contribute. There can be few people in Dissentis who do not begin, and end, each day in company with them. How familiar must they be with the ways and the wants of the egoistic pig, of the self-asserting, restless goat, and of the gentle, patient cow! The book of nature, too, is always open before them, and they are ever interested students of its pages. From hour to hour they observe the changes of the heavens, and consider what they import, for to them they import a great deal. How their little crops, too, are looking they note day by day, for the time that will be allowed for bringing them to maturity will be so short, that the loss of sunshine for a few days causes some anxious thoughts. This dependence upon, and close contact with, nature is a large ingredient in their education.

August 3.—Opposite to my hotel was the public fountain of Dissentis. The functions of a Swiss fountain resemble those of an Eastern well. To it come daily all the women of the village for the water they will require for their families. It has, however, other uses besides that of supplying the water that will be needed within the house. The linen, the milk vessels, and the cooking utensils of the village are for the most part washed at the fountain, for it would be hard work to carry home all the water that might be wanted for these purposes. Here, too, the daily news of the village is discussed, and put into circulation. This morning there was a stranger seated on the bench in front of the Hotel de la Poste, observing those who came to the Dissentis fountain. As to their personal appearance, it was evident that the hard work and poor fare of many generations had not dwarfed the race, for those who came were generally above what we should regard as the middle height. Their features, however, as might have been expected, were somewhat hard. Their dress was sombre : they are not a people who much affect colour. Their *coiffure* was simple : upon it not much time or care had been bestowed. Their *chaussure* at this early hour was with most of them that of nature. In their manner there was not much of liveliness, not, I suppose, because that would have been deemed unbecoming in public, but probably because they might not have been disposed to it. The hardness of their lives must bring with it some hardness of manner. These good women had already been up some hours, milking the cows and goats, and providing their husbands' and children's breakfasts; and this might have taken out of them some of that freshness of feeling that would have been in keeping with the freshness of the morning. They might, too, have been desirous of getting as quickly as possible to the hay-field, and the prospect of the hard work there awaiting them might have had something to do with making them grave and taciturn.

The telegraph bureau is on the ground floor of the hotel. Here the instrument, as is generally the case in Switzerland, was in charge of a young woman. What would the last generation in the valley, or the abbots and monks of their forefathers' time, have thought of a young woman of Dissentis earning her livelihood by keeping Dissentis in instantaneous communication with all Europe, the new world, and the antipodes? When the locomotive and marine engine were invented man began to move to and fro upon the earth. This movement, however, is still only at its beginning. When the electric telegraph was invented all the world was enabled to converse with all the world. This conversation, too, is still only at its beginning. And yet it is to these two agencies that we must attribute the rapidity with which events march in these times. But as this rapidity is so great at the beginning what are we to suppose that it will be a century hence? This is what no man can imagine. The astounding character of the last war in Europe was due to the railway and the telegraph. Whatever at this moment most engrosses attention, and agitates thought, as for instance the organization of the working classes, the rapid combined action of the leaders of aggressive Ultramontanism, and even the recent development in 'leaps and bounds' of the commerce of the world, are mainly due to the same causes. And if one of these causes is more potent than the other, it is that all the world can now converse with all the world, because it is this that in these days enables for any purpose a whole kingdom, a whole continent, or the whole world, to organize itself. We may compare the rapidity with which these inventions have been turned to account with the snail's pace at which letters, the most fruitful of all human inventions, have been manifesting their powers and uses. For how many thousands of years have they been working for the overthrow of ignorance, superstition, and injustice! It is true that in this work mighty advances have been made: yet when we survey the whole field we see that hitherto only so much has been done as to give assurance that a great deal more will be achieved in the future. What has been accomplished gives us ground for the hope that it is but a glimpse of what is to come. They have done, or at all events have rendered possible the doing of, almost all that has been done for us. What we notice is that it seems to have been done so slowly. Perhaps the electric telegraph by collecting and disseminating intelligence, and enabling people everywhere to converse with each other, is destined to lighten this reproach of letters, that they have not been so rapidly or widely fruitful as might have been expected.

At Dissentis the magician who manipulated this instrument of instantaneous communication with all the world, was a little body, very little, with very gentle voice and manner. By the side of the instrument she was working had been placed a bouquet of flowers, white marguerites, and red geraniums, with a carnation or two—a flower you see everywhere in Switzerland, generally in a pot, or box at the *châlet* window, for the Swiss are as fond of it, and tend it as lovingly, as the modern Greeks. These flowers much brightened the aspect of things, and took off from their office look. On my asking for a *billet* for the 10.30 A.M. diligence for Coire, the little body filled it in, and handed it to me made out in my proper name. The traveller, presuming on a previous conversation, commented upon this. 'Now I see that you are in every respect a little Fairy. You know everything.'

Little Fairy. 'It is that in these days little Fairies must learn to read, and yesterday evening your *sac* was left for some time in my bureau.'

Traveller. 'Yes. But in learning to read letters they have not forgotten their old skill in reading what is meant by a present of flowers.'

Little Fairy. 'Flowers fade, and so sometimes does their meaning.'

On the opposite side of the road to the hotel *Condrau de la Poste*, is, to the left of the fountain, the hotel *Condrau de la Couronne*. The latter Condrau is the editor of the Romansch newspaper which is published at Dissentis. I was told that he was a well-educated man, had for some time been tutor in a French family, and was entitled to write himself Professor. I took away with me a copy of that week's impression of his paper. I found that it was not difficult by the aid of Latin and Italian to make out the meaning of the printed Romansch of Dissentis, though probably, if I had heard it read, I should not have understood one word in ten.

At 10.30 was under weigh for Coire. The day was fine, and the conductor arranged a seat for me on the roof upon the luggage. The drive was pleasant and interesting. I can, however, only give of it such generalities as might have been seen from my seat on the roof. Of course the mountains most obtrude themselves on the eye. They vary much. Some are grassed, some are wooded to the top; some show much naked rock; of these some terminate in jagged points, some in rounded domes; some that you see through gaps in the bounding ridges gleam with sun-lit snowfields. As a rule the valley is wide, and so its bounding ranges stand back to such a distance that they can be well taken in by the eye from bottom to top, and in combination with their neighbours. They can be leisurely and sufficiently seen.

Another point observable in this grand long valley is the regular improvement in the vegetation which accompanies your descent. This has been already noted as far as Dissentis. In reaching that place yesterday afternoon we had passed from the treeless Alpine zone of altitude down to that of late maturing wheat. When you reach Coire, thirty-eight miles lower down, wheat has been superseded by maize, and you are among vineyards, which had begun to show themselves seven miles higher up at Reichenau. Between Dissentis and Reichenau different kinds of fruit trees, and of garden vegetables successively appeared on the scene. As the fruit trees began to come in, the frames for drying wheat, and other kinds of grain, began to die out. Above Reichenau are some naked glaring ravines cut deep into the white calcareous soil. Here the bottom land has so widened out as to give space for knolls and hills, some in wood, some in grass. As you descend an improvement, corresponding to that in the vegetation, is simultaneously observable in the houses and villages. As nature becomes more kindly and bountiful, human life becomes more varied, more easy, and more embellished. Long before you reach Reichenau good roomy substantial houses begin to appear in the small towns. Many of these are surrounded with gardens, of which you see nothing in the higher part of the valley, but which after they have become possible continue to improve all the way down. At last at Coire there is about the main street an air of something that gives it a not quite unfamiliar aspect. It seems as if a third-rate piece of Paris had been transported to the valley, and there dropped between the mountains.

At Coire, if you have some time before you, and nothing else to do, you will perhaps go to the Cathedral. You will there hear the old story of Saints and wonders, as if there had been better men and greater wonders a thousand years ago than there are now. Here the Saint was a British king, of a date when there were no kings in Britain. You will have met with British and Irish Saints elsewhere. You ask why these legends of British and Irish Saints of that day, but no Saints now? Have we degenerated so much from our fathers? I trow not. We are not worse than were they. We may, perhaps, be somewhat better. How, then, has it come to pass that these islands have ceased to be a factory of Saints? Is it because other people have at last come to know us? No longer are we so separated from them by the sea as to be in their eyes almost another world; and as they have come to know us they have arrived at the discovery that we are very much like themselves, at all events in not being more productive of Saints than themselves. In those times people wanted the idea of a nation of Saints. This they could not imagine of their wicked selves, or of any of their still more wicked neighbours, for they very well knew of themselves and of their neighbours, that they were always trying to overreach, and plunder, and knock on the head, and oppress each other; and so they localized this idea beyond sea, and the British Isles became a kind of realized Christian Atlantis. Tacitus, because the Romans were vicious, invested the distant Germans with a halo of rude virtues. For much the same kind of reason did the ages of ignorance and violence go to the British Isles for so many of their Saints.

CHAPTER III.

THE SCHANFIGGTHAL—PEIST—THE STRELA—DAVOS AM PLATZ.

> Where rose the mountains, there to him were friends ;
> Where rolled the ocean thereon was his home ;
> Where a blue sky, and glowing clime extends,
> He had the passion and the power to roam ;
> The desert, forest, cavern, breaker's foam
> Were unto him companionship.—BYRON.

August 4.—My Grison circumnavigator—for he had gone to Sydney by the Cape, and returned by the Horn—had been due at Coire last night at 9.30. A violent storm, however, on the Albula, and which had extended to Coire, had delayed the post till past midnight, and so I had gone to bed before his arrival. At 6 o'clock this morning he introduced himself to me. The first impression was not quite what he intended it to be. His general get-up was elaborate, and far in advance of mine. Everything upon him was new, from his stylish billycock hat, which afterwards he told me he had bought in Paris, to his boots which were fitter for the carpet than for the road. His outer apparel was of good broadcloth. His umbrella was of silk. As I was noting these particulars at the first glance, he improved their effect by telling me that he considered the 10 francs a day, for which he had agreed to carry my *sac*, insufficient. This I at once cut short by assuring him that I was of a different opinion; and that, if he had any intention of accompanying me, he must be ready to start for the Strela as soon as it ceased to rain. At 10.30 the sun burst through the previously unbroken canopy of dripping cloud, which withdrew with a magical rapidity that made one wonder what had become of it, and where it had gone. There was no corresponding promptitude in the appearance of the circumnavigator, for the sun had been shining half an hour when he again presented himself at my hotel (I had not seen him since the interview at 6 o'clock), and with overdone complaints of the cost of his breakfast, and with a bad grace, having taken my *sac* in one hand, his silk umbrella being in the other, we were off.

It is a good practical rule to be prepared for the worst, without at all taking it for granted that it will come to that, for things need seldom turn out as bad as they may be made to look, or as they may be forced into becoming. So I began by assuming that all was just as it should be, and would so continue. Our road was at first up hill, and the sun was full on our side of the valley. This, and the moisture with which the air was laden, for the wet on the surface of the ground, and on every dripping object, was being rapidly evaporated, made it unusually warm walking. I foresaw the good effect this might have, for I anticipated that it would bring my circumnavigator to a consciousness of his unfitness for his work, and so probably would lead him to correct the estimate he had lately been setting forth of the value of his prospective services. What I had anticipated was not long in coming. He soon had to take off his broadcloth coat. Within an hour he called a halt. Before the second hour was out his boots had become so pinching and galling that he had begun to limp. He never again was so beaten as on this day; indeed, he continued to improve during the whole of the time he remained with me, though to the last he was far from having acquired the power of doing well an ordinary day's work; and this often obliged me, as it did to-day, to end the day's march short of the point to which I should have been glad to have extended it; but from this time nothing more was heard of his having underrated the value of his services.

From Coire to the Strela my road this day lay along the Schanfiggthal. As to the road itself it was still in process of construction. The first moiety had for some time been completed, but not much used, as was evident from the metal not yet having been compacted together. Here the construction had been easy. The latter moiety was in a very incomplete state, for here the difficulties in the way of constructing a road had been great; and, as we saw to-day, there will be still greater difficulties in the way of its maintenance. The heavy rains of last night, and of the foregoing week, had made this manifest to the contractors, for in some places, where the new road had been merely gouged out of the flank of the mountain, it had been entirely swept away; and this had been so done that it would be far more difficult to replace it than it had been to form it in the first instance. The mountain side is here composed of small incoherent slaty *débris*, inclined at the greatest angle at which such materials, when aided by the turf and forest upon them, are capable of withstanding the wash of the rain torrents. In forming the road the turf, or forest, had been cut through, and the angle above and below the road enlarged. Both the angle, therefore, and the retaining conditions had been made less favourable. Of this it was a necessary consequence that when the rain torrent came down it should in many places cut through the road, as it would through so much sand; indeed more easily, for the small incoherent slaty *débris* is more pervious to water; and should leave incipient ravines sometimes across, sometimes even in the direction of the road. In some places, too, where the road had been built up, the substructions had been swept away. All this which was disastrous to the contractors was not without some interest for those who now had to pass over it, for it presented good opportunities for observing the nature of the soil, and the action of running water upon it, and so made clear what it was that gave to the valley its peculiar character. On a long new slope where the road, in consequence of the removal of the turf, had been completely carried away, and the whole mountain side set in motion, I had to find my way across the steep, loose *débris*, where if I had stumbled upon it, or it had slipped beneath my weight, I should probably have rolled down many hundred feet to the valley below. Again in a ravine, where a bridge was to be built, the late flood had so cut away the further side as to leave a perpendicular face of some twenty feet in height. From the left corner of the bottom of this to the right corner of the top I had to walk up a diagonal ledge, nowhere wider than the width of the foot, this being all that the workmen had for the present thought it necessary to make for themselves. If I had slipped from this ledge, or if it had given way under me, I should have fallen on the rocks of the torrent: of its giving way, however, I had no fear, for I saw that some of the workmen must have tried it with two or three more stones weight than I had to place upon it. Of this road one may say further that not only will it be very costly to maintain, but that the population of the valley is so small, that if it is not carried over the Strela to the Davosthal, it can never be much used. We may, however, be sure that if maintained as far as Langwies, to which point it will soon be completed, it will not be allowed permanently to terminate there; for the Swiss are very wisely, and with much skill and cost, rapidly opening up to the traveller every valley that can be taken in hand by the engineer. This is one of the conditions of the continued growth of their prosperity. Every valley that is opened soon has its hotels; and the increase of travellers the hotels attract, and the concomitant increase in the value of the land of the valley, before long many times recoup the cost of the road. No people understand so distinctly as the Swiss that to improve means of communication, whether footpaths, post roads, or railways, is to improve the most indispensable of the material conditions of progress.

And now a word about the Schanfiggthal itself. If not unique in its character, still it exhibits so interestingly the characteristics of the class of valleys to which it belongs as to make it well worth a visit. What you first notice is that the new road, it was so with the old horse path, is always at a great height, perhaps never less than 1,000 feet, above the bottom of the valley. A little observation soon reveals why you have here, and must have, a high-level road. The valley is formed on each side by a long precipitous *talus* of the loose *débris* already mentioned. These slant from their respective ridges down to the channel of the Plessur, in which they meet. The question then arises, Why is not the road here, as in other valleys, on the banks of the stream? The answer is that it is impossible to carry it along the bottom, or anywhere near the bottom, because every small affluent, or torrent, that descends from the lofty ridges on the north or south side, has cut in its rapid course down to the Plessur a deep ravine. Some of these ravines are of an extraordinary depth, and they all become wider and deeper the nearer they approach to the bottom. A road, therefore, is only possible at such a height as will enable it to turn, or cross, these ravines, where they have not yet become of an impracticable depth and width, and where it will not be liable to be carried away every spring, or at any time by any storm that may occur even at midsummer. Hence the necessity of the high-level road. That it is something peculiar is forced on your attention by the scenery throughout the valley being presented to you from an unusual point of view. The Plessur is generally quite out of sight and hearing. You are always looking down slopes of prairie or forest, which are seldom open to the bottom. And the point blank of the opposite ridge is always its middle height. All this is new to you; and will give in your memory a character of its own to the green, well wooded, ravine-seamed Schanfiggthal.

Another particular of interest the Schanfiggthal supplies is an instance of what geologists call earth-pillars. Some of these I saw by the wayside in the last ravine before entering Castiel, or St. Peter's, I forget which: the locality, however, may be so described as to be readily identified. They are to be seen from the new road about 200 yards beyond the chief ravine it crosses in its whole course. It had just made a bend to the left to cross this ravine, and then had faced to the south to recover the line of its general eastward direction. Just before it resumes this direction, that is to say just as it is about to leave the left side of the ravine, there are visible, some way below you, on the opposite side of the ravine, several of these earth pillars. Some appeared thirty feet, or more, in height. Some had still on their tops the boulders which had led to their formation. Of course they are situated so high above the torrent of the ravine as to be quite out of its reach, even at the times of its greatest rise; for had it ever touched them it must have undermined and washed them away. Obviously their formation is due exclusively to the action of rain. It must commence the work on the side of a ravine, above high torrent mark, by washing away the soil around a boulder. A beginning having thus been made, the storms of centuries continue the work; the water of every rainfall runs off the boulder, and cuts down a little deeper into the soil beneath, carrying down into the torrent below what has been cut away. This action does not cut down the soil beneath the boulder-cap quite perpendicularly, so that as the height of the pillar increases, or rather as the soil is more cut into, the base of the pillar becomes somewhat enlarged. Its form, therefore, is that of an exceedingly steep-sided cone. The interest of these earth pillars is not confined to the fact that they are a result of so long a continuance of rain action, for as we look at them we cannot but be reminded of some other conditions that were requisite for their formation, such as suitableness of situation, and soil of the requisite texture. Other instances of the formation are to be found in Switzerland elsewhere, and there may be some others even in this valley; I believe, however, that nowhere in Europe is it exhibited on so large a scale, and with such lofty and perfectly formed specimens as in the Tyrol, in the neighbourhood of Botzen.

To one coming from Coire the first village of the Schanfiggthal is Maladers. The maps letter the name conspicuously to indicate the importance of the place. We, however, passed through it, or by it, without seeing a house. We now, in the afternoon, passed through Peist from end to end without seeing a soul. It was now the height of the busy season, and all the people were up or down the mountain making hay, and the shutters of all the houses were closed. As to the little inn, or *châlet* which occasionally does duty for one, it, as is frequently the case in the Grisons, had no name or sign; and so we had looked at it, as at the other houses of the place, without observing in it any indications of likelihood for the discharge of this function. At last an old woman, who had heard our shouts, put her head out of an upper window, and gave us the information we needed.

This unobtrusive inn was on the old road parallel to, and a few paces below, the new road. We were admitted by a young woman who had been left in charge of the house. The room into which she showed us was small, low, and square, with two very small square windows in the Grison, that is to say the embrasure, style. The little light they might have admitted was lessened by the favourite branching carnation, and a plant of ivy, in pots. Our first question was what could she give us to eat? Her reply was, 'meagre cheese and dried beef.'

'Of course you have milk.'

'No.'

'Can you get some?'

'Perhaps.' For she knew of a neighbour who might have a cow at home in the village. All the rest were on the alpe.

In about half an hour the meagre cheese, dried beef, and milk were set before us, for I saw that in such a house it would be better that I should invite the circumnavigator to take his meals with me: it would be soothing to his Australian sense of the dignity of man, and would save trouble to the good people. I afterwards came to a similar conclusion with respect to the second bed in my bedroom, for I could not suppose that there was any other room in the house available for guests to sleep in.

As to the meagre cheese, and dried beef, during the following three weeks, as must be the case with every pedestrian through the byways of the Grisons, I had many opportunities of weighing their merits and demerits, undisturbed by any simultaneous consideration of other comestibles. The meagre cheese is made of skimmed milk in places where a market can be found for butter. Peist sells its butter at Coire; and so the good people of the place, and their few visitors, have to content themselves with cheese from which the butter has been extracted. It is not positively bad; but this negation of badness is its only merit. The dried beef is a production of the Grisons, for which they are indebted to their climate. At the altitude of their valleys, the air is so dry that for nine months out of the twelve meat has no tendency to decomposition. Availing themselves of this favourable condition they kill in the autumn the beef and pork they will require in the ensuing year. It is slightly salted and hung up to dry. Nothing more is done to it, except eating it. In three or four months time it is not only dried, but also cooked, that is to say the air has given it all the cooking it will ever receive. It has become as dry and hard as a board, and internally of the colour of an old mahogany table. Externally there is nothing to suggest the idea of meat; it is covered with cobwebs, dust and mould, and is undistinguishable from fragments of the mummies of the sacred bulls taken from the catacombs of the Serapeum at Memphis. When your host brings from his cellar the leg of the mummy of a Grison cow, shrunk to the dimensions of the human limb, and tells you that it is to be your dinner, you are disposed to advise him to take it to the trustees of the British Museum. He is, however, about to prepare some for your repast, and you watch the process with curiosity. It is a very simple one: the material is cut across the grain with a very sharp knife in shavings no thicker than writing-paper. Were it cut the length of the fibre it would be as unmanageable in the mouth as a piece of whipcord, or a fiddle-string. Curiosity again, somewhat stimulated by necessity, for the only alternative is the meagre cheese, at last impels you, with many misgivings, and after much deliberation, to carry one of the shavings to your mouth. After a week or two's experience you will begin to think that it is not badly flavoured, nor unusually repugnant to the process of digestion.

It was not, however, my first essay in dining on mummy beef which brought me to this negative estimate of its qualities. My dinner, therefore, to-day was but a frugal one. While its remains were being removed, our host, to whom in some way or other our arrival had been communicated, entered the room, and seating himself on a chair which he had placed in the middle of it, lighted his pipe, as a preliminary to conversation. This presented an opportunity for inquiring whether the resources of the village could be made to supply a supper that might in some degree compensate for the shortcomings of the dinner. To every question a decided negative was returned. There was, however, one suggestion the good man could make. A neighbour had a hen; she might not be unwilling to part with the creature for a proper consideration; and there would be time to make it into something for supper. I was horrified. I looked on the author of the suggestion, seated in the middle of the room, in his blouse and with his pipe in his mouth, as an ogre, and who, besides being an ogre himself, was offensively taking me for a brother ogre. That this unprepared hen, the pet of the children, and the familiar acquaintance of all the village, should have its days, and its career, too, of usefulness, cut short; that it should be put into the pot before the life was well out of it, merely to make a very doubtful addition to my supper! The blood of the poor bird would be upon me. The first mouthful would choke me; and that would be only what I had deserved. I peremptorily forbad the repetition of so shocking a proposal.

It was now the daughter's turn, and her suggestion was soup and a salad. This was a delightful suggestion; and there could be no doubt but that the soup and salad would at seven o'clock prove as good as the suggestion sounded charming. But of what was the soup to be made? Curiosity could not but be awakened, though I suppressed it for the present, thinking it better to give the soup that proof which a pudding is known to require. In due time the opportunity came for applying this proof : but all that it enables me to say unhesitatingly is—this I say only to those who can participate in what was my own curiosity—that herbs, onions, spices, and milk were among the ingredients. I even lean to the opinion that nothing more had been put into the pot. First, because these were all the elements of the composition I could detect, either by the eye or palate ; and next because there was nothing else in the village that could have been added except mummy beef, and I cannot believe that these frugal people would for a moment have entertained the thought of expending any of their little store of that precious material for such a purpose. No : I believe that it was rigidly a *potage* of herbs ; and that there was in it no element that would have disqualified it for being placed, at their great annual festival, before the President of the Vegetarian Society.

The beds and bedroom were as clean as one could wish. The basins were coloured pie-dishes ; the goblets were black wine bottles. At five o'clock the next morning we found that the goodnatured contriver of the soup had managed to procure some butter from the alpe for our breakfast. The coffee was quite up to the usual hotel mark. The bill for dinner, supper, bed, and breakfast for two persons was 2*s.* 8*d.*; that there may be no mistake, 3 francs 20 cents.

August 4.—At Langwies, where the new char-road

ended, the path for the first time began to descend towards the valley bottom, which was reached a little further on. In some places beyond Langwies the horse-track was quite overgrown with long grass and nettles. This indicated how little the Pass of the Strela is used. The scenery had now begun to assume a new aspect. Up to this time an unusual amount of bright green grass, and of dark green pine, had been universal. We were now approaching the head of the valley, and the grass was assuming the more sober green of upland pasture, while the forests became less vigorous in growth, and less profuse in foliage. The rock, too, where exposed to view, was no longer dark crumbly slate, but had become of a hard compact texture, and of a gray tint. At last the stream was reached, but not crossed; for after keeping upon its northern bank for a short distance, we had to turn our backs to it, and to ascend a grassy glade with forest on either side. The eastern direction, however, was soon resumed, which soon carried us beyond the last trees. After a time we had to cross a swollen stream on the trunk of an unsquared pine, the wooden bridge having been carried away two days back. Then passing some Alpine *châlets*, and skirting a lofty mountain, both on the left, over good Alpine pasture, we reached the head water of the Plessur. For stepping across this, upon the stones which form its bed, you must yourself select a spot, for just hereabouts there cannot be said to be any pathway. Immediately beyond the stream you begin the last ascent. Here a good path, over rock-strewn, and unusually flowery turf, conducts you up a steep ascent, that for half an hour will shrewdly try your lungs and legs. By that time you will have reached the top of the Pass of the Strela. You will now have lifted yourself nearly 6,000 feet above Coire, and will be at an elevation of nearly 8,000. Grand, naked, rocky summits, free from weather stains, will rise some thousand feet higher on your right and left. At first your way lies over a good expanse of turfy plateau, with some precipitous rock-faced ravines on the right and on the left. Before you is a troubled sea of mighty ridges and multiform summits, many capped and streaked with snow. Everything is in strong contrast to the somewhat monotonous green of the two long ranges of the Schanfiggthal. A little advance brings to your feet the long valley of Davos, 3,000 feet below you. At its head, to your left, you look down on the blue-green surface of the glassy Davoser see. On a quiet cloudless day you marvel at its reflection of the aerial azure. The mountains stand round about it, and the woods come down to its margin, except on the side nearest to you, where the prairies of the valley reach up to it. Amid them is the little town of Davos Dörfli. Somewhat further down the valley, which soon spreads out to a goodly expanse of softest tinted grass is the larger town of Davos am Platz, covering much space, for its houses are much dispersed. With that full before you, you no longer care to keep to the horse track, but taking the cattle tracks down the alpe, which carry you through a fine old larch forest, you again strike the regular path just before you enter the town. For a moment, if you have come from the Schanfiggthal, you will feel some surprise at finding so many good houses, so many large hotels, so considerable a town, and so excellent a road, in such a place. The Kurhaus is an enormous establishment. Being repelled by its name, and not attracted by its size, I went on to the hotel Rhätia, at the further, or southern end of the town, having passed some other hotels by the way. It was now twelve o'clock, and as the *table d'hôte* hour was near at hand, I stayed there for dinner. Chairs were set for 116 guests. The landlord told me that among them all were but three English parties. German was the only language I heard spoken. My experience has brought me to the conclusion that where this is the case the table is more bountifully provided, and the charges are less, than in hotels that are frequented chiefly by English and Americans. Germans will not submit to be badly served, or to be overcharged. Englishmen are generally indisposed to assert their rights in matters of this kind. And if they had the disposition, they seldom have sufficient command of the language to enable them to wrangle glibly with hotel authorities.

The contrast between the valley I had left and the valley I had now entered, as I have just said, was great; but still greater was the contrast between the human life of the one and of the other. There was an awning along the south side of the hotel. At one end of this, where it was of considerable depth, the seats were arranged in a square: this part of the space, now that dinner was over, was occupied by ladies and children. The other end, where there was only a single bench against the wall, was assigned to the gentlemen, who, as they took their after-dinner cigar, were conversing upon the condition of Europe, and other questions of the day. In the road was a constant succession of parties, departing, some on foot, and some in *chars*, for an afternoon excursion. The contentment of rest after exertion, aided by the narcotic leaf, disposed to dreaminess, and would not allow present objects quite to overpower and obliterate recent impressions. The bloused landlord of Peist, with his short pipe in his mouth, and his good-natured daughter, who had earned their three francs and twenty cents with so much unaffected kindly attention, and the villagers, who during the long winter meet to spin in each other's houses, that they may effect some little savings of firing and lights, and at the same time have a little talk about the affairs of the village, their world, would not be displaced from my thoughts. Each order of impressions somewhat deprived the other of reality. Each became a concurrent dream, or the two together formed themselves into a single confused dream.

The fantoccini figures of the one story jostled those of the other story for possession of the stage in the brain. For the time one felt no longer as an actor in life, but merely as a spectator of life. Human concerns became a spectacle, which only suggested evanescent fragments of half-formed thought.

CHAPTER IV.

DAVOSTHAL—ALVENEU—THE SCHYN—THUSIS—
HOHEN RHÄTIEN.

How poor are they that have not patience!—SHAKESPEARE.

THE cigar mentioned at the close of the last chapter had come to an end. This brought me to the question of where I would go next? Where and how? Had I stood alone in the world, that is to say, on this afternoon at Davos am Platz, without having to consider the incapacities and wishes of so uncertain an instrument as my neophyte porter, I should by whatever conveyance might have offered have sent my belongings some dozen miles down the valley, and have followed them on foot. Now, however, I was tied to him, and there were symptoms that he was not disposed for any more work to-day. First he had in the morning complained much of the ascent of the Strela; and again when we had arrived at Davos am Platz, I had told him that we would have a halt of two hours, and would then decide on what was to be done with the rest of the day: but he had allowed nearly three hours to pass before his reappearance. This I interpreted to mean that he wished to shorten the afternoon's work as much as possible; or, if he could so manage it, to prevent anything at all being undertaken in the afternoon. These, then, were disturbing elements in the question: if I were to proceed on foot, he might be somewhat crippled for future work, or demoralized from a consciousness that his devices had been seen through and thwarted. I decided, therefore, to go on that evening to Alveneu Bad, $16\frac{1}{2}$ miles, by *char*. We soon found that at this time of day our inquiries were too late: all the public vehicular resources of the place had been taken up by the numerous afternoon excursionists. I then bethought myself of trying its private resources in this matter. In this, by the assistance of the porter of the Kurhaus, I was successful; and at 5 P.M. we started for Alveneu Bad in the private carriage of one of the magnates of the little town. The carriage and harness were quite new, and the horse was, evidently, well cared for. The good man and his wife stood by to see the departure of their lately acquired turn-out, and to impress to the last on the driver the necessity of care and caution. When we had been gone about half an hour, a passing shower drifted down the valley. I hoped that those drops did not reach as far as Davos am Platz, that they might not be felt by the anxious old couple, though I was sure that even in that case their hearts would revive within them when they thought of the 22 francs they were to receive tomorrow morning.

There is a new and excellent post-road all the way to the Bad which is on the new Albula road. This new Davos road is a continuation of that of the Prätigäu. It is carried at first along smooth prairies, backed by lofty wooded mountains. The stream by its side is the Landwasser, which as it drains many valleys has a considerable volume of water. At last the mountains close in, and completely squeeze out the prairies. There is then no more room for the road, which is, therefore, at this point carried up and over the mountain on the right bank of the Landwasser to Wiesen. Beyond Wiesen the road runs along the mountain flanks above, and some way back from, the Landwasser. This gives you commanding views of the ranges and summits to your left between the parallel valleys of Davos and the Engadin. The scene is impressive. Below you is the deep valley of the Landwasser. Towards the bottom on the opposite side are bright green prairies and dull green pine woods; these are overtopped by lofty mountains, streaked by long deep slaty-coloured *couloirs* from top to bottom. Other mountains, behind these, seen through gaps, after showing a zone of black rock, were capped with snow from which the rays of the western sun were now gleaming. One in particular appeared to invite climbing, for its zone of black rock slanted up with what seemed to be a practicable slope to the snowy summit: of course, however, till a trial has been made one can only speak of such appearances as possibilities. In several places along the valley the new road, though only just completed, had already led to the erection of new houses and hotels. This will go on everywhere in Switzerland; and by the time all the available sites are occupied there, tourists will have begun to flood the Tyrol and overflow into the Carpathians.

Our horse was willing, and the driver not unwilling, and so we reached the Bad before dark. I found here about fifty people just seated down to supper. I was told that they were chiefly Swiss, many of them from the eastern cantons. Family parties, in which the middle-aged element largely entered, were in preponderance. It was evident that they had much to say to each other; and saying this probably did them as much good as drinking the waters.

August 6.—Having been delayed three quarters of an hour by the dilatoriness, or the scheming, of the circumnavigator, did not get under weigh till 5.45. As we left the house a funeral was passing the door. To us this might seem an early and a cold hour for taking a deceased relative to his last earthly resting place. We might almost feel as if there was in such an arrangement something hurried, some impatience, an unfair curtailment of his last glimpse of the sun.

But, then, it reduces to a minimum the demand which the ceremony must make on the working hours of the mourners' day. We were now on the Albula road. It here skirts the stream of the Albula, which our late companion, the Landwasser had now joined. In a little more than an hour, Tiefenkasten was reached, where the Oberhalbstein Rhine enters the Albula. In an hour more we were on the bridge of Solis. Upon this part of the road we crossed a long array of diligences and *chars*. They were from Thusis, which had been reached from Reichenau on the Coire-Andermatt road, or by the Splügen; and were on their way to the Engadin by the route either of the Albula, or of the Julier.

At the bridge of Solis you cross the Albula, chafing and fretting below you at a depth of 250 feet. From this point you enter on the new Schyn-strasse, a grand piece of road, and similar in character to its neighbour, the Via Mala of the Splügen route. For three miles, or more, it is grooved out, or built upon the side of a narrow deep ravine, several hundred feet above the rushing, tumbling Albula, and with several times as many hundred feet above the road; sheer and sharply shelving precipices below and above; and with the corresponding opposite parallel side of the ravine closely confronting you, to demonstrate to you how utterly impracticable was the construction of the road along which you are walking with unusual ease, for it has throughout been engineered, with scarcely any gradients, on one general level. Of course a road of this kind must have some tunnels, and, in places where it is crossed by *couloirs*, galleries to protect it from being occasionally buried, or carried away; and its bridges must be made capable of withstanding storm-swollen torrents. Some will think it worth while to give a passing glance at these bridges to see what were the difficulties the engineer had to contend with, and the dangers he had to provide against. In one place I saw that provision had been made below a bridge, to prevent the torrent from deepening its bed back to the bridge in any direction except at right angles to a line drawn across the centre of the arch of the bridge, because a deviation from this line to the right, or left, would have destroyed the foundation of one or other of the piers of the bridge. A torrent towards the western end of the Strasse had cut the strata of rock over which it fell into a somewhat regular flight of steps. The layers of rock were two or three feet thick, and each was cut down perpendicularly by the stream, some three or four feet in advance of the one which was above it. So almost down to the bridge, where the stream entirely disappeared, in consequence of the stratification having here been abruptly tilted into an inclination that was not far from perpendicular; and here the torrent had formed for itself a channel by eroding only one of the layers of rock, and that to such a depth that the layers on our right completely overlapped and concealed the stream which had been carried down some way below in the eroded layer.

The ravine of the Schyn nowhere admits of any kind of cultivation, not even of an occasional patch of grass. Pines are its only produce. Among these I saw towards its western extremity many fine specimens of the silver fir, which I had nowhere previously noticed. I do not see why the Douglas pine, one of the most rapid in growth, and valuable as timber, of all the conifers, should not be grown largely in Switzerland. Some of its moist and sheltered valleys would seem to be the very stations that might in every respect be exactly suited for it. It has been proved that it will grow rapidly in such places. In this, as in many other ravines, a track for removing the trees that have been felled below the road, is out of the question. If, therefore, they are to be used for fuel, they are cut into pieces, six feet in length, and pitched into the torrent, which transports them rapidly to their destination. Fuel that has been torrent-borne in this way may readily be distinguished, as it stands piled against the walls of the houses, by the manner in which the ends of the pieces have been bruised and frayed. If, however, what has been felled is to be used as timber for building, the length required would make it impossible to float it down such narrow, rocky, and tortuous streams. In this case winter must be waited for, and when it has frozen the torrent, and buried it beneath the snow, the hardy and industrious peasants avail themselves of the temporary pathway nature has provided, and haul their timber along it. But these winter pathways are not free from danger, for it sometimes happens that a rock, detached by the frost from an overhanging summit, falls on those who are at work below.

As you descend from the Schyn to Thusis everything is changed. You again find yourself among prairies, fruit trees, and scattered dwellings. A broad green valley lies before you expanding to the right and left, in which are the towns of Sils and Thusis; and beyond the valley is lifted up the broad shelving expanse of the eastern side of the Heinzenberg, a wide, unbroken expanse of trees and prairies, enlivened with many villages, and innumerable detached *châlets*. You see that every rood of it is turned to the best account, and that it is on the spot supporting a large and industrious population.

As you descend you pass the still solid remains of an old castle on the right, perched on a cliff overlooking the Albula. Another is above you on the mountain side. At the foot of the descent you reach the little town of Sils, separated by three-quarters of a mile of bottom land from Thusis, which you see on the first rise of the opposite bank, beyond the Hinter-Rhein, the stream of the valley. A third old castle, that of Hohen Rhätien, looks down on Thusis from the brow of a cliff, 400 feet above the stream, on what is still your side of the valley. As you cross the bridge, on its up stream side you see the Rhine rushing beneath it in a flood of whitish green. Immediately below the bridge the inky Nolla, more inky than the Tyne at Newcastle, its blackness is that of the skin of an unfledged rook, pitches its torrent of defilement into the whitish green stream. You feel that this is an act of disrespect to a main branch of so famous a river. Two hundred, or so, yards further on you pass a second bridge, that of the Nolla itself. You now see above the bridge what a vast amount of small black shaly *débris*, the cause of its inkiness, this stream brings down in its course from the summits of the Heinzenberg, and of the Piz Beverin. You had also just noticed some acres of this dark *débris* outspread on the broad, and now dry, sides of the channel below the Rhine bridge. The Nolla, then, you will remember as a kind of natural ink factory; and may think, too, that it has been pouring forth its torrent of ink from a date long anterior to the Chinese or Egyptian manufacture of the pigment.

Thusis commences a few steps beyond the bridge of the Nolla. The first house on the right side of the long street of which it is composed is the chief hotel of the place. We walked up to the door, and stood on the step. A four-horse carriage was about to start for the Splügen, and the landlord was impressively reiterating his adieux, and his wishes for a pleasant journey, to its occupants. For two or three minutes I waited, but as he did not think it worth his while to salute with a word the coming guest, or to beg to be excused for a moment, that he might pile up still higher his good wishes for his departing guests, I asked the circumnavigator to resume his burden, and went on to the hotel de la Poste, at the further end of the opposite side of the long street. Mine host that might have been now saw that, though it was well done to speed the guest parting with four horses, it was ill done not to welcome also the guest arriving on foot. But in this case the coming guest hardened his heart, and no place was given for repentance. The hotel de la Poste had its advantages. It was not yet 12 o'clock, and as my companion had been limping for the last hour, I saw that I should be obliged to sleep at Thusis; and when you have nothing to do, it is something to have even the arrivals and departures of the diligences to look at. Some of those who come, or who are waiting to go, by them will perhaps have something to say ; at all events you see something of what manner of people they are. And then the telegraph bureau is at hand, and you can, which it is always pleasing to do, in a few moments ask your travelling friends what they are about, and tell them where you are. This is very different from, and far better than, writing and receiving letters. It is so near an approach to direct, actual conversation. Letters belong to quite a dif-

F

ferent category. By the time a letter is received all your plans, or those of your friends, may have been altered. You may be going in an opposite direction to that announced. Your feelings may have become the reverse of those described. Regrets, or rejoicings, may have been called into being on grounds that never came to have any existence. But telegrams, which tell friends where they respectively are, and how they are, at the moment, are present indubitable realities.

Being then obliged to remain at Thusis for the rest of the day, I went in the afternoon to see the old castle of Hohen Rhätien. The ruins of one of these mediæval strongholds cannot, generally, be regarded with much interest, because gratitude is no ingredient in the feelings which the sight of it awakens. The stage of history to which they belong was rather a painful interruption, than a satisfactory continuance, of the progress of human affairs. Its units, represented by these castles, were small fragments of rude force; and these were but ill-compacted into rude wholes, that hardly deserved the name of states. The strong owners of these castles were prompted by a consciousness of their strength to lives of violence and oppression, and the weak were obliged to attach themselves to the strong, only to be oppressed. The physical ruled the moral and intellectual without disguise and without mitigation, except so far as it was counteracted by what soon became the moral and intellectual tyranny of the Church. Of the evils of this system we even suppose that we have not yet reached the end, but that we are still in some degree suffering from them. For reasons of this kind we are indisposed to see in it, what history tells us we ought, the first step in the new order of things to which we belong, and which we may hope has grander possibilities for us than the preceding order of things in the old world had for those of its day; or, indeed, to see in it anything but an assertion of force and injustice, which for a long period altogether forbad, and the consequences of which may be still somewhat hindering, the advance of society in the direction of fair and reasonable institutions. It is with very different feelings that we contemplate the monuments of Greece and Rome, and even of old Egypt; for they do not, as these do, remind us of mere individual brute force. They were works of organized societies, whose wants were of a more human and cultured kind, and whose mistakes and misdeeds, as their consequences are now no longer felt, are almost lost to memory. At all events we owe them much. The very ruins of their buildings remind us of one part of the debt. But we cannot, or will not, feel in this way towards the owners of these old castles. In passing, therefore, the remains of one of them many of us have no wish to inspect it. It is not sacred ground to us. What pleases us most in, the matter is the fact, visible in passing it, that it is in ruins.

For such reasons as these, while a little before midday I had looked up at the ruins of the old castle of Hohen Rhätien, I had not thought them worth the hour or so that would have been required for going up to see them; but now in the afternoon, having nothing else to do, I inspected them with some attention. To get to them I had to recross the two bridges. I then, about 200 yards beyond that over the Hinter Rhein, crossed a small mill-race running parallel to the road, and went straight up a steep timber-slide, which is visible from the road. At the head of this you come on the regular horse-track, from Sils to the castle. Three or four hundred yards of this bring you to a steep turfy slope, where you may desert the horse path which winds round the summit to the top, and in five minutes you will be on the top among the ruins. They consist of several detached buildings. The first is a square tower with thick walls. It has no door, or constructed entrance, in the walls that now remain, the only access to the interior being by a hole in one of the angles. We may, therefore, suppose that this was an advanced outwork, that was entered either by a subterranean gallery which connected it with the castle some hundred yards off, or by a ladder which was applied to some aperture in an upper story which has now disappeared from the walls. It may also have been useful as a storehouse for provisions of some kind or other. Next to this is a structure, which evidently was a small church. It is in good preservation. The tower still stands. Alongside of the tower is a chamber with a groined ceiling, which may, possibly, have been the chancel. In line with, so as to be a continuation of, this chamber is the nave of the church. The two windows that alone lighted it are very narrow; but, then, in this part of the world windows are made as small as possible, for to admit a sufficiency of light would, for the greater part of the year, be to admit an intolerable quantity of cold.

Close to the church, in the direction of the castle, is a building about twenty feet square. The walls are about three feet thick. Their stones in some courses are laid horizontally, in others in a slanting, or herringbone, position. Close to this is another building similarly constructed, but more dilapidated. This is not quite so wide as it is long. It has remains of a floor above the ground floor.

Just beyond these two last mentioned buildings is the true castle. It is of very solid construction, but of no great extent. I paced it, but do not remember its exact dimensions. My impression is that it is not so much as a square of forty feet. Neither the door, nor windows, were arched. The latter are in the form of embrasures, much recessed, of course to admit to the interior as much light as possible through such small openings, and to enable its defenders to command as much space as possible outside. The lowest of these embrasures is at a considerable height from the ground. Half the basement is occupied by a spacious excavation in the living rock, which doubtless was the cellar. This is the first necessity in every dwelling place in this part of Switzerland, where the winters are so severe, and some days in summer very hot. If the cellar of a house does not prove good, that is to say, if it should prove incapable of keeping wine, cheese, milk, beer, meat, and in these days potatoes, from the cold of winter and the heat of summer, the house itself is of little value. This large rock-cellar doubtless answered well the purpose for which it was designed. I pictured it to myself stored with hogsheads of wine, barrels of flour, salt beef and bacon, and tiers of cheese, against the annually recurrent siege of winter, or an expected summer siege from the lord of some neighbouring castle. There was plenty of everything, for those were days when rapid digestion waited upon vigorous appetite, and eating and drinking were the great business of life. There were three stories. The large stone fire-place of the first of these remains. Its chimney is carried up, and against, the inner wall, almost as if it had been an afterthought. Does the existence of this chimney throw any light on the date of the structure? We can hardly suppose such a chimney of earlier date than the fourteenth century, but as it appears to have been applied to the wall, and not constructed in it, the wall may be of much greater age than the chimney. There are no traces of chimneys elsewhere in the building. A court-yard surrounded the castle. This included at the angle, between the two precipitous faces of the extremity of the mountain, a space that might have been a garden, or a yard for the live stock in troublous times. It is now laid down in grass for mowing. The castle itself did not stand upon the edge of the precipice. Between it and the precipice, indeed on the very edge of it, are the remains of some small buildings. These, as probably did the three other buildings first mentioned, must have supplied the stabling for horses and cattle, and storehouses for provisions and hay in ordinary times. The church could not have been intended for more than thirty or forty people. This, and the small dimensions of the castle itself, furnish us with some data for forming an estimate of the wealth and power of its original builder, and of his successors. One cannot suppose that his retainers comprised more than about a dozen families. And perhaps the same may be said of the retainers of those who possessed the dozen other castles of the immediate neighbourhood. In descending I took the regular old road down to Sils, for I wished to go the way the old feudal chief and his retainers had used. To one either going to, or coming from Thusis, this way is quite a mile longer than the timber slide.

These may, as we are told they are, be the remains of the oldest castle in Switzerland; but their situation, as well as their character, demonstrate that the explanation given of the name is erroneous.

Livy tells us that, at the time of the settlement of the Gauls in northern Italy, the Etruscans they displaced moved off to, and took possession of the district of which the Grisons of our day form a part. In classical times it was called Rhætia, to explain which name, a leader of the emigration of the name of Rhætus was invented. This tradition is supposed to be supported by the assumptions that the name of Thusis is derived from Tuscia, and that the name by which this old castle is now known has come down from the times of Rhætus, its presumed original founder. The tradition, however, affirms an improbability. No invaders, settling themselves among a dispossessed and hostile population, would have constructed so small a fortress, which could have given shelter to only a very small garrison. Nor would they have placed it in such a situation: for there being then no road below Thusis, it would have been at the bottom of a *cul de sac*, and any one who could have held and devastated the valley, would have starved out the little garrison of the castle. We may, therefore, pretty safely conclude that it belongs to the same date as the church, that is to say, to the times, when feudal lords, who under the conditions of the period implied castles, were a necessity. The great number there was of them at that time in the valley was a kind of common insurance to each against some of the risks to which they would otherwise have been exposed.

We read a good deal in Swiss histories of the way in which in many places the peasants rose against their feudal lords, expelled or killed them, and dismantled or burnt their castles. At all events there was once an abundance of these lords, and we cannot suppose that they voluntarily abandoned their strongholds, and their lands. We see the ruins of a great many of these strongholds, and we see the peasants now in possession of the lands which once supported these strongholds. This, if like things are to be called by like names, is neither more nor less than what French, German, Italian, and Spanish Internationalists are aiming at. Here, in these valleys, as far as the land is concerned, their scheme has for many generations been thoroughly carried out. Lands which feudal lords once held peasants now hold. The substitution of one proprietary for the other was in many cases brought about by the direct use of physical force, in others by the peaceable, it might have been, expression of the will of the community, backed, however, by physical force: which comes to precisely the same thing. And now this peasant proprietorship has had several centuries to develop its nature completely, without any retarding, or disturbing causes operating against it. Whatever merits, therefore, and whatever demerits the system may have, may be seen here, for no one would assert that it can be without either the one, or the other. Some estimate of each I endeavoured to make in my first 'Month in Switzerland' of two years back; and in my second 'Month' of last year, I endeavoured to direct attention to the history, and to the present action, in this age of capital, of the Allmends, or commonable lands of Switzerland, which in the days anterior to accumulations of capital were, in Switzerland at all events, a necessary appendage to peasant proprietorship. All that I now wish to remark is that that portion of the land which is held as private property, has for a long time been divided into such small holdings, and from absence of settlements, trusts, and charges, has been so completely at the disposal of existing proprietors, as would probably satisfy the most extreme Internationalist, who was in favour of permitting any private rights at all in the land.

In human affairs, however, nothing continues long in one stay; and their progress has at length given rise in these valleys to a new and enlarged development of one of the instruments of production, which formerly existed in them only in the germ, but is now seen to have greater capabilities than have hitherto been found in the land itself: at all events it is one to which the uses of, and the property in, land must now accommodate themselves. This disturbing element, this instrument of production, the powers of which have of late been so much enlarged, is capital in money. And neither the Internationalist, nor anybody else who interests himself about the mixed questions of economics and politics, can arrive at any safe or workable conclusions, unless he so far understands its uses, action, and power, as to see that without it society would collapse, and revert to barbarism. We may, perhaps, get a little glimpse into the question of what are its uses, action, and power, if we divide the inhabitants of these thriving valleys into those who are supported by capital in money, and those who are supported by capital in land, and then endeavour to see how each class is living. I propose the division in the above form, because I suppose that ultimately, and in the nature of things, there is no scientific ground for the assumption, implied in popular usage, of there being a fundamental difference, when they are regarded as means of production, between land and money, or even between either of these two and labour. They are all I imagine, in a broad and true generalization, capital. They seem to be all means of production, and so only different forms of capital. Still the division proposed is one with which we are familiar, and which is intelligible, at least to the eye. To proceed, then, with it: it is clear that a man, and one, too, who was the son of a peasant, can now live here, and live better, than any of the peasant proprietors have for generations lived, without owning, or occupying, a *klafter* of land. Many are doing this. Every year a greater number do it. What is required for doing it is thought, knowledge, the power of seeing far, and of combining divers facts and considerations, energy, perseverance, and character. It is to be done not so much by the hands as by the brain. That is the chief human instrument to be used. The field to be cultivated is not a little piece of land for supplying directly a man's own wants, but his efforts must aim primarily at the supply of the wants of others, in a sense of the world. This, however, is only possible through the existence and the use of capital in money. For this purpose money has two distinct functions. First it is the common measure not only of all the useful and exchangeable productions of the world and of man, but also of all that contributes to their production, whether the human means as labour, skill, and knowledge, or the material means as the land and the requisite tools, implements, and machinery: in short, it renders both the human and the material means of production, and the commodities produced, all commensurable. In the second place it enables us, practically, to store up surplus produce of any kind in such a form as to be reconvertible at will into produce of any kind, or into the means of production. In these ways it correlates all the wants and all the capabilities of the whole family of man, dispersed over the world, putting each country into reciprocal relations with all the others. It enables each to produce whatever it may have any natural capacity for producing, and to exchange it for whatever it may want. And this it does not only between different nations, but also between the different individuals of the same nation, and of the same neighbourhood. This is a field, the cultivation of some part of which generally yields to its cultivator a far greater return than can by any amount of individual labour be extracted from two or three acres with some appurtenant rights of fuel and pasturage. And now if we turn to those who are living on the hard-won produce of their few acres, we see that their lives, too, have been greatly elevated and embellished by the existence and applications of capital in money. It might be shown that to it they were indebted for their education, and for the opportunities they have had for starting their children in the world. It has given them the means of travelling very cheaply at the rate of twenty miles an hour; it has given them the means of communicating with the world by the post and by the telegraph; it has brought to their door opportunities for earning something from the travellers that visit their neighbourhood; to it they owe their newspaper; it, too, has enabled them to procure coffee, sugar, wine, cheap clothing, and many other minor advantages. Annihilate capital, and every man throughout these valleys, and throughout the world, is debarred from access to the products of the world, and reduced to the miserable life that is limited to what he can produce with his own hands. Increase capital, which means ultimately, and in its largest sense, the store of useful commodities the whole world may be made to yield, and the human and material means requisite for production, and for distribution, and then there is opened to every man the possibility of entering by his own labour, or skill, or knowledge, up to the amount of their productiveness, into the possession of everything he needs, that any part of the world is capable of supplying. The way to enter on their possession is at all events opened to him, and the command over them to which he may attain will depend mainly upon himself, that is to say, upon the way in which he was brought up, and what he was taught. Whether he is ever to rise to the possession and management of any portion of the money capital of the world will depend almost entirely on how he was brought up, and what he was taught. When all this shall be seen more distinctly than it now is by some of us, the Internationalist, who is himself a creation of money capital, will not perhaps have so much to say as he has at present about the tyranny of capital.

But to go back to our Swiss valleys. It is clear that there has issued from the peasantry, who till recently were their only inhabitants, a class of men who are living a higher life than the peasants, that is than the landed proprietors. It is the life of those who accumulate capital in money, and who live upon the employment of it. And this capital in money is, under the circumstances of the country, within the reach of every one to far higher amounts in value than is the land, the old form of capital. What is needed for its acquisition is cultivated intelligence, and certain moral qualities. This is precisely the point to which the attention and the efforts of the Internationalists should be directed. If society takes care, and it is endeavouring to do this in Switzerland, to give to all its members as fair a chance as is possible under existing circumstances to attain to this culture of the intelligence, and to these moral qualities, the majority will more or less avail themselves of the opportunities offered to them; and so, having numbers, wealth, intelligence, justice, and moral character on their side, will be too strong to be disturbed by the *residuum*. The son of an Upper Engadin peasant, who had gone out into the world like most of his countrymen, there learnt German and French, and made some money, and now, having returned home with what he had made, was turning it to good account, remarked to me, 'Our education is improving, but already we have enough of it to enable those, who are disposed to avail themselves of it, to get on in the world. The rest are brutish, and must live by brute work.' For a moment I was shocked at the hardness of the statement: but I made no reply, for I saw that it was no more than the action of the inexorable law of natural selection applied to moral and intellectual life. It would not be a law were it not inexorable. The analogy, too, of nature requires that it should be applied to man as well as to the lower animals and to plants; and, indeed, if exemptions from it were admissible in any part of the general scheme, they would be admissible least of all in the case of man, for it is of more importance to guard against deterioration that which is highest and best, if we may so speak of any part of the general scheme, than that which is of inferior value—at all events than that which to us appears to occupy a lower place in the scale of being.

CHAPTER V.

THE VIA MALA—SCHAMSTHAL—ANDEER.

> Living things, and things inanimate,
> Do speak at heaven's command to eyes and ears,
> And speak to social reason's inner sense
> With inarticulate language.—WORDSWORTH.

August 7.—As I foresaw that I should not to-day get beyond Andeer, I breakfasted in a leisurely style at seven o'clock, without at all feeling that my loins were girded, and my staff in my hand. The head waiter, a very incarnation of good nature and harmless vanity, availed himself of the opportunity for trying to persuade me to delay my departure till the evening, or still better till to-morrow, that I might see General von Göben, who, as he impressively informed me, was to arrive to-day with a party of seven, and had taken the whole of the first floor. At Dissentis I was told that Von Moltke had been there; and at Pontresina, and elsewhere, I heard of other German celebrities. At the places where we ourselves most do congregate we find many Germans; but as they do not much desire our society, and do not go to Switzerland for precisely the same objects as ourselves, we must not judge by the proportion of them we find in these places of the number of them who are travelling in Switzerland. The elders and middle-aged among them much affect Bads. At such places as Davos am Platz and Tarasp they may be counted by the hundred. But even at these places we do not see their largest contingent. That is composed of the young and active, who wish to see the mountains, and who do all their work on foot. These are dispersed, like an army of skirmishers, over the whole country. In my excursion of this year, which took me on foot over between three and four hundred miles, and fifteen so called Passes, I nowhere met on the road a single Englishman, (had the Passes been difficult ones my experience, perhaps, would have been different,) but I seldom, if ever, passed a day without meeting several Germans, generally in parties of three, without a porter. We may to some extent judge of the degree to which Alpinism has penetrated the German mind by the fact, that, while our Alpine Club numbers 300 members, theirs numbers 3,000. I have no means of verifying these figures. I only give them as I found them in a Swiss newspaper. The same authority informed me that the Swiss Alpine Club now counts 1,700 members. Still what there may be of fact in the above statements indicates that mountaineering is not only a more accessible, but also a more popular, pursuit with them than with us. There must be some reason for this. Can the reason be that among them culture is both broader in itself, and more widely diffused than among ourselves? These people, too, are more gregarious and sociable than we are; perhaps some causes of repulsion that are operative here may not be felt among them; and so they may travel in larger parties than are common with us.

At 7.30 started for the Via Mala. A cloudless morning. The freshness of the air, the clearness of the light, the depth of the blue combined to stimulate the nerves both of body and mind, and prepared me for feeling all the effects of the expected wonders of the scene; or as it is unwise ever to expect anything, for appreciating highly whatever the walk might present to me. As I walked along, looking down precipices between lofty pine stems, as straight and round as if they had been turned in a lathe, to the broken foamy thread of the Hinter Rhein in the bottom, and then up 1,600 feet of opposite black precipice, on the summit of which, here and there, a lofty pine broke the sky-line, but showing at that height no bigger than a hop-pole, the circumnavigator, understanding how my mind was engaged, and perhaps himself a little touched by the scene, propounded the only remark he made on the scenery during the eight days he was with me. 'If a man,' quoth he, 'Sydney-way, had this gully on his run, he might make any amount of money by showing it. Any amount!' For the moment I was a little taken by surprise; but it was no more than an unexpected application of his governing idea—which I had already had served up in many forms, and those not always quite *à propos* to what was before us—that the only good of anything in the world was its capacity for being turned into money. Having been brought up to work at his trade from 5 A.M. to 8 P.M. for seven francs a week, (the wages paid at Poschiavo in those days,) he had come to hate and despise labour; and his Australian experiences, acting on a Swiss substratum, had made him an ideologist, but of one idea, that one being that the one sure way to the one great object was to buy cheap, and to sell dear. Again and again he had repeated to me that this was the way in which all the money in the world that had been made honestly had been made. But he never could explain how the money that was given in the good price had been made, except by the same process of selling dear. Those, he maintained, who had been most pre-eminently successful in life were those who had most thoroughly carried out the rule, perhaps without an undeviating regard for honesty. He had not succeeded at Sydney, because ice was so dear there; that is to say because ices could not be made without ice. The liquor trade had great capacities, because there are other things in the barrel besides liquor. The world, and its money-making inhabitants were to him only an enlarged edition of the two American lads, who during their journey in a railway car, without leaving their seats, made each of them a large fortune by an incessant repetition of the process of swapping what they had about them. I had little to say just now to his remarks, for what of the world was before me indisposed me to transfer my thoughts to the antipodes, or even to say anything on behalf of labour and thrift, and of honesty, in reply to his narrow and unfavourable experiences of life.

The Via Mala though of the same character as the Schyn is both more diversified and more astonishing. The roadway itself is wider, and of more solid construction than that of its neighbour; nor is it all on one general level, for, as you advance along it, you are generally ascending or descending. It also crosses from side to side, being carried over the stream by bridges, which here it has been necessary to build at a great height above the stream. The ravine, too, is not so uniformly wedge-shaped, but in places the opposite side will appear to be almost, or perhaps will be quite, perpendicular. There is indeed one instance of its actually leaning towards you. The hammers and chisels of the old world would never have made this road. Gunpowder it was that rendered its construction possible, and we may almost say that made the want of it felt. It first made the old castles indefensible, and the man-at-arms as good a man in the field as the armoured knight; in other words it first helped to sweep away such impediments to production, freedom of exchange, and accumulation as the Hohen Rhätiens of mediæval Europe; and when they were gone, and in consequence production had increased, and facilities for communication became necessary, what had aided in abolishing the castles was found capable also of aiding in the construction of the road. We may suppose that the inventors of this explosive, as has been the case with most inventions, had no glimpse of the good work it would accomplish. They could have had no anticipations of its disestablishing feudalism, and constructing roads through the Alps. And even now we seem to be only feeling our way to some guesses of what will be the kind of work it will do in any future war, that is to say what effect it will have on the history of the future.

I observed as I was advancing along this Via Mala, in what good keeping with the sombreness of the ravines was the monotonous form of the pines. Were its trees of the kinds that are spreading in limb, and varied in form and foliage, it would imply that nature was more benignant than the other features of the scene suggest. But as it is, you find that only one kind of tree can live here, and that a little thought shows you is so constructed as to enable it to withstand the heavy snowfalls and violent gales of winter. Its branches are so short, perhaps somewhat shorter than they would be with us, and, too, so constructed, that they never can be called upon to sustain any great weight of snow, and the trunk tapers so regularly, like a well-made fishing rod, as to enable it to sustain the most sudden and violent storm blasts. The top yields to the pressure, but does not snap, because the stiffness of the stem is gradually increasing; and this, before the bottom has been reached, has increased to such a degree as to prevent any strain being felt by the roots. As you observe this adaptation of form and structure, the hardness of the conditions of the station that are inferred deepens the effect upon your thought of the hardness of the conditions that are seen.

At Thusis we had been told that the storm of the previous Sunday night had so swollen the Hinter Rhein as to have raised the water to within a few feet of the crown of the arch of the bridge. At the other extremity of the Via Mala—the place is called Reischen—we found that a bridge had been swept away. This had interrupted the traffic for twenty-four hours, when those who had charge of the road succeeded in laying some pine trunks across the chasm, and forming upon them a roadway of transverse squared slabs. We stopped a few minutes to see the diligence pass this improvised structure. The three leaders were taken out, as there was some chance that the dancing and rattling of the loose slabs might scare them. With this precaution the passage was effected easily.

I have already mentioned that on the first afternoon of this excursion I inspected the deep perpendicular channel of the Aare on the eastern side of the Kirchet to see if it presented any indications of its having been formed by any other agency than that of the stream that is now running through it. Every indication seemed to imply that the channel had been eroded by the stream, and by it alone. Every deep channel I passed, throughout this excursion, I looked at with the same thought in my mind, and I nowhere saw anything to suggest the operation of any other agent. And in this ravine, the most perpendicular and deepest of them all, I saw nothing that pointed to a different conclusion. Here a single arch is sufficient to carry you over the stream at a height of 300 feet above it. It is impossible to suppose but that the whole of these 300 feet were excavated by the stream that is now fretting at the bottom of them. If, then, you are certain that it cut out the 300 feet below you, what, except your niggardly ideas about the extent of past time, is there to prevent your supposing that it cut out the 1,300 feet above you? Believe the evidence of your eyes in this matter, and it will add a hundredfold to the interest with which you will contemplate this grand example of the method in which nature makes a stream cut a channel for itself through a mountain of solid rock. You will think how long she has been engaged in the work, and that she is now carrying it on with the same instrument, and applied in the same fashion, as thousands and thousands of years ago. The reason why in these gorges the rock is cut with comparative rapidity is that in them the stream is always both rapid and confined. Because it is rapid it is working with the greatest possible power, and because it is narrow that greatest power is applied at the greatest possible advantage, that is to say it is confined to the central straight line of the narrow bottom, for all the sand and stones are turned in from each side to that central line. Hence the rapidity, narrowness, and directness of the cutting action. When, however, the stream has passed out of the gorge into more level ground, it becomes diffused: it cannot, therefore, cut any longer at the bottom; and for its former tendency to directness of course is substituted a tendency to meandering.

In Switzerland you read much of the past and present life of this terraqueous globe. So indeed you may on the alluvial flats of our eastern counties, if it is there that your lot has been cast; but with this difference, that in them the characters of the writing are small and indistinct, while in Switzerland they are in Roman text, and are held up before you, as it were on a signboard, to attract your attention. The life of the globe, like that of a plant or animal, is the result of the forces that have acted, and are acting within it, and upon it. In Switzerland you behold what was their action in past times in the mighty mountains they have upheaved; and in the stratification of these mountains you behold what preceded their upheaval; and then you go on of yourself to consider what preceded the deposition of those strata. You are reading nature backwards, as you might a Hebrew volume. In the igneous rocks that you see have been intruded you read another chapter that reveals to you the action of other forces. The shivering of mountain pinnacles tells you something about lightning, storms, and frosts. Excavated valleys, and lakes, polished rocks, and striated mountain flanks, and old *moraine* mounds are a lesson to you upon glacier action, and its greater activity in former epochs. Excised ravines, filled-up lakes, avalanches of *débris*, mountainside slips, burying villages and blocking up valleys, roads you are traversing cut through, and bridges you were to have crossed carried away, fields buried, or washed away, or lately formed, are chapters on the action of running water. Forests flourishing on all but naked rock, greenest prairies on a soil but an inch or two deep, earth-pillars, threads of water on every mountain side, and a glancing stream in every valley, oblige you to think of the relation of oceans, clouds, winds, the varying capacity of the atmosphere for retaining moisture, and of rain, to the vegetable and animal life of the land. Fragments of mountains hurled into valleys may remind you of earthquakes. And the interest of all this is intensified by thinking how it has shaped the life of man, and is at this moment, while you are reading the lesson before you, affecting its every day. Manifestly it is these operations of nature which have provided him with his station here, and manifestly he must conform his life to the conditions of the station he inhabits. It is so, of course, everywhere. But here in Switzerland it is more readily seen and felt that it is so.

On emerging from the ravine of the Via Mala the transformation of scene has some resemblance to that on the St. Gothard route, when one passes from the Devil's Bridge by a few steps through the Urner Loch into the Urserenthal. In the case of the latter the transformation is more sudden and complete. There the change of form from pointed ruggedness to wavy smoothness, and of colour from gray and black to soft green is so instantaneous that the feeling produced is almost that of being transferred in a moment from darkness to light. Here the change, though complete, is not instantaneous. You are prepared for the valley of Schams, its fields, chiefly of green, but with some gold, its villages, its churches, its scattered *châlets*, its busy inhabitants by a mile, or so, of intermediate improvement. The scenes are not shifted, or reversed, before you know what is being done, but one melts into the other. It is a diorama in which the valley of Schams takes the place of the ravine of the Via Mala. Still, if you are at all susceptible to effects of this kind, the change in the nature of the impressions will be felt to be great. My feeling was that I was a musical instrument possessed of consciousness, but not of free agency; and that nature was playing on me what, and as, she pleased: first something rude, simple, and clangorous; then something soft, soothing, and varied.

From Zillis, the first village of the valley, where we stopped at the hotel de la Poste for half an hour, I counted five villages over the grassy slopes around me, and seven churches, generally on more or less conspicuous knolls. I was seated outside in the sun on a bench against the wall. The presence of a stranger soon attracted the curiosity of some children that were playing about in the street. A few cents secured their attention. I asked them why they were not at school. The schools here were not open, they told me, except in winter. During the four months of summer they are closed, in order that the children of these industrious peasants may learn to labour, as well as to read and write; and that the schoolmaster, too, may have as well as other people, time to get in his hay, or in some way or other to earn what will enable him to buy hay, for in this part of the world none can live without a cow.

And as it is with attendance at school, so is it to a great extent in these valleys with attendance at church: it is affected by times and seasons. I once asked a woman who was describing to me the rigour of the winter in one of these high valleys, whether she was speaking from experience? Did she live up here in winter? Of course she did. Where else had poor people to go?

'What do you do to pass the time?'
'In winter we go every day to church.'
'Why do you not go every day now?'
'Because we have now something else to do.'

The custom, then, of going to church, as I have often suspected is the case with prayer three times a day in the East, does not owe its existence and its maintenance exclusively to motives of a religious kind. It in some degree rests upon its giving people something to do, who otherwise would at the time have nothing to do, and upon its enabling them to indulge their sense of gregariousness. There is nothing mischievous, or reprehensible in this. Quite the contrary; for why in our efforts to keep alive our sense of the Unseen, and our moral sense, should we reject what aid may be obtained from the action of motives which, though not religious in the ordinary meaning of the word, are quite natural and very beneficial?

I found that in this valley, as is the case in most others, there are very few families who do not reside in houses of their own, and very few owners of houses who are without a bit of land of their own. This very much increased the interest with which I regarded the seven villages, and the multitude of little patches of green, and of gold, which tesselated the area around me of about a mile and a half in diameter, walled in by its amphitheatre of rugged mountains. To live in a house that is your own makes life pleasanter, and to cultivate a field that is your own makes labour lighter.

The thoughts, the feelings, the lives of peasants who live in their own houses, and cultivate their own land are of a higher order than the thoughts, the feelings, the lives of those who do not ; and where this underlies the picture, the scene is a pleasanter one to contemplate.

Having loitered much by the way it was mid-day when I entered Andeer. This is the chief place in the valley. It possesses many roomy substantially built houses, and is quite a little town. From its extent you would suppose that its population must exceed the 600 it is said to contain. All these towns, however, cover more ground than towns of equal population would with us from the fact that almost all the dwelling houses have annexed to them cowhouses with the hayloft in an upper story : and these cow-houses with haylofts over them are not readily distinguishable from dwelling houses. The hotel Fravi, at which I put up—I do not know whether there is another in the place—rehorses the diligences and carriages, which go to and fro over the Splügen. It is therefore a large establishment, making up many beds, and having stabling for about forty horses. The thickness of the walls of the hotel, nearly three feet on the third story, reminded me of the severity of the winter these 600 people have to get through, somehow or other, with their scanty means and humble appliances, when their houses are for months together half buried in snow, and they are walled in, as it were in a prison, with mountain-high snow barriers right and left, and every breath of air that reaches them is charged with most benumbing cold.

On this day, however, there was nothing to suggest the severities of an Alpine winter, except the preparations these good people were making for its advent. The depth of colour in the blue abyss, unflecked by cloud, and undimmed by a suspicion of mistiness, was such as we can know little of here in England. It was one of a succession of sunny days, that was following a spell of wet; and so every man, woman, and child was out making, or bringing in, hay. The shutters of almost every house in the town were up, indicating where their inmates were, and what they were about. Later in the day the results of the work of the day, and of the few fine ones that had preceded it, began to be seen in the streets. There was a constant succession of little trucks drawn by oxen, some on wheels, and some on runners, loaded high with fragrant hay. Those who could not afford oxen drew these trucks themselves, the mother and the little people often pulling it along together; and, to go a step still lower, those who could not afford the trucks, carried their hay in large bundles on their own backs. The sun was at the bottom of all this life and successful labour; and the warmth he was pouring down into the valley to-day would keep these industrious families alive in the winter. The amount of air, too, was just what was enough for their haymaking. To one sitting outside the hotel, close by its row of poplars, watching the arrival of the hay harvest, the breeze appealed to four senses at once. You felt the contact of its crisp freshness; you heard the rustling, and saw the quivering of the aspen leaves as it moved by them; and it brought to you the fragrance of the new hay. Later in the day when the hay was housed, and the fields were wet with dew, you heard the blacksmith's hammer repairing the damages the good people's tools had sustained, and the wood-cleaver's axe preparing to-morrow's fuel. For in this part of the world all trades work till 8 P.M., having begun at 5 A.M.; two hours in the middle of the day being appropriated to rest—two sacred hours, the sabbath of each day—which are most religiously observed everywhere, even at the post-office bureau. And these men who were now working on till eight, had been at work all day in the hay-field, from which they had only been driven by the heavy dew of such an evening, following such a day, at such a height.

CHAPTER VI.

AVERSTHAL.

> Will Fortune never come with both hands full?
> She either gives a stomach and no food—
> Such are the poor, in health; or else a feast
> And takes away the stomach—such are the rich
> That have abundance, and enjoy it not.—SHAKESPEARE.

August 8.—By the stratagem of inviting the circumnavigator to breakfast with me this morning at 4.40 was enabled to get off at five. As we passed down the main street of the little town—the hotel Fravi is at its northern end—I again heard, as I had up to eight yesterday evening, the blacksmith's hammer and the wood-river's axe; for there was at this early hour too much dew on the grass for their hay-making. If, as the monkish saying tells us, to labour is to pray, then the life of these poor peasants, at all events in summer, is both continuous and earnest prayer. It is prayer in deed, in support of the prayer in word of their long winters, about which we were told something in the last chapter. Their prayer in deed must have a good moral effect upon them, for it is doing their utmost under such conditions as oblige them to feel that the success of their efforts will after all depend on unseen causes over which they have no direct control. It is also through a dumb, yet still a most eloquent appeal to those unseen causes.

Above Andeer our valley, which is now approaching the Splügen, begins to close in. The Splügen, however, was not my destination. The aspect of things in, as we are told, the highest inhabited valley in Europe, and a glimpse of the life of its inhabitants, had more attraction for me; and so my route to-day was to be up the Aversthal, debouching, whenever the time might come for that, at Casaccia at the foot of the Maloja, on the road from Chievenna to the Engadin. My plan was to get as far as I conveniently could in the first half of the day, and to spend the remainder of it in looking at whatever there might be to see at whatever place I might then have reached. I did not expect much encouragement in my efforts to push on from my companion. Still I would not begin by anticipating difficulties and disappointments: at all events I had yesterday given him very little to do, and plenty of time to rest; and some of that little to do he had shuffled off by entrusting my *sac* to a return carriage, and some of that plenty of time for rest he had turned to account by sleeping through the greater part of the afternoon in an empty diligence in the coach-house of the hotel. At about two miles above Andeer the stream of the Aversthal falls into that of the Hinter Rhein. Immediately beyond the point of junction the path for the Aversthal starts from the right bank of the Hinter Rhein, and takes the left bank of the Averser Bach. There is no mistaking it, for at first, and for some two or three miles up the valley, as far as an abandoned smelting-house, it is an old cart track. After this it becomes a horse path. In some places between the binonymous hamlet of Inner Ferrera or Canicül and Campsut it has of late been so damaged as to be for the present available for pedestrians only. But these good people have so much of the wisdom of the ant and of the bee in repairing damages, that we may be sure that the road will soon again be made practicable for horse traffic.

As this is undeservedly a not much frequented way, I will give some particulars of it. It begins in a pine wood with the Averser Bach, or Averser Rhein as it is more grandiloquently sometimes styled, blustering by on your left over its rocky bed in no inconsiderable volume. After a time you cross to its opposite bank. The stream has now, in correspondence with the increasing grade of the ascent, become more rapid and noisy. The rocks, too, over which it tumbles having become larger—some of them are large tables of rock—give occasion for several small waterfalls. There are lofty mountains by the side of your path, and others still loftier are at times visible in the distance. Sometimes your path lies over the outspread rock-fragments brought down the mountain side by storm torrents. You see that it would be bad to be caught here while such work was going on, for you would have but little chance of keeping your feet against the descending stream of commingled rocks and water. After this the valley widens into prairies, upon which are a few *châlets*. This is the village of Ausser Ferrera. Beyond this the path, still on the right bank, takes you through a stretch of pine wood, which again terminates in prairies. This time the expanse is larger; and here is Inner Ferrera, or Canicül. You now have to recross to the left bank, and to ascend through a pine wood, which continues as far as Campsut. Along this part of the way the scene is often grandly hard and rugged. The near and distant mountains are mighty masses. The iron-faced precipices awe you. The stream is impatient to get away from them. At about a third of this stage of the way we had to cross, not much above the stream, some steep inclines of freshly brought down mountain rubbish, which had in some places buried, in others carried away, the path. This brought us down quite to the level of the stream, where its course describes a curve round the end of a lofty precipitous mountain. We were on the inner side of the curve. Here nature had given no space for a path, and so it had to be formed partly by excavation, and partly by the construction of a narrow wooden roadway supported on king-posts and struts, just out of the reach of floods. On the opposite side of the Bach, in the precipitous face of the mountain wall, which formed the outer side of the curve of the stream here described, was a deep ravine: to form it the mountain wall had been as it were split in two, or rent asunder. Through this ravine poured the Starlera Bach. As soon as we had rounded the curve, being still not many yards distant from the Starlera ravine and its torrent, we came on a corresponding ravine and torrent on our side—those of the Val de Lei. We crossed them by a wooden bridge. Beyond the bridge is a little level space of three or four yards square. Standing here the scene was singularly impressive. The only sound was that of the three torrents rushing together. The only sight that of the three deep, steep, ravines they were rushing down, each torrent between two lofty precipitous mountains. Three troubled streams, and six iron-faced lines of mountain precipices, and the little space of unfathomable blue above: these were all. Had I been alone, or had there been with me one who possessed an inner sense capable of being touched by such a scene, I would gladly have loitered at this point for some little time. The feeling that came over me was that which the desert engenders—that you have intruded on a scene not meant for man. There it is stillness, desolateness, absence of life; here it is mountains closing in around you, and torrents blustering by, and no place for anything else, that warn you off. The iron-faced precipices will advance a little closer, the torrents will rise a little higher, to resent your intrusion. I wished to surrender myself for a little time to the impressions of the moment, to commune a little with the *genius loci*. As it was, I was hurried through this home of the spirit of the Brocken, and still wonder the monster did not show himself, to make me understand that that was no place for such feeble creatures as the children of men.

Beyond this point we found that the road had again been carried away. A straight-sided gully had lately been cut through it to the depth of about eight feet. Four men were here at work making a cutting for the road down to the bottom of the newly-formed gully. In such a place it would have been of no use to refill the excavation, because the incoherent material used for this purpose would be carried away by the next rain. They had instead of this sunk the road to the bottom of the gully on the lower side. Up the perpendicular eight feet of the upper face, which they had not yet begun to make practicable, we had to climb by the aid of a few projecting roots. If our hold of the roots, or the roots' hold of the soil, had failed—of course there was but slight chance of either of these possibilities occurring—we should have tumbled down about sixty feet into the Bach, for as the road was along the edge of a precipice, a fall from the face of the gully would have been a fall down the precipice also.

The path now in good repair, and on the descent, continued through pine woods, and in about an hour conducted us to an open grassy space, where we crossed the stream to the right bank. Here was the village of Campsut. We were now at an elevation of 5,000 feet, where nothing could be grown but grass. As we were entering the village, a little girl, of about ten years of age, a rosy *brunette*, who was running to join her friends in the hay-fields, almost came into collision with us. She was so confounded by this sudden rencontre with strangers, that for some little time she was unable to answer our questions. When we released her, she started off again like a wild animal that had been suddenly disturbed by a more than doubtful apparition. At the further end of Campsut we got a rare draught of milk. It was presented to us in a little circular wooden tub with two small handles formed by the projection of two of the staves. This milk was deliciously fresh and rich; and as to the little wooden tub, that was so spotlessly clean that it was a pleasure to look at it. The dame to whom we were indebted for this draught was above the common height, and, like the little girl, had remarkably good features, and a ruddy brown complexion. Hard work, rough weather, long winters, and simple fare, had had as yet their issue only in health and strength. I tarried over the tub of delicious milk, not only for its sake. A little talk with such a donor of such a draught was a pleasant interlude. The order and cleanliness of everything in the *châlet* showed that she had such ambition as Campsut admitted of.

Beyond Campsut a charming bit of smooth turf interspersed with large rocks, and detached larches, some little height above the brawling stream, with grand mountains right and left, and still grander mountains in front, brought us to Crot—a village of a few scattered *châlets*. You have to descend to the stream. Before you lies the sombre green, treeless Madriserthal, to be entered after crossing the stream by a bridge. Our way, however, was not across the stream up the Madriserthal; so just beyond Crot, having crossed the Bach of our own valley, we turned away from the Madriserthal, and ascended a steep, grassy slope on our left. This after a time became rocky, with, among the rocks, larches and cembras. Having reached the summit of this rise, with our Bach on our left, we advanced for some way, along the flank of the mountain, through an ancient open forest, and then crossed the stream, now in a ravine, by the second of two bridges, about a mile from Cresta. On the Cresta side of the ravine is no wood : at first only very rocky alpe, and then, when the village is reached, upland prairie. At about half a mile from the village we met a chubby little urchin of about ten years of age, with head and feet bare, clad in strong thick homespun of hemp and coarse woollen. He came up to us with an easy self-possessed air, knowing very well what we wanted, and announced that he was the son of the *Pasteur*, and would conduct us to his father's house, which is for travellers the recognized inn of the place, as he is their recognized host.

It had been part of my Machiavelism for this day to take with us nothing to eat, in order to ensure our getting at all events as far as Cresta. The stratagem had been quite successful, for having stopped nowhere by the way, except for the tub of milk at Campsut, we reached Cresta at 11.30 A.M. And fortunate it was that we had started early, the result of the other successful little ruse I have already mentioned, and had had no delays on the road, for we had not been at Cresta half-an-hour when it began to rain, the rain being diversified only with snow for twenty-two hours.

During the afternoon there was no going outside the door. But there was enough within for an afternoon. First there was the *Pasteur* himself, a well-built man of about forty years of age. He wore coloured clothes, in which it was clear that he did much out o'door work. This, from the situation of Cresta, must have been restricted to cutting, fetching, and riving wood for fuel, and making hay. On Sundays, of course, his working clothes are exchanged for the clerical black and white, with the portentous collar and bands of the Swiss Reformed Church. He kept himself no cows, only goats. The goats, however, would require hay, and he could assist his neighbours, too, in making their hay. Cow's milk, I suppose, can always be bought in such a place, where the number of cows must be great in proportion to that of the villagers. He spoke German, French, and Romansch, and was a man of observation, thought, and intelligence. He is also the schoolmaster of the Commune, which is that of Oberland Aversthal, which reaches from Crot to Juf, a place some way above Cresta. His pastoral duties, I understood, extended down the valley below Crot as far as Inner Ferrera, or Canicül. To these employments must be added, as I have already mentioned, that of entertaining such travellers as would prefer what he has to offer to what they would find at the little village inn.

The good man's wife was not now visible. She had for some months been suffering from a serious illness, and had not yet seen a medical man; nor, whatever turn her illness might take, was there much chance of her seeing one, because it would require two days for one to come and return, St. Moritz in the Engadin being the nearest point from which assistance of this kind could be had. Here, therefore, medical advice and medicines can only be received through the post. The poor woman's illness threw much of the work of the house upon him, in which, however, he was aided by a sturdy Romansch-speaking damsel.

Then there was the view from the window. This, from a height above the stream of about 500 feet, commanded the valley and the opposite range. The lower half of this range was covered with the open forest of cembra, a part of which we had passed through in the forenoon. Above the forest was Alpine pasture. All along the ridge the line that divided the forest from the pasture was perfectly straight: nowhere did the forest encroach on the grass, or the grass on the forest. On entering the forest above Crot we had seen some larch, but there was none, I believe, opposite to Cresta, nothing but cembra. Nor were there any young trees in the forest, though the old ones stood at such a distance from each other as to give sufficient pasturage for a herd of cows I could just make out as I stood at the window. I could also make out with a glass a flock of goats in the forest, and that accounted to me for the absence of young trees. I had often observed that the goat cannot kill the young spruce, of which the forests generally consist. Of course they bite off the new terminals of the leader, and of the laterals, but not quite to the bottom of the new wood. The terminals, therefore, of the laterals, though bitten back every year, still gain an inch or two every year; and as this makes the plant grow into a very compact and bushy form, the time comes when the goat can no longer reach over the compact mass of laterals to bite off the terminal of the leader. That was only to be got at so long as its enemy could reach over to it. Every year the enemy is forced back a little; and so in a dozen or twenty years it is no longer able to reach it. The terminal of the leader then advances in safety, and a tree is quickly formed. All that has happened is, that it was delayed some years in making its start. But during this period of delay the roots were spreading far, and establishing themselves with a good hold of the ground; when, therefore, the start at last is made, the growth is very rapid. You may always distinguish the trees that had in their early days been kept back for a time in this way, for the lower part of their trunks, the three or four feet nearest the ground, are always crooked. This indicates how they had been maltreated by the goats. So it is with the ordinary pine of the Swiss forests. Of the cembras, however, I observed that they could not escape the goats in this way, or in any way; either because the bite of these animals is at once destructive to them, or because having been bitten back they have not the power of forming a compact bush, and so of rising eventually out of harm's way. At all events the goats kill the young trees of this species; and this will account for so many forests of cembra having died out, or now being in process of dying out. One would suppose that this cause of their destruction would be guarded against in these lofty Grison valleys, some of which are rendered habitable only by the supply of wood furnished by what remains of ancient forests of this species, which is the only Swiss conifer that grows at such heights. But in this valley of Oberland Aversthal there is some peat; its inhabitants, therefore, are not entirely dependent for fuel on their single forest of cembra opposite to Cresta. Their dependence, however, upon it for material for the construction of their houses is complete. When, therefore, their one forest shall have been consumed they must either take to building with stone, or abandon the valley as a place of residence.

It was interesting to watch the effects of the snow storms, which throughout this afternoon alternated with showers of rain, and will continue to do so till 10 A.M. to-morrow. On our side of the valley, which, as it faced the south, had been heated by the sun of the forenoon and of yesterday, the snow never lay on the ground. On the opposite side every fall of snow completely whitened the Alpine pasture above the forest, but rarely extended any way down into the forest; and on the few occasions when it did was very soon gone. When we left the place the following day all the pasture above the forest was white, but the turf between the trees was free from snow. Of course the ground beneath the trees is somewhat warmer than in the open, as every animal knows when it chooses its night's resting-place; still the visible difference between the two suggested the questions of whether there is not what may be roughly regarded as a line for the snow that falls in summer, and whether it is this supposed line of summer-falling snow which defines the upper limit of the forest by preventing above that limit the germination of seeds or by killing the young plants in the tender stage of their first growth.

Of course there was a great deal of talk with our host. He was, naturally enough, glad to have some one to talk to—a feeling which his guest, as might be supposed, was ready to reciprocate. This was his second year at Cresta. This year, up to the date of my visit, several Germans, and two Americans, had stopped for a night at his house, but not one Englishman. His continuance in his present position depended in equal degrees on his parishioners' good pleasure and on his own choice. The liberty of the two contracting parties was equal. They could bid him go, if so minded; and he, if so minded, could bid them look out for another *Pasteur*. Romansch he thought was dying out in the neighbourhood, being hard pressed by German on the north and to some extent by Italian on the south. As respects the schools there was a general leaning towards having German taught in them, on account of its superior utility for business purposes, even in places where the religious instruction is still given in Romansch.

The school of Oberland Aversthal is held in his house. A large room on the ground-floor has been fitted up for this purpose. Considering how poor the peasants are, I was surprised at the excellence of the fittings. The room had double windows, and an excellent stove, which was of such dimensions that I was at a loss to imagine how it could have ever been brought up the valley. There were good desks and benches, master's desk and blackboard. In short, the apparatus was as good as could be wished. All this is accounted for by remembering that, though it is provided by the peasants, it is provided for their own children. Every family in the valley has a strong personal interest in the school; and this concentration of personal interest upon the school-room issues in its being the best furnished room in the commune. And as the minister is the master, we may suppose that the teaching and tone of the school is correspondingly good. Of course here, as elsewhere in these parts, the school is open only during the winter months, which, however, at an altitude of 6,400 feet, that of the schoolroom—Juf is some hundreds of feet higher— must comprise nine months of the year.

Off the schoolroom was the guests' chamber, whose wants had been taken into account in the construction of the house. In this everything was brightly clean. It contained two beds, and about a dozen volumes in German. Behind these two rooms was the hall, or store-room, of the house. Above the school-room was the sitting-room. On either side of this was a bed-room. Behind these were some small rooms, in one of which my porter was berthed.

The Canton had been desirous that a road should be constructed through the valley to connect either the Upper Engadin, or Casaccia, below the Maloja, with the Splügen road; and with a view to this the preliminary surveys had been made. The proposal, however, was so distasteful to the peasants, that it had been withdrawn for the present. This reminded one of the opposition that was made to the Great Western Railway by the authorities of a famous University; an opposition which has left its mark on the railway map of England, for it diverted the railway from its intended course, both to the cost of the shareholders and to the inconvenience of the University. The unlettered ignorance of the peasants of Oberland Aversthal has come to the same conclusion as did the learned Doctors of Oxford. They both alike argued, we are no part of the world; the world is wicked, and will invade us; we are no match for the world. Fortunately not. The result in the case of Overland Aversthal will be what it was in the case of the famous University. The wicked world will in the end have its way, and the opponents of the wicked world will come to acknowledge that it is not a bad way, and that they are none the worse for accommodating themselves to it: in fact, that they are themselves a part of the world, and cannot do without it.

One little matter I noticed this morning cannot but work in the direction of opening the eyes of these naturally conservative peasants to their true interests. Some time after we had entered the valley—it was at about 7 A.M.—we met a walking postman with a bulky bag on his back. There was much in that bag.

It contained the wants, the hopes, the schemes, the feelings of Unterland and Oberland Aversthal. At about the corresponding hour in the evening, as I was looking from the *Pasteur's* window at the aspect of things in the rain, I saw the same man arrive on his return journey. He had on his back the same bag. In it he had now brought back the reciprocation of that terrible outside world to the wants, hopes, schemes, and feelings of the valley. All this only means that these good people have dealings with, and friends in, that terrible world, dealings without which they could not possibly exist, and friends who are very dear to them, and affection for whom constitutes a large ingredient of their inner life. Every family must every year sell a cow, and a young bullock or two, and so much cheese, to buy coffee, and brandy, and scythes, and many other things it cannot do without; and arrangements for these sales and purchases are made through the post; and every family may have a relative seeking a livelihood in the outside world, some far enough off in it, and it does them good to hear of that relative's welfare. Well, if it is desirable that these transactions, and this intelligence, should be facilitated by the walking postman, would it not be desirable that they should be still further facilitated by a good road? It would, practically, enhance the price they would get for their young bullocks, and surplus cows and cheese, and lessen the price of the coffee, the brandy, the scythes,

I

and their other necessary purchases. It would, too, increase the value of every *klafter* of land in the valley. And it would bring many travellers into the valley, in catering for whom some money might be made. Some of them would get a better living, than any of them get now, by acting as guides and porters. They would see more of the world, and the world would see more of them ; and just as the world would be the better for knowing something of Aversthal, so would its good people be the better for knowing something of the world. No one of them would now wish to go back to the ante-post times. The silent, but inevitable action of the post will lead on to the road ; and then no one will wish to go back to the ante-road times.

But the above-mentioned bag, full of such beneficent magic, for it was magic that disclosed to every family what their hearts were yearning to know, and what their business required, was not on this afternoon the whole of the walking postman's load. There was also on his back an osier basket for our host. He had made preparations for its reception ; but the chubby little fellow, who had conducted us to his father's house, was the first to announce its arrival. He and his father were soon out in the rain, opening it carefully so as not either to injure the basket, or rudely to shake its contents, I should have said its inmates, for on raising the lid there were revealed to their delighted eyes three geese—three live geese. A little enclosure had been got ready for them, to which they were forthwith transferred, the good man carrying two, and the chubby little fellow the third. They already had half-a-dozen chickens: the only ones I saw in the village, or, indeed, in the valley. This, then, was a great and interesting addition to the live stock of Oberland Aversthal; though now, on recalling the conditions of the place, I cannot imagine how they were to be kept through the winter, or, indeed, how they were to be kept at any time out of harm's way: for they needs must sooner or later get down to the Bach, from which there would not be much chance of their coming back alive, as they would probably, in their first attempt to navigate it, be dashed to death against the rocks. But whatever might be the issue of the experiment, the good opinion of our host I was already disposed to form was further strengthened on my finding that he was fond of tending animals. It was, too, an experiment that might, I wish I could say must, add to the companions and the resources—there is a little jar in that word resources—of his neighbours, whose lives up here above the clouds are somewhat wanting in objects of ordinary earthly interest.

The Romansch-speaking damsel was setting the table for supper at the time when this new form of animal life arrived at Cresta. The *Pasteur's* half dozen fowls hearing the stir outside came forth from the shed, in which they had taken refuge from the rain, to see what it was all about. They were of a small breed, for it costs too much to keep large fowls in a place where their maize has to be brought a day's journey on a man's back. I chipped off a few crumbs from a roll that had just been placed on the table—they were detached with difficulty—and threw them down from the window. The proud little cock—it was a proceeding we must all many a time have observed—took a piece up with his beak, but instead of swallowing it—what self-restraint! summoned his seraglio for the delicious morsels, depositing before the first arrival the one that was in his beak. That surely, the thought flashed upon me—for at Cresta one sees things in a new light—is not instinct; or if it is, then the ordinary definition of instinct ought to be somewhat enlarged. It is self-denial, politeness, policy, gratitude, affection. Whether it looks to the past, or to the future, there is something wonderfully human about it. It is true that all chanticleers do this; but if they do not understand now, which is what I do not believe, then their progenitors must have once understood, so this supposition only removes the fact some steps back, that under the conditions of their position, that is under the relations in which they were standing to their seraglios, it was the right thing to do. The conditions and relations of the position must have been understood, and what under them was profitable and becoming must have been seen. Either then, for that is our conclusion, reason is less mechanical in them, or else more mechanical in ourselves, than is generally supposed; or, to put it in another way, their reason and ours are more closely akin than is generally supposed.

But the arrival of the geese by the post carries us back to our argument that the post is a preparation for the at present much dreaded road. Will not these good people some day come to see that if it is advantageous to have a path that admits of the postman bringing to them three geese in a basket, and other such things, that it would be more advantageous to have a road that would admit of the diligence post, or the carrier's cart, bringing them many other things they want, but which are beyond the carrying power of the postman? This is a question we may be sure will occur to them, and be discussed, in their long winters; and, too, we may be sure that the young people, who will have been brought up by the minister in the well-appointed school the old people are maintaining, will upon this subject for the most part be of a different way of thinking from the old people.

As to the supper, (the preparations for which supplied us with those crumbs, the grateful, or judicious, appropriation of which made us wish to improve our knowledge of what we call instinct,) it was the same as our dinner had been with the addition of butter, and the substitution of coffee for Valteline wine. The meat was again the mummy beef with which I had first become acquainted at Peist. To this was now added mummy ham. The bread had been baked at Silva Plana in the Engadin, and was a month old. It was the petrified fossil of bread. No traces of moisture remained in it, and it was as hard to masticate as it had been to cut. Those who know what are the habits of Swiss swine in summer, when kept on the mountains about the *châlets* where the cows pass the night, will not be able to bring themselves to touch pig in any form in Switzerland. As therefore I was obliged to reject the mummy ham, and had not yet discovered the merits of mummy beef, I dined on bread and cheese and wine, and supped on bread and cheese and coffee. Not so, however, the circumnavigator. At dinner I had been somewhat shocked at the vigour of his appetite, for he left nothing on the table; and now at supper, seeing that the same process was being repeated, and knowing how hard those comestibles had been to come at in this part of the world, and seeing also that the good *Pasteur* had set before us what he must have supposed would have left a large margin for discretion, I rose from the table in a way to intimate to my companion that I thought it time for him to do the same. He would not, however, take the hint. I, therefore, reminded him that these things were hard to come by up here, and that I had no doubt but that they were in consequence used frugally, and wound up my little speech with the dictum that enough was better than too much. My facts, however, reflections, and platitudes had no other effect than that of extracting from my voracious attendant the remark, that he always began to suspect that he was not all right when he found that he could not feed well. I could not help retorting, 'Then just now you must have the satisfaction of feeling that you are unusually well.' But this, like what had preceded it, glanced off from his thick skin, for he continued doggedly at work, till there was not left on the table a crumb of anything, of beef, ham, cheese, butter, sugar, or bread, wherefrom to draw any further sanitary inferences. I now poured out on him the last dregs of my disgust by telling him that it was fortunate for him that he had not to live up here, for if so he would have few opportunities through life for ascertaining the state of his health. It would have had a pleasant flavour of revenge, if I could have made him pay his own shot for this supper; but from that he knew that he was safe, because if for any reason—my reason in this case was the wish to save our host some trouble—you bid your man take his meals with you, you must of course pay for both.

Besides his experiment in live stock, the good man was making one in gardening. He had enclosed a little space, about half-a-dozen yards square, facing to the south, and had sown in it white beet, the leaf-stalks of which are eaten, cabbages, turnips, and lettuce. This was his first summer at Cresta, and so he had lost no time in endeavouring to ascertain how far the sun could help him in this matter. But on this, the 8th day of August, the prospect of success was far from encouraging. The turnips showed no tuberous tendencies, and had formed each but a few small leaves. The foliage of the cabbages and lettuces was in much the same condition. The peculiarities of growth in those plants could still be known to his neighbours only by what they might have seen in that much dreaded outside world. A little might be expected from the white-stalked beet; but as there was only a fortnight more for the continuance of the experiment, and it was even then snowing, I cannot think that it will be repeated next year. Or if so, it will not be for the sake of any contributions the little garden may be expected to make to the *Pasteur's* table, but for the sake of his recollections of the world below to which he once belonged. The thought, however, crossed my mind that this little garden had been made not so much as an experiment, but in the hope of pleasing his sick wife by exhibiting to her its products.

The fact is that nothing can be grown here but grass, for Cresta is some way beyond the last cembra on its side of the valley; and if one of these highest-climbing of Swiss conifers could be coaxed into living on such a spot—I saw a stunted oldish-looking dwarf of the kind in the lower part of the village—it would require a century to overtop the *châlets*. No human food, therefore, can be produced except what is supplied by the goats and cows. Here everything is transmuted grass. No tribe of wandering Tartars ever lived so exclusively on their flocks and herds. Not a potato, not a stem of hemp, can be grown. Nature has been far more bountiful to the most hard pressed Kirgishes. Their steppes are a Paradise of fertility and variety compared to Cresta. Indeed we must go somewhere near the Arctic zone to find a parallel to its climate; and even that will not do, for Iceland will not give it, because there a few turnips and potatoes, of the size of walnuts, may be grown. For what we are in search of we must go beyond Iceland, and enter the arctic circle, and perhaps at last the latitude that presents an equivalent to its altitude may be found in Lapland.

What a life does this imply! What a weary winter! What dreary confinement to the small comfortless house, with the snow piled up to the windows of the first floor, month after month! How must the returning warmth of the sun, and the first glimpses of the green grass be hailed! How must every hour of the few days of their little summer be prized! In that brief space they have to provision the garrison of each home for the ensuing nine months. Their chief care is for their hay, the one store upon which ultimately the lives of all, both man and beast, depend. We may be sure they do not lose an hour of daylight. It is fortunate they cannot cut their grass by moonlight. If they could, there would be some probability of their working themselves to death. They could not cut it by moonlight, because, though thick enough on the ground, much of it is only a few inches long—not longer than what I have often seen the mowers leaving behind them in English meadows. You see no waste of that kind here, for these careful people mow very smooth, and very near the ground. And then they know that their few days of possible summer are always more or less abridged by summer snow-storms. How then must they be rejoiced in their hearts when two or three bright, breezy days come together, and enable them to get up what had been previously cut! How heavily are they weighted in the race they have to run for their lives against time!

Where the cow, a little aided by the goat, is the one great means of support, the humblest family cannot exist with less than five or six. They ought, indeed, to have not less than seven. Milk and cheese are their mainstay, with on high days and holidays a shred or two of mummy beef, or pork. Everything else they eat, or drink, or that they clothe themselves with, or use in any way, must come indirectly from the same source; that is to say, every family must every year sell one cow (the price last year was twenty napoleons), and a young bullock or two, and what cheese they can spare, to purchase with the proceeds rye or maize flour, potatoes, brandy, coffee, hemp, wool, tools, and whatever else they may require. Even the few pigs they keep can be turned to some account only by the aid of the cow. No kind of grain, or of roots, can be had for this purpose. When summer, therefore, has come, piggy must follow the cow up into the high pasture, where the cheese is to be made. The whey, that will be expressed from the curd, will be his share. Upon this he will thrive moderately. When he will descend from the mountains with some little weight of flesh upon him, he will be taking his last walk. He is about to pass into the mummy condition. But how will those that are to be retained for stock be kept during the winter? For several months there will be nothing for them to graze upon, and not one mouthful of anything convertible into human food will be available for them. Every pedestrian in Switzerland will have observed in front of the mountain cheese *châlets*, where the cows have for generations passed their summer nights, and often, too, by the side of the cow-houses in the villages, beds of a large-leafed Alpine dock. Where the accumulations of centuries from the cows have made the soil too fat and greasy for grass, this plant luxuriates. It delights in rankness. It also affects moist places, as does in this country its congener, the water dock. The leaves, and leaf-stalks of this dock, these careful people collect in summer, and having scalded them, seasoned with a sprinkling of salt, nettle-tops are sometimes added, the mess is tubbed or barrelled, for the winter. This is the pig's winter food; his sour krout. His daily meal of it is served to him warm.

That the Swiss pigs have to ascend and descend the mountains together with the cows accounts for their form. They are large-framed, and clean-limbed; they have a long back, and long, bony legs. If built at all like our pigs, they would be unable to do their long journeys, and their climbing. In colour they are generally more or less, sometimes entirely, of a rusty chesnut.

There had, then, been much to do, and there had not been much time for doing it. There was the wood for fuel and for repairs that had been felled in the previous winter, and that had to be brought in before the hay was made. And there was the turf, too, that had to be stored; and that also had been dug before the hay was made, that every hour of sunshine might be utilized for drying it, and for making the hay—the precious hay, to which everything must be subordinated, for upon it everything depends. And that, too, after many delays and anxieties, has at last been won, and is now safe under cover. The whey-fed old sow, or the full-grown hog, in about the condition they would be with us when put up to fatten, and the old cow now past milk, have returned home for desiccation. The cows, whose day is not yet done, are being comfortably housed. The rye and maize flour, the potatoes, the brandy, the coffee, the hemp and wool for the women to spin and weave, are all being provided as expeditiously as possible. But time is running these preparations hard, even if it does not show a-head of them, for the snow has already fallen so deep that the ground will be no more seen by the peasants of Ober Aversthal till next year. The long dreadful winter is again upon them.

CHAPTER VII.

JUF—THE FORCELLINA—THE SEPTIMER—CASACCIA.

> Yet still e'en here content can spread a charm,
> Redress the clime, and all its rage disarm.
> Tho' poor the peasant's hut, his feast tho' small,
> He sees his little lot the lot of all.—GOLDSMITH.

August 9.—Up at 5 A.M., but nothing could be done out o' doors. The only difference from yesterday afternoon was that the amount of the rain had diminished while that of the snow and sleet had increased. The downfall of one or other was incessant. Such is Cresta in the dog days. The good man of the house, however, was of opinion—the circumnavigator did not present himself and his opinion till past seven—that the weather would improve before midday. At ten his prognostications were verified, and we started for Casaccia by way of the Forcellina and the Septimer. Every one yesterday, and this morning, recommended us to go to the Engadin by the way of Stalla on the Julier, as the shorter and easier route. But as I was not due till midday to-morrow at Pontresina, where I was to meet my wife, and the little boy of my two former *Months in Switzerland*, there was plenty of time, if only the weather would permit, for the grander Pass of the Forcellina, the old paved road of the Septimer, and the Maloja, all of which I wished to see; the shortness, therefore, and easiness of the alternative route were only deterrent considerations.

The valley immediately beyond Cresta begins to widen and flatten its bottom prairie land. We walked over the grass rejoicing in the returning gleams of sunshine; and all the more because we knew how deeply every soul around us was stirred by the same feelings, for did not those warm rays of light mean well-being for their families during the long arctic winter that was already not far off? These first gleams, however, were shockingly short-lived, for before we had reached Pürt, the first village beyond Cresta, the sleet had again returned, and we were driven to take refuge in a large hay-grange, which it was pleasant to find nearly full of new hay. Upon this we sat for some twenty minutes, noting, through the open door, the women of the place scouring their wooden milk vessels, and setting their small white meagre cheeses on the window sills to consolidate. Each piece was about the shape, size, and colour of a marmalade gallipot. The sleet having nearly exhausted itself, a second start was made. As we went along we counted a herd of about fifty cows on the lower flank of the opposite range. Among them was a large flock of crows; on our side we saw a pair of hawks, and a pair of choughs. The feathered fauna of the Grisons is to the eye of the pedestrian far more abundant both in species and in individuals than that of Central, or of Western Switzerland. We passed through two more villages, and as many more scuds of sleet, and at midday reached Juf, the last village of Oberland Aversthal, and the highest village in Europe that is inhabited throughout the year.

Here it was necessary that we should halt for dinner. Designedly I had taken nothing with us, in order that we might be thrown entirely on the resources of people who live at an elevation of 6,900 feet, that is to say 500 feet above Cresta. The *châlet* we chanced to enter was that of the shoemaker of Juf. At first we found in it only an ancient dame. Before, however, we left we had to receive a levée of some ten, or a dozen of the inhabitants of the place. The ancient dame would gladly do for us anything in her power. Milk, of course, she could supply; but she insisted on our having it warm: for who ever offered any one cold milk when sleet was falling? For this it was necessary that a fire should be lighted. She also had some black rye-bread, and two kinds of cheese: a piece of last year's fat cheese, and plenty of this year's meagre cheese. This was all. I, however, was quite satisfied. Was it not the best these good people had to offer? and was it not what they had themselves to be satisfied with? The sitting-room was very low—hardly more than six feet in height. This was, first, to economize the wood of which the house was built throughout, and all of which had to be brought from below Cresta; and then to make the most of the heat of the stove, the fuel for which, whether wood or turf, was very costly to them; every piece of the latter having been paid for with so much of the precious time of their brief summer, and of the former with very large demands upon the muscular tissues of their own bodies, while cutting it in winter, and getting it across the ravine opposite to Cresta. The stove was a large structure, and filled about a fourth part of the room. The object of its size was that it might have as much heat-radiating surface as possible. It was fed by an opening not in our sitting room, but in the kitchen behind it. At last the milk was warmed, brought in, and placed on the table in a large bowl. In this was placed a wooden ladle to dip out the milk with. The bowl was flanked on one side with the loaf of black rye-bread, which, as it was moist and fresh, was preferable to the desiccated wheaten bread of the *Pasteur's* establishment; and on the other side with the two kinds of cheese. Of these the fat variety was so old as to have almost lost its consistency, and with its consistency had almost gone its goaty flavour; the meagre variety had the texture of new soap, while its flavour was that which may be imagined of soap which has somehow or other become somewhat insipid. I asked for a knife to cut the loaf and the cheese. Had not the Herr a knife of his own in his pocket? No other kind of knife was used at Juf. This being their practice with respect to knives, of course forks were altogether unknown. The Herr happened to have a knife in his pocket, and was not sorry that his not having thought of using it had thrown some light on the table arrangements of Juf, which do not admit of anything that would require a fork, or any kind of knife, except that which is carried in the pocket. These particulars do not seem inviting, but it must be remembered where we were, what was the *entourage*, and what the conditions of the situation, and it will then become intelligible how it could have been that this Juf dinner, if that word may be used for what was before us, would not have been left, if one had been called on to make a choice between the two, for a Lord Mayor's banquet in the Egyptian Hall.

We, and our ways, appeared as interesting to the Juffians, as they and their ways to us, if we might judge by the attention with which we were observed by the levée of old men and old women, and young women too, who came in, and took possession of the benches fastened against the wall, which surrounded the room, except in the stove corner. The room contained no other seats than these benches. Among our visitors was a poor fellow who had broken his leg on the mountains; and, the fracture not having been properly reduced, he was now sadly crippled, and complained of the pains he felt at moving, and at every change of the weather. He never then, I thought, can be long together up here, at all events at midsummer, without having his sufferings aggravated by the latter cause. From what I understood of what we now had to do, I was sure that my porter would be quite unequal to his work, I, therefore, made inquiries for one who would act as guide and porter across the Pass. A venerable senior among the company had a son, who, he assured me, was exactly the man I was in want of; and so he went to fetch him.

I paid five francs for our entertainment. I estimated its fair price rather by the satisfaction it had given to myself, than by what it had cost my hostess; that satisfaction was heightened at seeing how her old weather-beaten, stove-dried features relaxed and brightened as she took into her withered hand the little flake of gold, which perhaps was the easiest earned payment she had ever received in her long hard life. The balance between the services rendered and the value of them to their recipient, having been thus adjusted to the contentment of both parties, and the youth who was to accompany us over the Pass having arrived, we recommenced our march at one o'clock. There was nothing about him to indicate that he had been cradled in so rude a climate. He was tall and slim, yet well and strongly built. His features were fine and regular, and his complexion fair, almost to girlishness.

Before us was the long *cul de sac* of the head of the valley. We had to ascend the left mountain diagonally almost from Juf to the visible summit, about two miles off. For the most part there was no path at all, or our young guide could do better than following it. His long, sure, smooth stride, as he glided up the slant of the mountain, seemed like some new kind of pace ; it was hardly walking. We found it no easy task to keep up with him, which we only did, in Irish style, by following him as well as we could. When we left Juf the sun was bright, but as we ascended higher we saw a dark storm advancing towards us from the direction of Cresta. It might not, however, reach us ; and for the present we had the sun, in the warmth of which even the marmots were rejoicing, for we frequently heard the shrill cries of their sentinels announcing the presence of an enemy, and saw those that had taken the alarm scrambling back to their earths. When we were approaching the summit, the diagonal direction of the ascent ceased for a time, and we had for three or four hundred feet to go straight up the mountain. This was the only bit of the Pass which at all required attention to what we were about. It was something like walking up one of the angles of the tower of York Minster, supposing that angle to have become so dilapidated as to give from bottom to top an almost perpendicular, irregular staircase. This is, I believe, what is called in mountaineering phraseology an *arête*, that is the edge of a mountain rib, or shoulder. Here the rib, or shoulder, was not far from perpendicular, and could not be crossed. It had, therefore, to be ascended, and its edge had been nicked into steps all the way up, partly by nature, and partly by the pickaxe. As I was going up this mountain staircase, and saw the storm below me, no great way off now, I hoped it would not catch me upon it. In that case I thought there will be some chance of my being blown off. We were, however, soon over this bit, which also proved almost too high for the storm, for not much of it reached up to where we were, about 1,700 feet above Juf.

This Pass presents a scene of solid, rugged desolation, of dreary grandeur, as approached from the Juf side. The way to the summit lies across one of the crateriform depressions, which are not uncommon in such situations, between two mighty peaks, with torn and shattered pinnacles. The whole scene is hereabouts so storm-beaten, and frost-bitten, as to be apparently incapable of supporting even a lichen. Everything on which the eye rests is in character— rocks protruded, and rocks shivered, of a dull dark colour, pools of water equally dark, and patches of new summer snow; the whole made more forbidding to-day by icy gusts and pelting sleet.

And now that we have traversed the whole valley from the junction of the Averser with the Hinter Rhein to the summit of the Pass, upon which we are about to step, we are able to understand how its Oberland comes to be the highest inhabited valley in Europe. But we will review the whole of it. Our way up has been through three well defined stages. It began with the Ferrerathal, the first stage. That is comparatively low ground; in respect of altitude it has no special interest. It possesses only the ordinary Swiss interest of being bounded by mountains more or less rocky and precipitous, of maintaining forests more or less shady and vigorous, interspersed at the mouths of lateral valleys with small pieces of grass-land, which give space for the support of their respective little villages. So, too, with the second stage from Canicül to Campsut. The difference here is that the forest has become far more damp and mossy, and the mountains, especially at the triple watersmeet, more precipitous and iron-faced, and the stream more impetuous, and that there is an entire absence of prairies, indeed even of margin. From Campsut, the third stage, the particular of inhabited altitude becomes interesting. This portion is divided into two parts, that from Campsut to Cresta, and that from Cresta to Juf. In the first the mountain ranges begin to recede from each other; and as the forest has been made to confine itself to the rocky mountain side, there is in the middle a good expanse of grass land, capable of supporting many cattle. But as to the cultivation of anything else we have now got too high for that. At Cresta, which is over against the last trees, there is for about a mile a narrowing in again of the valley. It then spreads out once more, and continues wide all the way up to Juf. In this last part lies its chief interest, for under ordinary Alpine conditions, though the grass might still be available in summer, so elevated a valley would be unfit for human habitation. What, then, is there here to counteract the ordinary conditions? The answer is the height and direction of the ranges. They run from east to west, closing in completely at the eastern end. The broad valley, therefore, is thoroughly protected from the cold winds of the north and east, completely open to the south, and no ray of sunlight with its accompanying warmth is intercepted. Still, notwithstanding, there might be a condition which would neutralize these advantages; for instance, if the valley were closed with a glacier, or had glaciers from either of the bounding ranges descending into it, the place would probably be unfit for human residence. There is, however, nothing of the kind; the head of the valley and the bounding ranges are not of such a height as to support snowfields and their glaciers. It is, therefore, the presence of the favourable conditions that have been mentioned, and the absence of the unfavourable ones, which make the grassy expanse of Oberland Aversthal the highest inhabited ground in Europe.

As you begin the descent of the Forcellina on its northern side you come upon two or three pieces of old snow. Beneath these—it may be about 700 feet from the summit—flowers suddenly become abundant; among many others the charming little Alpine forget-me-not, a purple pansy as large as a shilling, and a clear dark-blue little gentian. About 400 feet more of descent bring you to a grassy bottom—there are no trees in sight—which is in reality the summit of the Septimer Pass from Casaccia at the head of the Bregaglia to Stalla on the Julier. In calculating the day's work I had supposed that, as the books spoke of the Septimer being a Pass on this route in the same sense as the Forcellina, we should have had to descend so much from the Forcellina as to have had to ascend somewhat on the Septimer. This expectation was wholly unfounded: for to those who take it from the direction we did every step upon it is downhill: to them it is only the descent of the Forcellina. To those, however, who take it reversely and who are also going on by Stalla to the Julier, and not by the Forcellina to Juf, it is a Pass, and one with a stiff ascent of at least two hours.

The way to Casaccia was now along an old paved road, said to have been constructed by the Romans. The pavement consists of blocks of gneiss, and is generally in good preservation. On the summit it is lost, either because it is now buried beneath the turf, or because in this part of it its stones were taken up to build the hospice the ruins of which you pass, and the wall that enclosed some space around it. There are some places, in which you would have expected to find it buried, or carried away by storm-torrents, but in which it is still in good order, and much in the same state as I will not say its first, because it is safer to say its last, constructors left it. For as we are told that German as well as Roman Emperors used it for the transit of their armies, we must infer that those who last used it for this purpose repaired whatever damages time had done to it. I saw pieces of it on the very edge of the stream, where it must sweep over it with great force, but which were still quite uninjured. I was surprised at its general width, as well as at the size of the stones with which it is paved. I say general width, because there are some interesting exceptions. These occur at points where the roadway could not have been enlarged to its general width without cutting through a projecting rock. That on a great military road the inconvenience—very great to an army on the march—of these narrow places was submitted to shows that it would have been very costly in old times to have cut away such rocks; a work which a few handfuls of some explosive would now effect in a morning. It also shows that if wheeled carriages were ever used on this road their gauge must have been very small. Some five miles of the old pavement still remain. I have seen very similar bits of Roman road on Judæan hills. The sight of this drew from the circumnavigator the sceptical remark, that it was a very good road (he meant too good an one) for those times.

In descending this old historical, but now deserted route, on which even a centrifugal tourist is seldom seen, I could not but think of its older and better days. Those granite blocks, on which I was treading, had felt the tramp of Roman armies marching, it might have been, to the Danube, to secure that threatened frontier of the Empire against barbarian aggression. The couriers who brought the intelligence of victories from which much was hoped, and of disasters from which much was feared, had traversed it with quicker steps than those with which I was then descending it. At Rome, and in the cities and villas of northern Italy, the despatches of which they were the bearers had been anxiously looked for. After a time the mind's eye could see hordes of barbarians swarming down its steep pavement to plunder, and to overthrow, the civilization, to aid in the protection of which it had been constructed. Time had turned the tables.

But probably there had been an earlier, and unrecorded chapter in its history. We know that there had been in almost prehistoric times an Etruscan Dodecapolis established in the plain of the Po, and which reached down to the Adriatic, an offset of the original Dodecapolis between the Apennines and the Tyrrhenian sea. The inhabitants of these confederations of cities were the earliest known organizers of commerce in Europe. That they were great in maritime commerce implies this, for maritime commerce presupposes inland and overland trade. Now in those times tin and copper must have been among the most coveted articles of European commerce, because it was from a combination of them that the best tools and weapons then procurable were formed; and there is a very high degree of probability in favour of the supposition that Britain was even in those early days the chief source for the indispensable tin, and if of the tin, then almost necessarily of some of the copper at that time so abundantly used; and as we can hardly suppose that the way to Britain through the Pillars of Hercules was then used as a highway of commerce, we are almost driven to the conclusion that they were brought down to the shores of the Mediterranean by overland carriage. Some of the traffic may have centred at some port on the Gulf of Lyons, perhaps at the point which afterwards became Massilia, for of course it was an inland trade that supported the maritime commerce of Massilia, and made it rich and populous, and powerful. That part, however, of the traffic, of which the Etruscan Dodecapolis of the plain of the Po and of the Adriatic was the *entrepôt*, in all probability came over the Julier and the Septimer. In thinking of those remote times the necessity of the existence of a very considerable inland traffic has been almost entirely lost sight of. This was far the most potent agency then at work among the barbarians of Europe, precisely in the same manner as ocean commerce is in these days of ours far the most potent agency now at work over the whole world. We have many indications of it in the trade in gold as well as in that of tin and copper. These commodities were widely carried about, and very generally dispersed. This active and continuous traffic implies the existence of certain well-established, and regularly used routes. And all this reached far back beyond any historical traditions. The traffic in the bulky article of salt also must needs have been of equal antiquity. That the inhabitants of northern and central Europe were tribes of barbarians is no argument against the existence of these kinds of traffic. They did exist. And as to the people who carried them on being barbarians, whatever that might have amounted to, they were not such savages as the negroes of central Africa now are; and we know that they can appreciate the value of the ivory trade, and of that in ostrich feathers, and gold dust, which commodities, under the guidance of Arab, and Banian, and Nubian traders, they collect at stations and marts in the interior, to be furthered to the coast, and thence to be dispersed over the world. And this they did also in the time of the Pharaohs, three and four thousand years ago, as we know from still existing Egyptian sculptures and paintings. The ivory that was expended in the decoration of the palace of Ahab and of the kings of Assyria was doubtless procured from this source, and in this fashion. The barbarians, then, of central Europe, aided and instructed by Etruscan merchants, might, though perhaps we ought to use a stronger auxiliary, and say must, have done the same by the tin, and perhaps the copper, of Cornwall. And this way of the Septimer was in all probability the route a part of their trade in these articles took. If so it cannot have been but that Etruscan traders were in those times to be seen every year in Britain. They had landed at Dover. They had trafficked at the British *entrepôt* of Londinium. They must have had some kind of establishment there. They had not stopped there. They had gone on to the mines from which the tin was extracted, and had looked out on the western ocean from the Land's End.

As I walked down the Septimer, constructing in my mind this chain of inferences, I saw by my side the large-boned, sturdy Etruscan trader, overlooking his party of barbarian porters, loaded with tin and copper, and perhaps with some amber, which he had been twelve months, or more, in collecting, and which he had paid for with the gold jewelry, in the workmanship of which those Dodecapoleis were so skilful, and in later times perhaps with iron knives, and daggers, and spear and arrow-heads. Again this trade must have had established routes, and for the eastern Dodecapolis the most likely route must have been the Julier and the Septimer; and it must have had some organisers and managers, and it is in these cities that we must look for them.

Commerce, then, first traced this road. Of course

it must have had some halting stations, and *depôts*, and these could only have been at such places as Casaccia, Stalla, Molins, and Tiefenkasten. Some of these, doubtless, were fortified, and made capable of maintaining a small garrison against sudden attacks of barbarians, just like the forts of our Hudson's Bay Company. Then came its imperial days, when it connected the capital and heart of the world with a threatened frontier. But commerce has now taken other channels, and empire has established itself in other seats, and the barbarians have become the foremost nations of the world; and this road is only traversed occasionally by a few northern travellers, descended from the barbarians, or from the kindred of the barbarians, it was constructed to keep back, but who now have no other object in traversing it than to see deep valleys and lofty mountains. For many centuries change has everywhere else been actively at work, but the poor herdsmen who dwelt round about the Septimer remained in much the same condition as their predecessors of the old imperial and commercial periods of its history. Hitherto there had been little change for them. It was only yesterday that they were as hard-pressed and as poor as their remote forefathers had been. Their only resource was still their cows, and what little their cows enabled them to get of the products of sunnier valleys, and of the plains below. Human societies, however, are now entering on a new phase of their long progress, the distinguishing features of which are that culture is becoming accessible to all, even to the children of these herdsmen; that mind can now find a station, and a market anywhere; and that new avenues to obtaining the means of living are being opened on all sides to all men, who have the capacity and the will to enter upon them. And what is changing the rest of the world has not been unfelt up here. Many now go out from these valleys into the world, and after a time return with the proceeds of their labour and thrift. And, too, the outside world having advanced to a point which enables it to take an interest in the aspects which nature wears up here, sends hither, yearly, many visitors. This also supplies means of living to some. Life has, in consequence, become easy to many, and less hard and narrow to all. And these advantages, which are far from being altogether of a material kind, at all events they both rest on and lead on to, what is moral and intellectual, are year by year being extended to greater numbers.

As I walked down the single street of Casaccia the contrast it presented in externals to Cresta and Juf was felt to be great indeed; but when I entered the hotel the contrast between its interior and those with which I had yesterday and this morning become acquainted was felt to be greater still. To one coming from the mountains—it seemed as if one had been sojourning among them for a long time—its single reception room had an air even of amplitude and loftiness. One noticed, as one might something that is not seen every day, that chairs and sofas had taken the place of benches against the wall. Table linen, too, had reappeared, for the table was ready spread as far as the usual condiments and appliances go. This indicated the possibility of such a supper as would require such aid. In this house—it is often so with small inns in Italy, and Italian influences begin to be felt at Casaccia—there was no attempt to shunt the kitchen out of sight. Here it had to be passed through to reach the stone staircase that led up to the bedrooms. The landings and passages were spacious for the size of the house; and so in a still greater degree was the bedroom into which I was shown. It had two windows; but, as they were small and deep-recessed, they did not admit a sufficiency of light; and the ceiling and panelling being of a dark coloured pine-wood, this scanty allowance of light was not made the most of. There was about the room, and its contents, a look of newness from disuse, or rather of oldness kept new by disuse. It had three beds. These it was evident were not frequently required, for the bed-clothes had been put away beneath the mattresses; and the washing apparatus for the possible occupants of the three beds was all arranged on one of the deep-recessed window-sills, as if it was regarded rather as something to be looked at than used. This also led me to infer that the windows were seldom opened: an inference which was not contradicted by a kind of solidity and ancientness in the atmosphere of the room. The lock on the door was very un-Swiss, and very Italian. Everybody knows that every lock on every door of every bedroom in every hotel in Switzerland is a little plain black iron box applied to the surface of the door. Here it was a highly elaborated specimen of the locksmith's art : all open iron-work, with a marvellously large and complicated key, and an equally marvellous arrangement of bolts. For some little time I despaired of being able to discover how the key was to be inserted, or used ; and feared that, if I should succeed in turning it, I might not be able to turn it back again. Such a lock would not have been out of place on the door of some floridly decorated old Chapter House, or of the banqueting hall of some mediæval castle. The good man of the house assured me that the room should be arranged for me immediately. It was then five o'clock. It was, however, not till night had come down on Casaccia that this immediate arrangement was taken in hand. On that day, at all events, he was the only person who was in the house, and so he had to obtain from outside the female hands that were needed for the immediate arrangement. At last he impressed for this little service two of his neighbours—I suppose to atone for the delay by showing that he was ready to do all that was in his power, even more than was really needed.

As to the good man himself; in his making, as in

that of the lock, there was nothing Swiss. He was altogether unlike the hardy sturdy people I had been among lately. The loss of a few thousand feet of altitude had made a great difference in the elements of the human composition. His figure was tall, but not erect. His muscular tissue was soft. His features were large without being coarse. His hair and eyes were of a jet black, though in the latter there was none of that twinkling rapidity of motion, which is characteristic of the children of the south. His face was quite smooth. His complexion was the bloodless and untinted, but not unhealthy, white of many Italian women, and of some Italian men. He had none of the volubility of utterance, or quickness of manner of the Italian. On the contrary; his voice and manner were as smooth as his face. Smoothness, indeed, was his pervading characteristic. His smile was smooth, but it was the smile of manner, not of the heart, and indicated not pleasure, but the wish to please, or rather to make, and keep, things smooth. His dress even was smooth, and studiedly so. To him would have been intolerable anything so rough as Swiss homespun. His step was inaudible as he glided in and out of the room. What he did for you in placing things on the table, or removing them, was done as it were by the shadow of a man. He would have deemed it barbarous to have disturbed, he would have shrunk from disturbing, you even with a sound. His business was to assist, and to please. I had asked him what I could have for supper? He had replied with the gentlest tone, with a forward inclination of his body, and with a half smile, 'Whatever I pleased.' 'Could I have mutton cutlets?' 'Certainly.' 'In half an hour?' 'Certainly.' In an hour and a half the supper was placed noiselessly on the table. It was announced in the form that the cutlets were served. They proved, however, to be of veal, as doubtless he had foreknown that they would be; but it had seemed to him harsh to tell a man that he could not have what he wanted. In like manner it was now deemed unnecessary to call attention to any deviation from what had been promised and expected; or to say a word that might imply that anything could possibly be otherwise than as you had wished. Did not his manner give you to understand that he had done all, and would continue to do all, in his power to supply your wants, and to contribute to your comfort? Everything was said and done so smoothly, that it was impossible for you by an exhibition of surprise, or of dissatisfaction to break the spell of smoothness that had been cast over you. We affect bluntness, and even roughness, under the supposition that they indicate honesty and independence of character. The Italian—and this Casaccian was Italian in mind and manner—does not value the exhibition of these qualities. He affects gentleness, mildness, blandness both for their own sake, and because they are means to his ends. This is his idea of civilization; and it is what we, perhaps, may come to when our civilization shall have become as old as his. Our manners may, then, have become more soft, more pliant, more politic. The time may arrive when we too shall consider it uncivilized to say or do what will produce needless mental jars. Our present ideas may indicate that we are nearer than the Italians to the woods and caves.

CHAPTER VIII.

THE MALOJA—THE UPPER ENGADIN—PONTRESINA.

There's place and means for every man alive.—SHAKESPEARE.

AUGUST 10.—As I had undertaken to present myself to-day at Pontresina in time for an early dinner, I engaged a *char* at Casaccia to take me as far as St. Moritz; and having walked to the top of the Maloja, was there overtaken by it. The Maloja has an altitude of only 5,941 feet, which makes it the lowest of all the passes by which Italy may be entered from Switzerland. Its ascent from Casaccia is over an excellent road, with a rise of 1,150 feet, the latter part of which is through well-grown pine woods. I reached the summit so much in advance of my carriage as to have plenty of time for contemplating the backward view of the upper reach of the Bregaglia over the head of the forest—a view which was well worth the time.

The books tell us so much of the peculiarities, interest, and beauties of the Upper Engadin, that every one who goes to see it expects much; and I cannot think that there will be many of those who see it, who will feel any disappointment. In respect of length, and of capability for supporting human life, it may be equalled, or exceeded, by other Swiss Valleys, as for instance by those of the Rhine, of the Rhone, and of the Ticino, but there are other particulars of interest in which it leaves them all far behind. The great point is that it combines an elevation above the sea, which is elsewhere found to be but ill suited for supporting human life with an amount of population which would in any other valley be regarded as considerable; and that this large amount of population is evidently maintained in circumstances of comparative comfort. Beginning at the height just mentioned, it descends at first so gradually that at St. Moritz, twelve miles down the valley, the stream is only 150 feet below the summit of the Pass; while the town of St. Moritz itself, which is 300 feet above the stream, is actually 150 feet higher than the summit of the Pass. And in the sixty miles of its course from the Maloja to Martinsbruck it only loses 2,598 feet. The effect, too, of its actual elevation upon vegetable, and therefore, upon human life, must be somewhat aggravated by its direction, which being to the north-east exposes it to cold winds, and renders it, moreover, somewhat unfavourable for the reception of sunshine. And, then, its temperature is still further lowered by the contiguity on either side of many snowy summits. These conditions make in its upper parts all kinds of cultivation, except that of grass, almost impossible. I saw this day at St. Moritz, and a little above it, some few potato patches, but as in every instance the haulm of these had been killed back by recent midsummer frosts, nothing this year would be got from them but disappointment. Still I found this part of the valley surprisingly populous, for it contains what almost may be called a chain of little towns, in every one of which are several good houses, and in not one of which is there the slightest indication of any approach to pauperism. The absence, however, of this form of wretchedness might almost have been expected, because where the winter is eight or nine months long no family can exist which has not some assured means of living. But this does not explain the well-to-do condition you must infer is the lot of many, whose substantial and neatly kept houses you see in every one of these little towns. Nature you conclude at a glance is too niggard here to maintain so many well-to-do families; you begin then to inquire how they are maintained? Whence come their means? What are they living upon?

The answer to these questions is worth obtaining not only for the sake of what it will tell us of the history of these people's lives, but also because it will remind us of a change that is now coming over the whole world. These good people are living mainly upon capital, either upon the interest of capital invested in good securities, or upon the dividends of capital employed in such ventures as are open to them. This is a fact of Grison life to which reference has already been made, and to which we shall have to recur again. The reader is already aware that my companion, the circumnavigator, who was now seated by my side, was one of those who had failed in the Grison method of wooing fortune; but the owners of almost all these good houses had been successful wooers, for the good houses that belong to old Grison families are comparatively few. You pass a house which appears to be a goodly mansion. It covers a great deal of ground, is solidly built, and of two, or possibly of three, stories. It may not, however, be quite so large a dwelling-house as it looks, for the ground floor, or part of it, is perhaps a stable for half-a-dozen, or more, cows, and a couple of horses—these are seldom kept in outhouses. And this house may also contain a haystack sufficiently large to maintain these cows and horses for seven or eight months. Still after these deductions have been made it is a goodly house, and much ornamented, for its owner is proud of it; and the question arises, Whence came the money to purchase the land on which it stands, then to build it, then to buy the land which supplies the hay, and last, but not least, of all to support the family in comfort according to Engadin ideas? The money required for all this must have been a considerable sum, and the valley of the Inn has hitherto offered no opportunities for making such sums. In the particular case now before us it was all made by selling little cups of coffee, and still smaller glasses of liqueurs, at Paris. And before its owner could begin this small trade on his own account, he had to serve some years as waiter in an hotel; for he took no capital with him to Paris except the determination to get on. That was then all his stock in trade, but it was of such a kind as to be enough for the purpose. It was ultimately upon that foundation that the big house was built. His pecuniary savings began in the hotel. By the time he had learnt the ways and the language of the place, he had saved enough to commence the sale on his own account of the little cups of coffee, and smaller glasses of liqueurs. With what care must the cent or two that was made by each cup, or glass, have been guarded! How rarely were any of them spent in self-indulgence! It was self-indulgence enough to look forward to the house in the Engadin, with the thought that its owner would become one of the aristocracy of the valley; and to find at the end of the week that the life-supporting prospect—the ambition of a life, was so many francs nearer to realization. The next house was built by one who had rolled up his francs by vending little cakes, and small confectionery at Vienna. The process had been throughout the same. You inquire about a third with a coat of arms over the door, and gilt lattice at the window. Its owner climbed the ladder by becoming a *bon-bon* maker at Brussels. After half a life spent in unswerving fidelity to their single purpose these keen accumulators of small gains had made enough to enable them to take their ease for the rest of their days in Paris, Vienna, or Brussels; but that was not what they had been slaving and saving for. Of the 100,000 francs each of them had made, each invested the greater part in some good security, and the rest he expended in buying a piece of land, and in building a house, in that valley that has the climate of Iceland; and this house and land together with the money invested, which enables him to live in the house, is his unquestioned patent of nobility. In right of his manifestly achieved success he assumes his place in the aristocracy of the valley.

This is a spontaneously formed, and self-acting system. The distinction is real and substantial, and the way to it is open to all, and must be travelled by all who attain to the distinction, and none who travel it successfully can miss the distinction. With us it is different. Here there are many ways of making money, and but few only of those who have trodden successfully some one or other of the many ways attain to the splendid summits of society. It is not so in the Grisons. There the man who makes the money in the hard and humble way open to him, and builds the big house, and lives in it, becomes *ipso facto* a Grison grandee. He climbed up to his Herrship by a ladder that was very difficult to mount, but was equally accessible to all; and every one that climbs it enters the charmed circle. Enterprise, self-denial, and patience; great enterprise, for it is that in a penniless peasant to go out into the unknown world to compete with the natives of some great foreign city, unflinching self-denial, and heroical patience are the only course open to them. If the same mental stuff is needed for the making of the Cæsar of the village as of the Cæsar of the world, then we may suppose that under different circumstances, these men would have risen to eminence through higher paths. They were made of good stuff. We see in them men, who had their lot been cast here, would have become Lord Chancellors, Admirals, Generals, Statesmen, Scholars, merchant Princes, perhaps even Bishops.

But these successful builders of big houses are not all the people; and we must not allow their big houses to hide from our view the small houses of these little towns, and the small people who live in them. All men have not the same gifts; and of those who have all do not exercise them alike and to like issues. Many may have had the enterprise without the heroical self-denial and patience, which in some cases may mean a narrow horizon and a hard heart, but which narrow horizon and hard heart were necessary for success in the case of such small traffickers. And some, too, may have had the self-denial and the patience in heroical degrees, and not been deficient either in the requisite enterprise, but yet were kept back from turning these qualities to good account by the goodness of their hearts. That may have kept them at home to provide for, and to tend, an aged parent in his chair-days; or an early affection may have influenced them to the same result. And so possibly there may be as good stuff, intellectually and morally, among those who have never left the village as among those who went forth into the world, and prospered. Chance, too, has a place in the affairs of men. Good fortune does not always mean good conduct, nor bad fortune bad conduct. Conduct that was both wise and good may have had ill-fortuned results. But we will set these cases aside, and ask if those who, because they stayed at home for good reasons, and so are now in no better condition than their fathers were, and those who went forth and prospered, find in any sense their rewards equal? Certainly not, if both of them measure, as the world does, all things by francs. Still each has his reward, and the reward of satisfied affections, and of a satisfied sense of duty, is great as it is felt at the moment, for at that time every consideration gives way to it; and it is great also in retrospect, which is the recalling of the feelings of that moment. We are glad, then, to witness the success of those who made the francs, and built the stone houses, and to talk with them of their experiences of the world in which the francs were made; but this does not diminish our respect for those who stayed at home, and who will live, and toil, and die in the same small wooden *châlets* in which their fathers lived, and toiled, and died. Indeed, our respect for them, and even our disposition to like them, are rather increased by the sight of the big mansions of the lemonade, and bon-bon, and coffee and confectionery lords.

So much in explanation of the big houses we find not only in the Engadin, but more or less in all the Grison valleys. We now come to the valley itself. The sun on this day was unclouded; but we were on the road from the Maloja to St. Moritz; these words, therefore, must not be taken to mean what they would stand for had they been said of a drive from Bath to Bristol. We all know what a cloudless day is here in the middle of August: in the Upper Engadin it is not quite the same sort of thing. With respect to what meets the eye: there is no trace of haze; the definition of every mountain and glacier outline is sharp and clear; the luminous blue is not blue, or luminous, in our subdued fashion; and even the greens and grays of the mountains are hardly less green and gray quite up to the distant sky-line. There is little toning down. Distance only blends the local variegation into an uniform colour. You cannot make out the variegation of the flowery turf, of the lichen-painted rock, and of the glancing foliage and shaded trunks of the forest, on account of the distance: that is all. The distance as it were fuses together the smaller differences; and then it puts a varnish over the whole: the clear bright air is the varnish. Then as to the appeal this diaphanous rarefied air makes to the sense of feeling : though, indeed, it is not air; that is a word that here would mislead ; it is a celestial ether ; and so with the sun, though it is hot, what you feel is not heat; it is a permeating, invigorating, life-creating warmth ; this warmth, then, which the sun imparts to this ether, pervades your lungs, your heart, and reaches to your very bones. It makes you conscious of a lighter, and of a quicker life than you ever felt before. Like the air of the desert it so rapidly, so instantaneously evaporates the imperceptible perspiration that the skin beneath your clothes as well as that of your face develops a new sensation. It has ceased to be merely a tough, half-dead integument, whose function is just to protect you from external rubs. As the flower expands to the light, and turns to it, from the satisfaction it has in absorbing it, so your skin has become sensitive to this ether, and feels the delight of being in contact with it. And a third sense has yet to be gladdened. Up here it is now the middle of hay harvest, and the air is pervaded with the fragrance of the new hay. And you are all the way passing by, or through, pine-forests, and the bright sun is constantly raising into the air from their trunks, branches, and leaves myriad molecules of their resinous exudations ; and this perfume also is wafted to you.

And then the scene has its peculiar features. In these twelve miles you pass four lakes ; the small lake of the Maloja summit, the Silser see, four and a half miles long, the Silva Planer see somewhat longer, and that of St. Moritz about a mile in length. Thus, throughout almost all the way, you are driving along this chain of lakes, on a road a little above them. Of the colour of these mountain lakes our English home-trained eyes know nothing. It must be seen to be understood. It is of the blue of the sky, only a shade less deep, and with some slight admixture of green. You wonder what the trout that live in them can find to live upon in water so pure, and which, in truth, is not water, but the lymph of the celestial depths—heaven's azure liquefied. Everyone feels the charm of water as an addition to the scene : but such lakes as these, which are not of water, but of some less earthly fluid, how great is the charm they add to this scene ! And the more so, if you have come upon them suddenly after some days of trudging and toiling in the mountains, where the eyes were wearied, almost wounded, with the continual recurrence of pinnacles and precipices, rocks and ravines, nothing but what was hard, dark, jagged, and torn. The impressions of sombreness, ruggedness, and terror that had of late been stamped on your brain, and seemed to be in it like things that were alive, are now laid to rest by the sight of the smooth blue : its effects are soothing and healing.

Another peculiarity of this road is the number of glaciers and snow summits that are seen from it. Of these, too, as it is with the blue lakes, you are hardly ever out of sight. You come abreast of a lateral valley; and as you look up it you see at its head a mighty glacier, the view of which seems so complete that you think you can make out its whole course, that is to say its whole life, from the snowfield out of which it is compacted, and by which it is forced on, till at last it issues, in another form, from its own mouth. Or a range before you recedes a little, or becomes depressed a little, and you see at this point a mighty snow-capped giant from behind peering over into the valley; and you feel the current of crisp air that is flowing down into the valley from the glacier, or from the giant's head—the breath of the glacier, or of the giant. And in the twelve miles you pass as many towns as you do lakes; one for every three miles: all clean, and flourishing: and not a dilapidated hovel in a land where nothing is grown but grass, and where there are nine months of winter and three of cold, with the exception of a few such days as was to-day! This absence of visible poverty adds much to the sense of satisfaction with which you contemplate the scene. Nature here has made it difficult for man to live upon his fellow man, for a man, under the conditions here imposed upon him, can hardly do more than support himself. Of course three-fourths of the population might be cleared off, and half the quantity of cattle maintained; but that is not the turn things took here. Every man, excepting the capitalists we have already spoken of, and no one grudges them their hard-earned accumulations, which besides do good to some, and no harm to anyone, everyone, excepting them, must work hard to live ; but to live here by his hard work a man must himself have the fruits of it.

The direction in which the stream by your side is flowing is often an ingredient in the thought of the wanderer among these mountains of central Europe. 'This stream,' he says to himself, ' is hurrying to join the Po, or the Rhine, or the Rhone.' On this day I said to myself, ' These charming lakes are among the head waters of the Danube.' The little stream we passed as it came racing down from Monte Lunghino into the Silser see is the furthest urn of the Inn. This makes you feel that you have passed into another region. The continent is now inclining in another direction. The Danube, and the Black Sea for a time become the goal of your thoughts of this kind. In this respect Lunghino along the eastern roots of which I was now passing, and the opposite side of which I had traversed yesterday, is pre-eminent, for it contains the diffluent urns of three great historic rivers, the Rhine, the Po, and the Danube ; of the Rhine by giving birth to one of the feeders of the Oberhalbstein stream, of the Po by giving birth to a feeder of the Maira, which joins the Adda as it is on the point of entering the lake of Como, and of the Danube by giving birth to the actual head water of the Inn.

A little more than a mile before you reach St. Moritz, you look down on the old monster Kurhaus, and a new and more monstrous one nearly completed. They are upon the alluvial flat at the head of the lake. As I saw by my side a patch or two of potatoes smitten by summer frosts, I thought it strange that any people, possessed of free agency, especially invalids, could be found to descend into, and to stay in, such a place. With what ice-cold vapour must the evaporation from that alluvial bottom load the air so soon in the afternoon as the sun is off the ground, and down there they cannot have much of him! And how cutting must the cold wind be down there! Is there anything that can compensate for these evils? I doubt much whether mineral waters can that sometimes are in fashion, and sometimes are forsaken. But there will always be plenty of people who will try anything of this kind, and there will always be some who will endeavour to persuade people to resort to such supposed remedies. One would like to know what is the proportion of people who go to these places a second time, not for the sake of the society they expect to find at them, but for the sake of the waters ; and whether the proportion of actual cures is much greater than of the cures effected by touching the bones, or the old clothes, of some supposed saint. If after two or three weeks at such a place as this a man finds himself no worse than when he reached it, he may infer that after all his system is not so far enfeebled but that air, exercise, and diet may do something for him.

The above wayside remark is made subject to correction from those who thoroughly understand these subjects. There is, however, another way of looking at this charming lake, with the green forest that descends to it from the opposite mountain, and beyond the lake the valley opening up to Pontresina, and with the long varied vistas up and down the main valley, and with the little town of St. Moritz, perched on its niche on the mountain side, close before you. There is so much variety, so many objects, so much colour, and everything is so clear and fresh, and so bright in the sunshine, that you can hardly think the scene belongs to the same world as you are accustomed to at home. It hardly looks real, the difference is so great. It looks like something got up to please and astonish you, and in this it quite succeeds.

We reached the Post *bureau* of St. Moritz at 11.30, and started at once for Pontresina, the Australian having shouldered my *sac*, or—to be accurate—having taken it in his hand, for from a feeling of self-respect he would never shoulder it in a town, lest this method of carrying it might lead to the degrading inference that he was a professional. The walk was a pleasant one of about four miles down to and across the Inn, along the lake side, and through woods and meadows. I was just in time to save my engagement. Of course everybody knows that time was made for slaves, but sometimes it is pleasant to be punctual, for instance when a long business, subject throughout to a variety of circumstances, has been brought to a close at a prearranged moment, for then you may fancy that it is you who are master of time and of yourself.

As I parted with the Australian he was sufficiently professional to ask for more than he had agreed to serve me for plus the present I added to the agreement. This demand I did not decline to comply with, for had I not now reached my destination for the time with some treasure of memorable sights and of pleasant thoughts for myself, and how could our journeyings benefit him except in this way of francs? And why by withstanding his request for more should I ruffle my companion, or be ruffled myself? Besides, too, in our last four miles I had begun to think him less burdensome, or more tolerable, than he had appeared to me at any time previously. In those four miles he had again, as he had frequently done on other occasions (but as now I was about to see him no more the incongruity seemed rather amusing than shocking) called the ravines gullies, the forest bush, my *sac* the swag, and the glaciers—how horrible, but how explicable in such a circumnavigator—the icebergs! And so after all we parted amicably, as it is best that people should, and with reciprocal expressions of good wishes for each other's welfare.

Pontresina consists of a long narrow street. At its northern extremity, by which those arriving from the Engadin enter it, the first building you pass is one of its two large hotels. The other is at its southern extremity. A few hundred yards beyond this is a second little town, Upper Pontresina, with its hotel. The two will soon be united into one long unbroken street of about a mile in length. This street is crowded at most hours of the day. There are people returning from their forenoon excursions, and others starting for their afternoon excursions. People arriving from, or leaving for the near towns of the Engadin, or from or for Italy by the Bernina Pass. After the early dinner, which had regulated my movements throughout the forenoon, and indeed for some days back, my wife and her little boy took me in hand, to introduce me to the sights of the place. 'There is the Roseg valley, and the Roseg glacier, with such and such peaks above it.' These could be seen from Pontresina. 'We will take you there to-morrow. This afternoon we will go along the main valley, and give you a look at the Morterasch.' And that was what they did. The road, like the street, only in a less degree, was alive with parties coming and going, for it is not only the way to the Morterasch and Bernina, but also the route to Italy by Poschiavo and Tirano. The evening was closing in when we returned to Pontresina. The crowd in the single street had now in the neighbourhood of the

Post *bureau* become almost a block. In the crowd I met an Englishman I had seen in the morning at Casaccia. His air was distracted. He had been for some time in search of a place to shelter him for the night, but was everywhere told the same story, that his search would be hopeless: even every landing and passage in every private house, where a shake-down could be placed, was already bespoken.

Bewildering was the stir in the narrow street. There were many Germans, but the English including the Americans, or as they might put it, the Americans including the English, were largely in the majority. The peculiarity of the crowd was that it included many children, and almost as many ladies as gentlemen. What was it that had brought together this concourse of people from many nations, and even from the New World? It was simply to see glaciers. The glaciers had been there from time before history, from the time, it may be, that man had trod the soil of Europe: it is scarcely, however, a dozen years since such crowds began to assemble here to see them. This indicates new thoughts and new sentiments about the world we live in, as well as an increase of wealth and of facilities for locomotion. It was never so seen of old times. In our fathers' times men and women flocked to London and Paris, as they had done in the old world to Rome, to see and to be seen. Society was the great attraction. For a little time a few had been attracted to Athens, because it was the centre of art, of culture, and of refinement, but that was a dawn of promise that was soon overcast. For some thousand years before that dawn so soon obscured, the greatest annual gatherings of men had been at Egyptian Thebes. The object, however, which had brought them together there had been the exchange of the commodities of Asia and of Africa. The attraction was first commerce, then social dissipation. Here men are brought together in a lofty Alpine valley, too cold to grow a potato, where there is no trade, and no society, to see mountains and glaciers. This is a higher, because a purely intellectual, purpose. In the first gatherings of the young world only one class of men took part, merchants and traders. In the next mainly those who had riches and nothing to do. Here we have, without excluding the rich, men of all professions, mostly not rich, and many of them with plenty to do. They come in multitudes; and the cry is still, 'they come,' that is in yearly increasing multitudes.

But the impulse that has carried the world to Pontresina, will not stop at Pontresina. At no distant day the children of these summer-tourists, when locomotion shall have been still further improved, will cross oceans for their summer excursions, and will climb the Andes, and the Himalaya, as their children may the Mountains of the Moon, going perhaps by the Soudan railway we now hear is in contemplation, and taking the sources of the Nile by the way.

People will not for ever, now that they have begun to look out on the world, be content with the moderate altitudes, and the sombre, monotonous pine woods of central Europe. The appetite for seeing nature is one that grows with what it feeds on. Those who have found pleasurable emotions result from seeing Switzerland will wish to see something more of this glorious world. They will long to become acquainted with grander mountain ranges, with nobler and more diversified faunas and floras than those of our temperate zone, and with other conditions and forms of human life than those which obtain among a portion of our near kindred circumstanced not very dissimilarly from ourselves.

The history of the recent spread of the love now so widely felt for nature is interesting and instructive. Clearly it had its rise in that increase in the knowledge of nature which belongs to our times. It is, however, obvious that it is not confined to those who have this knowledge in the form and degree which would entitle it to be regarded as scientific. They are few, but the desire is felt by many, almost, indeed, by all who have received any culture worthy of the name. It seems, therefore, to have spread from the few to the many by a kind of infection, which shows that it is a natural taste, which former conditions kept in a state of repression. From what we see we may conclude that the acquisition and possession of the images and ideas, which the contemplation, or if that is too strong a word for the case of those who have been debarred from any scientific acquaintance with nature, then which the mere sight of the forms and phenomena of nature supplies to the mind, is a source of delight. Of course, the delight would be far greater, had the previous knowledge been wider and deeper, that is to say had the mind been better fitted for the reception of the images and ideas; but still it is felt, and so strongly as to give rise to a desire for more extended fields of observation. Even in old times there are indications of this pleasure having been felt. It was not absent from the awe and wonder which accompanied the observation of the starry firmament, and of the phenomena of the great deep, or from the attempt to co-ordinate the details of the natural scene as depicted in the hundred and fourth Psalm. Solomon's collection of facts and observations about animals and plants—for his works on these subjects must have been something of this kind—was suggested by this pleasure. And as these emotions had such issues among the ancient Hebrews, we cannot suppose that their kindred neighbours were strangers to them. We know, too, that by the Greeks and Romans they were still more strongly felt. From these early observations and impressions, accompanied by pleasurable emotions, as from a small germ, but one that was full of vital power, has arisen the distinctly aimed effort to grasp in one intelligible whole all the phenomena and forces of nature, and all the forms of life the world has to show us. What was long ago dimly divined is now clearly understood that the world, and all it contains, are very good; that precisely it, and nothing else is the great external gift of God to man—man's great inheritance; and that it is only by seeing it, and understanding it, that he can enter on the possession of it: for there is no other way in which he can make it his own.

But the picture which the world presents to us for contemplation is not composed merely of land and water, ranging through different zones, with their respective floras and faunas, and physical phenomena: the soul of the picture is the observer himself—man; not the individual observer, but the race. Man it is that imparts dramatic life and interest to the picture. Not that this globe is without a progress, that is a history, of its own. It has that, but its history is devoid of the highest element of interest, that is the moral element. It is by viewing the world in connexion with man that the picture becomes invested with this, the highest source of interest. And if an extended view of the world, inclusive of man's place in it, and relation to it, be taken, whether the extension be in the direction of space, or of time, it will be seen in each view with equal clearness—and the inference from one view proves and confirms the inference from the other, for they are identical—that in the long drama of human history it is increase in the knowledge of nature which has led to increase in man's dominion over nature, and it is increase in his dominion over nature which has led on to, and given rise to, those conditions which have resulted in a richer and higher moral life.

CHAPTER IX.

ROSEG GLACIER—PIZ LANGUARD—LA PISCHA—MORTERASCH GLACIER—PONTRESINA.

> Ah! that such beauty varying in the light
> Of living nature, cannot be portrayed
> By words, nor by the pencil's silent skill;
> But is the property of him alone,
> Who hath beheld it, noted it with care,
> And in his mind recorded it with love.—WORDSWORTH.

August 11.—At 8.30 A.M. got under weigh for the Roseg glacier, piloted by my two new guides. The morning was bright, the air quiet and fresh, and everything level to their wish that what they had to show might be seen to the best advantage. As you turn your back on Pontresina, and cross the rocky channel of the Bernina Bach, which carries off the outflow of the eastern and northern sides of the Bernina group, you command the upward view of the valley of the Roseg. It is not of the narrow ravine kind, but has some little space of wooded bottom, generally open enough to afford a little pasturage. You are 6,000 feet above the sea; the forest, therefore, is composed of larch and cembra. On either side are grand mountains. The western is steeper than the eastern wall, and is still in the morning sun. The eye ranges over the valley to rest on the great snow-field at its head, which commences its rise at a distance from you of six miles. It is of the purest white, and this is not to any great extent scarred and broken by protruding rocks and summits, for the naked rock faces of its ridges look not in this, but in the opposite, or southern, direction. It closes the head of the valley, and is a wide field that satisfies the eye with its amplitude of expansion, its pure white, and its majestic rise to the sky-line.

A walk of five miles through the forest brings you to a little plain, which is evidently the site of an old lake long since filled up with glacier *débris*. At the near end of this is a little inn, kept by a little Frenchman, who will talk to you about the empire, the commune, and the republic, but with some reserve. At the further end, about half a mile off, is the foot of the glacier. My guides, in the exercise of a wise discretion, did not take me upon the glacier itself, but by a path along the flank of Piz Corvatsch, for about a mile or more, to a very commanding position, a little beyond the *châlet* of the alpe. This point, which is sufficiently above the glacier, is opposite to a dark protruding eminence in it, yclept Agagliouls, below which its two main ice-streams meet. And here, like the Lord Thomas and fair Annet of the ballad we sat a while on a hill. They sat all day; and when night was come, and sun was set, they had not talked their fill. We, not having the excuse they had for being forgetful of time, after half an hour began to retrace our steps, though we had hardly looked our fill. Still we had looked enough to be able to carry away with us a mental picture, that might be recalled at will, of the topography and aspects of the grand scene—the widespread uptilted snowfield, and its component parts, and the named summits, and their relations to each other, and respective effects on the whole, and upon the glacier in particular, which is the outcome of the whole. A peculiarity of this scene is its bounded completeness. It does not in any direction suggest the infinite, as it might if you were on a central, or commanding eminence, with snowy heights all around you, reaching away to distant horizons. It has near, definite boundaries. You seem to take in the whole of it, when it is looked at from our to-day's point of observation; and when looked at from Pontresina, as all other objects are there excluded from your view, the effect is almost that of a picture set in a frame. One marked feature of the scene, from our point of observation on Piz Corvatsch, is the lofty, precipitous, slate-coloured, *couloir*-streaked Piz Tschierva, with its dark hanging glaciers. It bounds our snowfield on the north.

As we returned we made a requisition for our dinner on the resources of the expatriated Parisian, the victim of political instability. It was verging towards evening, when, after a day of pleasant loitering, we again found ourselves at Pontresina. The greater part of the evening I spent in a long discussion with the head of one of the old patroon families of what was once New Amsterdam, and is now New York, on the suitableness, or the reverse, of the principle of free trade to the present industrial condition of the United States. Of course the logic of neither had any effect on the other.

August 12.—Out at a few minutes before 5 A.M. We contemplated the ascent of the Piz Languard, and whatever else the day might admit of our doing. The masons and carpenters employed in building on our side of the road a large new hotel, and on the opposite side a *dépendance* to the existing hotel, were already seated around on pieces of timber, and heaps of stones, waiting for the moment when they were to commence the labours of the day. The horse that was to carry the little man as far as the foot of the cone, and the guide we had engaged for the day, arrived as we were emerging from the door of President Saratz's house, in which we had been so fortunate as to obtain our lodgings, and we were started by the clock of the church across the street striking the hour. Upper Pontresina was soon passed by our taking a short cut up to the forest through a prairie or two, from which the hay had just been carried. The ascent may be roughly divided into three stages, each requiring about an hour. The first is through the forest, and is somewhat toilsome.

The second lies beyond the trees, and is about an hour more of open, rocky, bleak, not steep Alpine pasture, along and up the valley of the Languard. Then an hour of stiff climbing up the cone by a grandly irregular mountain staircase. Here steps have been made in the rock, here slabs of rock have been fixed for steps, here an impracticable rock so barred the way that the path had to take half the circuit of it before the staircase could again ascend. All this is on a perfectly naked, precipitously steep incline—truly the side of a mountain cone.

The summit which is sufficiently level affords standing and sitting space for perhaps half a dozen parties. There might have been as many upon it before we left it. It is composed of huge blocks and slabs of rock tossed together in disorder, but so as to give many natural seats, and some shelter from wind.

But what of the view? On this morning it was not seen to the most advantage. There were clouds rising from many of the valleys; and these, though they were neither continuous, nor fixed, interfered much with the view, for they obliged us to watch for an opportunity for seeing all that was to be seen in any direction, and made it throughout impossible to see the whole panorama connectedly at a single glance round. In time, however, we managed to see the whole in detail, so as to be able to put it together in the mind. The view takes its character very much from that of the region. It is the peculiarity of this region, as compared with other great mountain districts of Switzerland, that, while the mountain tops are not so lofty as elsewhere, the valleys are far loftier. For instance, the Finster-Aarhorn rises to an altitude of 14,026 feet, Monte Rosa of 15,364, Mont Blanc of 15,781, but the Piz Bernina, the loftiest of the surrounding heights, rises only to an altitude of 13,294. And if the small group to which the Piz Bernina belongs be excepted, the height of but few of the summits of the encircling ranges is greater than the 10,715 of the Piz Languard itself, that is to say of your point of view. And as to the valleys: while Interlaken is depressed to 1,863 feet, Brieg to 2,244, and Chamouni to 3,445, St. Moritz and Campfer, the only points in the valley of the Engadin visible from our observatory, do not descend below 6,000 feet. Here, therefore, we have to look at a ring of lower mountains springing from a far higher level. The consequence of this is that they have not sufficient altitude to develop any very marked peculiarities of form. This will be seen at a glance by comparing any part of the panorama of this view with any other: the two will resemble each other very closely. And if the whole view be compared with that from the Gorner Grat, the Eggischhorn, or the Rigi, its general sameness will be again perceived. What we here have is a multitude of apparently small summits, a large proportion of which are snow-capped, but none of which are distinctly featured; and they all appear to be at about our own level. The effect is almost the same as that of an agitated sea, the waves of which are of about the same height, and many of them crested with foaming white. The only exception to this is the Bernina group close by, into which you look: but even here the summits which stand out of the snowfield appear to have no striking varieties of form. There are no Wetterhorns and Shrekhorns, and Finster-Aarhorns, no Weisshorns and Matterhorns among them. What in this group is really grand, and which we saw well to-day, is that the whole of the snowfield that is visible from right to left, and from above, converges to the Morterasch glacier. There is in this the unity of a picture. It is held up to you who are on the Piz Languard, to be looked at, just as a picture might be, and just at the right distance for taking in the details of such a picture. It has the completeness, limitation and definiteness, which, from this side, belong to views of this group. And, too, its pure field of unsullied white, contrasts well with the dark rusty brown of the cliffs and ravines immediately around and below you, which are themselves one of the most striking and interesting features of this view from the Piz Languard. They are the foreground, and have an impressive and awe-inspiring aspect. Beyond them, all round the horizon, excepting the Bernina group, is the ocean of petrified waves, many crested with petrified foam. Just in one place an opening enables you to look down on St. Moritz and Campfer, the only point in the vast panorama, at which you can find a trace of man, and of his works — all the rest is but mountain summits innumerable, a world to the utmost horizon of rock and snow.

In descending the cone, you may find near the foot of it a low inconspicuous signboard, not two feet out of the ground, as if it had been intended that it should escape observation. On it is inscribed the word Bormio. The little man, who, during his stay at Pontresina, had been constructing in his mind a map of the neighbourhood, knew very well what this meant. It pointed in the direction of the Pischa Pass to the Val del Fain. There below us, to the left, was the Western spur of the snowfield of the Pass; and snow appears to have an irresistible attraction for youthful minds, as it has also for feminine in the Alps. A debate, therefore, instantly commenced whether it would not be better to take to the snow. In this debate I did not join, in order that the other members of the party might decide for themselves according to their own wishes, and their own estimates of their own powers. I had, however, no doubt of what the decision would be. It took but a little moment to arrive at it; and then we turned our backs on Pontresina, and made for the snow. First we had to get to the bottom of the valley: that was quickly done; and then to ascend it to the snow over blocks and fragments of rock, each of which was as clean as if it had been boiled in caustic lye. They were also so tightly jammed together, that you might walk a hundred yards, or more, upon them without one slipping, or so much as moving, under your feet. How came they to be of so clean a surface, and so tightly fixed together? They are clean because there is little up here to soil them—no dirt, no dust; and being buried deeply in winter and spring under the snow, there is not much chance for lichens to form upon them; and whatever soil, or stain, might commence to adhere to them, is washed away when the snow is melting in the spring. And as to their being so firmly fixed together, I believe that is a consequence of their being every year rammed together by a rammer, that has to a London paviour's the ratio of Nasmyth's steam-hammer to a blacksmith's. And this rammer that is brought into operation here is that of the avalanches that break away from the overhanging heights. They fall on these streams and beds of fragments of rock with hundred ton blows, compressing and jamming them together, when the blow is direct, and, when they slide, sweeping off the pieces that cannot be infixed in the compacted mass.

After the clean macadamized rocks came the snow: first about three-quarters of a mile of gradual ascent; and then, when the actual Pass was reached, a steep incline of snow up the mountain on the right, and on the left a more level field on a lower stage. The two were separated by a kind of ridge of snow about

250 yards long. A slip from this to the lower stage would have been easy, and might have been serious: there was, however, footing enough on the ridge, if only you would look where you were going to set your foot, and not at the lower snowfield. From this we stepped off to a glacier on our right; the glacier of the Val del Fain, or Heuthal. It is of no great length, and is uncrevassed, but has rather too great an incline for direct descent: we, therefore, took it diagonally. The stream from the glacier is not seen to issue from it, but as you walk over the stream of rocks, that continues the stream of ice, you hear the stream of water rushing by beneath your feet. The books I see say that this is a Pass for experienced mountaineers; I should rather say that, when it is as it was this day, it is a charming bit for lady beginners, who have got so far as to know that they can, under not very trying circumstances, trust to their feet and heads.

Having left the glacier you find yourself in a depressed area of some little extent surrounded with jagged summits, on which, wherever it can find a lodgment, snow is resting. The central area is not flat, but composed of knolls and pools. As we were standing on one of these knolls—it had a flattened top—noticing how hard, and cold, and dead, was everything around us, we espied at our feet, growing here and there on the scaly rubble on which we were treading, several plants of the *Aretia Glacialis*. To find unexpectedly upon such a surface, and with such surroundings, so charming a form of life could not but give a little thrill of pleasure. Each plant was a compact round patch of mossy foliage, singularly even and smooth, and firmly set together, perhaps half an inch high, and two or three inches in diameter. Out of this little green cushion stood up about a dozen, or more, little pearl-coloured stars, not in one cluster, or in several, but each star singly on its own stem. The pearl-coloured stars were interspersed with some that were of a waxy white. The pearl-colour was the hue of youth, freshness, and vigour; the white told of age and incipient decay. This discovery led to our looking about for something more; and our search was rewarded, for on the next knoll we found several tufts —that is the shape it assumes up here—of the golden dwarf *Papaver Pyrenaicum*. These two lovely plants did not on this day waste their beauty on the desolate scene. Their flowers are now gone, and they are themselves buried in snow; but what they were on that August day still lives in the mind. The little pearly stars, and the golden cups, have still an existence. Their form and colour, now that they are creatures of the brain, are the same as they were while they were expanded on the shaly knoll, protruded through the snow, on the top of the Pischa, quickened by the warmth, and drinking in the light, of the sun that was smiling on them. There, too, in the brain, they must have some substance, for creatures of the brain must be of the substance of the brain. The difference is that now they exist in another medium, and are cognisable by another sense; but in that new medium they still have their original form and colour, and still possess the power of giving pleasure.

If then any lady beginner in Alpinism shall have been brought here by a desire to add to her Alpine mementos these two plants (I left them undisturbed), gathered after such a walk, and on such a spot; she will find, after she has secured her mementos, that what she has next to do is to effect her descent into the Val del Fain. The first stage of the descent will be found somewhat steep, and very incoherent. We, having done this piece, and reached the turf-grown side of the mountain, instead of continuing straight down into the valley below, along the bottom of which lies the path to the Bernina House (not the Hospice), descended the flank of the long mountain diagonally from the point where we first came out on its side all the way to the Bernina House. It is worth while to take the Val del Fain in this fashion, because, although it may give you somewhat rougher work, the added amount of rougher work will be repaid tenfold by the astonishing variety of beautiful flowers you will see on the mountain flank. The stations, as botanists call them, vary much, the ground being sometimes wet, and sometimes dry, sometimes good and deep, and sometimes shallow and stony. Indeed, this valley is celebrated for its flowers; and I am acquainted with no other in which they may be found in greater variety and profusion. As we approached the Bernina House—about half a mile from it—the air was loaded with perfume. The *Edelweiss* abounds on these ridges. Some days back, my two unprofessional Pontresina guides had found many specimens of it up the valley, only at a point further up than we were to-day. While we were at dinner at the Bernina House our professional guide ascended in search of it the dark cliffs at the back of the house, beyond the stream, and was not long in returning with a large *bouquet.*

The dinner just mentioned we had earned, for we had been on the move since 5 A.M., and in that time had ascended the Piz Languard, and crossed La Pischa. Nor was the dinner unequal to such antecedents; for it consisted of trout, beefsteaks, Poschiavo potatoes, Valtelline wine, *omelette aux confitures*, a *compote* of pears, and cream at discretion. The charge for this for three persons, was 9 francs, 20 cents. I give these particulars because it is a kind of ingratitude, when you have been treated well at an inn, not to have a word to say upon the subject. After you have paid your bill, the only way in which you can encourage well-doing of this kind, and make a return for the good services by which you have been benefited, is to make them known.

We now set our faces towards Pontresina—somewhat more than 5 miles distant. Our way lay along the excellent Bernina post-road. At about a mile, or a little more, from the inn we were abreast of the falls of the Bernina. As the rest of the party knew the road well, having this summer, and last, made many excursions along it, I here left them to find their way home, while I diverged from the road to see the falls, and to get a near view of the lower part of the Morterasch glacier. As to the falls: the rocks over and upon which the stream tumbles being in unusually large blocks and slabs, and of a dark colour, and the tumbling water being much broken, and in consequence very white, and the overhanging larch being of a tender green, make them a favourite bit with painters, and on this sunny day there were several easels beside them. As to the glacier: it has a very distinctive character. The point of view from which I was now looking at it was a rock just above the last trees on the mountain side. Here it has the appearance of descending by a rapid and short course (in fact, however, it has a descent of 7 miles), from the snow-clad ridges above you, which, as seen from this point, do not appear of commanding elevation, nor do they present any very distinguishing features. The characteristics of the glacier are its breadth and massiveness. At the point I took for viewing it, its eastern half was hid from sight by an enormous central *moraine*. As I afterwards saw from the road this enormous *moraine* assumed on the lower part of the glacier the form of a Brobdingnagian Ray or

Skate, with its tail upwards, and its broad shoulders just reaching to the termination of the glacier. As you continue your contemplation of the scene, you may fancy that you are taking in at a few glances the whole life and history of the glacier, from its first beginnings on those heights, throughout its course opposite to where you are seated, and down to its termination at the head of the small filled-up lake you crossed, as you were coming up through the wood below you. As to its termination at the head of the old filled-up lake, that alone is well worth turning out of the road to see; for this is not a glacier which thins out, and dies away feebly, as the fashion of some is, but is one of those which end grandly and abruptly: few, indeed, more so, for it emphasizes the conclusion of its course with perpendicular ice-cliffs some 200, or more, feet high. This near view I have been speaking of must necessarily be very incomplete, but you will to some extent be able to supplement its incompleteness by what you will see of the glacier from the road, and by the general survey of it you will take from the top of the Piz Languard.

I got back to Pontresina at 5 P.M., having been out twelve hours. This may seem a long day to those who are killing themselves by their sedentary habits. But if a lady, and a child who had not yet numbered as many years as these hours, could go through it without suffering that amount of fatigue which is implied by the expression of 'being knocked up,' we may be sure that a great many of those who might pronounce it beyond their powers, would be very well able to do it ; and would be all the better for a month's excursion, which would give them such a day once a week. Such a month every year might perhaps add a dozen years to their lives, and enable them to do each year a great deal more than they will ever otherwise be equal to, and to do it better.

Our guide of this day was a young man by trade a carpenter. He told us that it was his intention, in accordance with the Grison custom, to go abroad for some years. His plans were already arranged. At the end of the summer he was to start for Chicago, where he understood that a great deal of building was going on. He hoped that he should be able to make and save some money, and, while so employed, to learn English ; with which money and language he further hoped in some half dozen years to return to Pontresina. How strangely do things come about, and combine ! Here we have a Grison peasant going to the New World to learn English, and a fire in a town on the border of Lake Michigan, at a spot where, in the memory of people still living, the buffalo quenched his thirst, creating for him an opening for going. But, then, this peasant can read and write, and so can his neighbours : had it been otherwise, he never would have comprehended the advantages, or imagined the possibility, of his learning English ; and never would have known anything about Chicago, and its fires; much less have been able to plan how he might turn the possibilities of the place to his own account. And this is only a particular instance of a wide general fact. The whole world is now in a very practical sense becoming the stage for the activity of all who are capable of doing its work; and in every field those who are better qualified will push aside those who are not so well qualified. For a long time this has been exemplified by the Scotch. Scotchmen were to be found not only in every large town in England, but in India, China, the West Indies, and more or less all over the world. So is it now beginning to be with the Germans. They are spreading themselves over the whole of the commercial world. They are to be found in this country, and in all countries, wherever any business is to be transacted. The reason is again the same. Germany is not favoured by nature with a rich soil, with any great variety of produce, or with good harbours: what is giving its people so large a share in the business of the world is that they have endeavoured to fit themselves for it. And in these days of general intercommunication, and of inexhaustible supplies of capital, nations follow the same rule as individuals. The nation that has become better qualified than others for producing anything the world requires, will take the place of those who have not kept themselves up to the mark. If its people have the other requisite qualifications they will never find any difficulty about commanding the requisite capital ; for it is they who will be able to employ it most profitably, and it is for profitable employment that capital exists. All the world is now open to all the world, and the principle of the selection of the fittest, which Mr. Darwin tells us rules among plants and the lower animals, will assign its place to each nation, as it does to a great, and ever increasing, extent to individuals. If it be a law of nature, it must be universal and without exemptions.

At Pontresina everybody complains of the dearness of everything. The hotel-keepers endeavour to persuade the grumblers among their guests that this comes of its being a place that produces nothing but milk and a scanty allowance of fuel. This is not the cause of the high prices. London, which has to provide for a million more mouths than the whole of the Swiss Confederation, does not produce even the milk and the fuel. Much of its bread is brought from California, Oregon, and the Antipodes. Much of its meat comes from Scotland and the Continent; and so with everything it consumes. The supplies, however, of Pontresina are drawn from central Switzerland and northern Italy—no great distances. I saw in its long street hucksters' carts, which had been dragged up from the Valtellina and the Bregaglia by the wretched animals then between the shafts. These carts were full of the most perishable kinds of fruit, which were being retailed by the men who had brought them, and who would soon be back again with another venture of the same kind: here, as everywhere else in the world, whatever is wanted is sure to come. The true reason of the high prices is one which would not sound well in the mouths of those who are naturally, and not reprehensibly, profiting by them: it is that scores of people more than the hotels can accommodate, apply for accommodation every day in the season. For every bedroom there are many applicants of this kind. The one, therefore, to whom it is assigned, is glad to have it, as each of the rejected applicants would have been, at rather a high price. It is the same with guides, horses, and carriages; the people who are anxious to secure them are out of all proportion to the supply. Every market is practically a kind of auction; and at an auction no one thinks it wrong that there should be much competition, or that there should be little. Here we have much competition, in consequence of the supply being very much in arrear of the demand. This is a matter which time will set right. President Saratz's new hotel, to be opened next year, will do a little towards trimming the balance. It will be under the management of his son, whom he kept in London for two years to learn English, and to make him a Master of Arts in hotel-keeping. The Charing Cross Hotel was the college in which he pursued these studies.

I have already mentioned that I saw this year

more birds in the Grisons than I had ever seen before elsewhere in Switzerland. To those who take an interest in ornithology, the President will readily show a collection of the birds of the canton, made by himself. He has well set-up specimens of a great many species. As might be expected from the altitude of the valleys our English species do not figure largely among them. He has besides, in a room in the basement of his house, two living specimens of the noble rock eagle—the Stein Orteler. These, I believe, he intends to add to his collection as soon as they shall have attained their full adult plumage. In his younger days he was a successful chamois-hunter, and he has preserved the heads of more than thirty of these antelopes as trophies of his prowess.

But to go back for a moment to the high prices now ruling at Pontresina. They press hard on the peasants. None of them have, or ever had, superfluities: enough of cheese, and of potatoes and rye-flour purchased with their surplus cheese, the fruits of very hard work, and a bare sufficiency of fuel, with no margin for reduction in anything, was pretty well all that in the general distribution of the good things of this world fell to them. And now the prices of these necessaries of life, and of the few other things they may be obliged to purchase, have been greatly raised against them, first by the general rise of prices everywhere, and then by the local causes of a great increase in the permanent population of the neighbourhood, and of the large summer influx of visitors, who are, as respects the peasants, merely a flight of locusts, that in their passage eat up everything. As, then, a Pontresina peasant, after maintaining his family from the produce of his little plot of ground, can have very little surplus to sell, it is evident that, if he cannot make his house fit for lodging visitors, or obtain some share in the new, highly-paid summer employments, his life must be much harder than it was before. To him that the world now comes to Pontresina is the reverse of a gain.

CHAPTER X.

EXCEPTIONAL GERMANS — THE BERNINA HOUSE — THE HEUTHAL — LIVIGNO — LAPLAND AT LIVIGNO — 'MINE HOST.'

To please his pleasure. — THOMSON.

August 13.—After breakfast walked to St. Moritz to replenish the fisc. As English sovereigns were reckoned at twenty-five francs only—the Swiss Post-office allows twenty cents more per sovereign on money orders from England—I did not understand, nor have I since learnt, why I was asked to pay for the transaction the little commission of two francs and a half.

Having returned to Pontresina I went to the Post *bureau* to despatch some heavy luggage to Lausanne. In the middle of the business, while the clerk was engaged in weighing the pieces, a German pushed his way through the crowd, and interrupting the business in hand, without a word of apology, took possession of the clerk. I once saw at Interlaken another gentleman of the same nationality act in precisely the same fashion. The action exactly corresponded—the comparison must be excused for the sake of its illustrative aptness—to that of a pig, who having come up to the feeding-trough a little late, instantly knocks aside those who are already in possession, and setting his forefeet in the dish, gulps down all he can. The German pig, however, goes further than this, for he plants himself lengthways in the narrow dish, so that the first comers who have been knocked aside, can have no more till he is satisfied. On both of these occasions the clerk submitted without remonstrance. I have also seen managers of hotels accept with equal meekness German animadversions long and loud on items in their bills, which I cannot but suppose they would have resented had they come from Frenchmen or Englishmen. Why this difference? Is it because the Swiss are used to this kind of Tudesque violence? Has much experience taught them at last that there is nothing for it but to wait till the storm has exhausted itself? Or is it because they are afraid of it? And, then, of these barbarians; as all the world knows that Germans are for the most part easy, good-natured, reasonable people, to what class do they belong? Are they junkers? Or are they specimens of the Allemanic variety of the *nouveaux riches*? Do they belong to the shopocracy, or to the Bureaucracy, or to the barrack? Do they come from Berlin, or from the Hercynian Forest?

This was my last day at Pontresina. My little guide had now to return to the college of Lausanne, where he would have to put in his appearance on the 15th. It was now the 13th. He, therefore, and his mother, must leave to-night by the 4 A.M. diligence. I would join them at Lausanne, but at present it was too soon for me to return; and so I determined to go by some cross-country way to the Stelvio and to the Ortler; and when I had reached Trafoi to think about where I would go next. My own idea for the start was to take the lakes Nero and Bianco on the way to Poschiavo; and then by Val di Campo, and Val Viola, to get to Bormio. But Christian Grass, a name well known in Pontresina, whom I had engaged to accompany me, was quite sure that I should find more to interest me if I went by the way of the Stretta to Livigno, and thence over M. della Neve, and by Isolaccia, to Bormio. I was easily persuaded, for so that we went I cared little what way we went. I knew we could not go a bad way. His advice was, that I should send on my *sac* to the Bernina House, by the Post this afternoon, and walk there in the evening; and then, at 6 A.M. to-morrow, by which hour he would himself, having slept at home, arrive from Pontresina, start for Livigno. As this was what I had myself thought would be best, so soon as the Livigno route had been decided on, I showed my confidence in him by telling him I would act on his advice.

About an hour before dark I reached the Bernina House. There is a bit of wet ground, three or four acres in extent, between the House and the Bernina Bach. It is completely levelled for cutting; but, as it is swampy, it grows hardly anything but the large-leafed dock, and other kinds of marsh-weeds. Still its produce is of much use in a country where there is no straw for littering cows, and horses. I now found in it a gang of ten men at work, cutting the weeds. Those who in these parts mow for wages, are generally Italians; the native men being employed on their own land, and in waiting in one way or another on travellers; or, which comprises a considerable proportion of the young men, have gone abroad for a time to seek their fortune. The pay of these itinerant haymakers, was, I found, two francs, seventy cents a day. As they live almost exclusively on polenta, they are able to save the greater part of their wages. I asked one of them what they did in winter. 'We go home,' he replied, 'and sleep like the marmots.'

A heavy shower drove me from the field into the house for the rest of the evening, for it soon became continuous rain without any intermission of the patter against the window. Under these circumstances, the landlady, who was also a not inconsiderable landlord proved a host as well as an obliging hostess. She was never long together out of the room, always having something fresh to tell about herself, the people, the country, the summer and winter traffic of the road, or something or other. The House is her own property. She has also between thirty and forty thousand klafters of prairie, or grass land levelled and irrigated for mowing, and fourteen cows. Fourteen hundred klafters are about equal to an English acre. I have already mentioned, as we found yesterday, that the good woman treats her guests well in respect both of what she gives them, and of what she takes from them. The bedrooms, of which there are six, are small but clean. They are over the stabling, on the opposite side of the way.

August 14.—It rained all night. At 6 A.M. Christian Grass, true to time, arrived. At 10.15 the rain having subsided to a drizzle, we started for Livigno. Our road lay up the Heuthal. We had been out half an hour when the sun finished off the attenuating clouds, and we had a most charming day for our walk. The marmots before us, and right and left of us on the mountain sides, had come out from their earths to salute, in their fashion, the return of 'the God of gladness.' Their sharp short cries we heard all around us. 'That,' said Christian, 'is the barometer of fine weather; as the descent of the chamois from the mountain tops is of a coming storm.' Who would not have thought well of the man who put local observation in such a form?

If one can be pleased with a long treeless valley, marvellously full of flowers (though, indeed, they abound more on the high flanks than in the bottom, where the path lies), and with mountains that are neither covered with snow, nor very rugged, he will be more than satisfied with his five miles' walk through the Heuthal. All throughout it that admits of being mown is assigned in lots to the burgers of Pontresina, for hay-making: the rest is good Alpine summer pasture. Of course, as in every Swiss valley, the music of a hurrying stream accompanies you all the way. Near the further end of it, you come on a little shallow tarn. 'What,' you ask, 'has created this tarn in this place?' Something must have excavated it. It seems itself to put the question to you; 'can you tell how I came here?' As I looked up to the mountain that overhung it, that seemed to give the answer. From its top down to the little tarn there was a steep side, in fact an unchecked slide, if reckoned vertically, of 2,000 feet. What enormous masses, then, of snow, must at times, probably every year, drop down to this very spot! Their momentum must be suddenly checked, and expended, just where the little tarn is. The expenditure of such a force must have an effect. The little tarn is the effect. Whatever in the soil is compressible must be compressed, and whatever is expressible must be driven out, by the blow. This is what the mountain seemed to say in explanation of the existence of the tarn. 'It is my work,' quoth the mountain; 'I excavated it.'

A little beyond the tarn, and on the same level with it, you suddenly, without any preparation, find yourself on the top of a lofty mountain, with a deep valley at your feet. In fact for the last five miles you have been walking up the western declivity of this mountain, without perceiving it, or giving it a thought, and latterly, without being aware of it, you have been walking on its summit; and now in a moment, you come to the brow of the summit, and the eastern side of the mountain, all but, as it seems to you now you are looking down, a mountain-deep precipice, is at your feet. One step more you think would roll you down to the bottom of it. You slept last night at a height of 6,735 feet. You are now on the summit of the Pass, at a height of 8,143 feet. So gradual, through your five miles' walk up the valley, has been your ascent. The peaks right and left of you are 2,000 feet higher, and the sight of them had assisted in keeping the true character of your position out of your thoughts. There in the deep valley of the Spöl below you, into which you now have to descend, lies your way to Livigno. The valley is at right angles to what has hitherto been the direction of your path.

Having got down to the valley we selected a halting place just above the stream of the Spöl, and below the brow of its bank. Here we were in the sun, but out of the wind; and having seated ourselves on the turf, with rocks for footstools, we spent three-quarters of an hour about what we called our dinner. We had breakfasted early, and had walked just enough to make us hungry. It was a very pleasant three-quarters of an hour. There was the bright, warm sun, the pleasant sensations of its brightness and warmth enhanced by the recollection of the cold, wet morning; there was the green valley before us, with a herd of cows grazing near, and a party of salt carriers returning with their asses to Poschiavo; there were the naked drab-coloured mountain-tops, three, or more, thousand feet above us; there was the motion and the music of the lively crystal stream, as it hurried by over its rocky channel at our feet, near enough to enable us to dip from it without rising, what we wanted for diluting and cooling our wine, that we might take it in long draughts; and then there was for me the conversation of a companion, who I knew was intelligent, and who also, I had every reason to believe, was a man of good faith.

One source of pleasure in such a three-quarters of an hour is the perception of its difference from your ordinary life. There is a present sense of the long thread that connects you with home. What is around and before you is not all that is at the moment in the mind's eye. Even the seas, the lands, the cities, the mountains that lie between are not altogether lost to view. The images it may be of your East Anglian Vicarage, and of all that you have lately seen between it and this charming little halting place below the brow of the bank, and just above the stream, of the Spöl, are recalled to mind. That within you which thinks and feels is quickened into its own proper life. The sense of life is the conscious enjoyment of the powers of life. And here, as you sit at rest on this sunny fresh-aired bank with so many senses of body and of mind so pleasantly appealed to, you have the sense of life abundantly—the sense of a living mind in a living body.

The rest of our way was along a gentle, almost unobserved descent; at times, as we passed along the silted-up beds of old lakelets, quite on a level. The rounded tops of most of the contiguous mountains showed where the materials had come from to fill up the lakelets. You see in thought the steps of the process; the frost disintegrating the summits, and the torrents from rain, and from melting snow, bringing the particles and pieces down to the lakelets; and then you see man appearing on the scene, and toiling through the short summer in burying and removing the fragments of rock that strewed the surface, and levelling all with what soil he could find, to make a bed for the carpet of turf over which you are walking, and upon which you see that all the life in the detached *châlets* and hamlets you are passing, ultimately rests: for here, that is the one means of supporting life.

The valley down to Livigno is generally broad and verdant. At 4 P.M. we reached Livigno. It is a large scattered village, perhaps a mile and a half long. Its houses are old, or at all events most of them have the appearance of age, for the cembra timber of which they are built after some years of exposure weathers to a rich black. This the people call sun-burning. The place has three or four churches. On a blocked-up window of one of these, I counted six tiers of swallow's nests. I saw here no gnats or musquitoes. This numerous colony, therefore, must be supported chiefly by the house-fly. The reason why there are so many house-flies here, and elsewhere in Switzerland, is that there are so many landed proprietors. The valley is broad, and is divided into little estates, each just big enough to support a single family. The land can only be turned to account through cows. Every house, therefore, in the long village has a manure heap at, or beside, its door. These manure heaps, one for each house, are coverts and preserves for breeding flies. If this part of the valley was in a single property, there would be but one fly-preserve; as things now are, there is a series of them a mile and a half long. The chain, then, of conditions is as follows; a broad grassy valley at an altitude of more than 6,000 feet; this is divided into small properties; each of these is devoted exclusively to the support of cows; the manure from each byre, for the eight months the cows are under cover, is heaped up at the door; these heaps are left festering in the sun throughout the summer, for the land, the hay not yet having been made, is not yet ready for the manure, and the people are too busy to remove it; in these heaps, innumerable flies are bred, these flies feed the martins that build on the blocked-up church window nests six tiers deep. If the whole valley were put into a few cheese farms, the reduction in the number of flies, and so in the number of martins, would correspond to the reduction in the number of proprietors. The number of flies is in correlation to the size of the landed properties.

The only attempt that I saw had been made in Livigno to grow anything except grass was that by the side of some half dozen houses in the village in little enclosures of a few yards square, white turnips and white-leafed beet had been sown. But in the middle of August, the former had no tubers, and the latter were very stunted. Some of the mountains right and left of the village, a little below it, have a peculiarity: those in the second range appear to have mountains of black rock placed on the top of what may be called the original mountain, in shape somewhat like the naves of titanic cathedrals without towers. One of these superimposed masses on the left is especially well formed and grand.

It was 4 P.M. when we reached the inn. An hour afterwards, the rain of the early morning returned. It soon, as the temperature continued to fall, changed into snow, which continued for thirty hours. This was a severe test of the resources of the place. I had heard that it was celebrated for trout. One might of one's self have supposed this, for we had for the last 9 miles been walking by the side of a stream, the water of which was nowhere too broken for fish. Of course, therefore, we ordered trout for our supper, which was to be served at 6 o'clock. The little inn has two little parlours. In each of these we found a party of card-players. The two parties were forthwith placed in a single room, that the other might be appropriated to the visitors. These card-players were elderly men, they represented the class who had in their younger days sought fortune in foreign cities, and in the degrees which satisfied them had found what they sought. They had now returned to Livigno to live on meagre cheese, mummy beef when a great occasion justified such an indulgence, and black bread, with a trout or two I suppose now and then; to be regarded as the aristocracy of the place; to spend a large proportion of their evenings in playing at cards for schnapps, and to lay their bones in the God's acre of one of the four above-mentioned churches. As we stood at the door of the inn, looking at the falling snow, and not forgetting that it was the middle of August, I asked one of these elders, 'What, when he might have lived in comfort elsewhere, had induced him to return to such a place?' His reply was, 'The memory of one's parents is a beautiful thing.' I felt ashamed of my question. I was rebuked, humiliated, and silent. In a moment his sentiment so natural, or if not, then something much better, so human, or again if not, then something much better, so tender, so pleasing, was confronted by the recollection of the brutality of the English wife-beater. What, I thought, can account for this world-wide difference? Why is this peasant's mind in this wretched Alpine recess a smiling garden, while had his lot been cast in smiling England it might have been a howling, outrageous wilderness? Can, I asked myself, can in the one case the general diffusion of property, the great educator, and the absence of it in the other, lead, through their natural consequences, and effects, to these two so widely opposite states of mind? Is this at the root of the difference?

As there was no going outside the door, and as the room assigned to us was, now that the snow had been falling some time, uncomfortably cold, I went into the kitchen for warmth, for company, and for something to see. The arrangements of the ground floor of the inn were as follows: the front door by which you entered, opened, throughout the day it was never closed, upon a hall about 25 feet long, and 18 wide. On the right of this were the two parlours; they were small square rooms, each with a small square window, which had, as is usual in Grison *châlets*, a strong family resemblance to an embrasure, the object of this unusual diminutiveness and peculiarity of form being to keep out the cold. On the walls were a few coloured prints on religious subjects, and a few photographs of friends and relatives. Of these two parlours the one nearest the front door was assigned to us, the other to the card-players. Opposite to our parlour was a small room without a window, strongly fortified against frost. In this was sunk the well, which in winter was the only source to the house for its supply of water. Opposite the other parlour was the door of the cellar. Next to the hall, this was the largest room in the house. It was somewhat sunk in the ground, and by placing the cow-house against it, and by other devices, all available means for keeping out the frost had been resorted to. It contained many vats, hogsheads, and barrels of various sizes, which are replenished each year, while the roads are still passable, or so soon as they become passable, but while there is no probability of the occurrence of some of the few hot days of a Grison summer. The hall has no window, and receives all its light from the front door, which must therefore be left open except in very severe weather, and from the embrasures of the two parlours. Against the wall of the hall, between the doors of the two parlours, stood a table, on which were two or three black bottles accompanied by some little glasses. This was the provision for supplying the villagers with schnapps of distilled drinks. Opposite to this table, against the opposite wall, between the doors of the pump-room and of the cellar, was another table, on which also were black bottles, but accompanied with small tumblers. This was the provision for those who preferred Valtelline wine to distilled schnapps. At the further end of the hall was, on the right, the staircase to the bedroom floor; and to the left of that, the entrance to the kitchen.

The kitchen had but one window, and that, again, as it was in the embrasure style, admitted a very insufficient amount of light, and that insufficiency was minimized by the blackness with which nearly a century of smoke had stained the ceiling and walls: for in these wooden interiors whitewashing is unknown. On a high stool on the right side of the fire, in the chimney corner, sat the aged father of our host. His hair was long, and as white as the snow that was falling. He wore a kind of full dress, a swallow-tailed coat, and knee-breeches, I suppose to indicate that he no longer made any pretence to do any kind of work. In front of the fire was the burly wife of our host, preparing the coffee, and frying the fish. The fuel used was the wood of the cembra. This is so full of turpentine, that no sooner does a chip of it touch the fire than it bursts into flame. It was by the aid of these chips that the good woman from time to time ascertained whether the milk was burning, the coffee had come to the boiling point, and the fish were frying to her satisfaction. Supposing that her visitor had come to see how things were done at Livigno, she took a large chip, and having touched the fire with it, held it up before me in a blaze of pure white flame, and said, 'Behold a Livigno candle.' 'Thanks, Signora,' quoth the visitor, 'I see that bountiful nature has well supplied your wants.' All the while the landlord, when not summoned to the hall to pour out a glass of schnapps—the wine to-day was seldom called for: it was too cold and damp for such thin potations—was constantly coming in, and standing by the good woman's side, watching her proceedings with deep, and generally silent, attention, as the eyes of a maiden might watch the hand of her mistress. He was not quite calmed by his reasonable conviction that the result would be a triumph, but he wished to have himself some share, however small it might be, in producing that triumph; so he would at times inquire, *sotto voce*, whether there was anything he could do Should she want any more wood? Any more milk? He would now bring the jugs for the coffee, and for the milk, and the dish for the trout. He would now warm the plates.

At last it was time for us to leave the scene of these preparations. The moment had arrived, when all that could be done had been done for the coffee and the trout. And now the good man's turn had come. No sense of social inferiority had he in serving his guests. Indeed in Livigno, his function was honourable, and conferred much distinction. He could not have served his guests with more observance had they come to his house direct from Paradise, for the purpose of opening to him the gate of Paradise, as soon as their supper should be finished. He was quite sure that the gate would be opened; and gladness, that stood in no need of words for its expression, filled his heart; but still something might depend, a little, but still something possibly, on his attention, and on the satisfaction his guests might receive from their supper. And now the coffee, the trout, the bread and cheese, and the butter are on the table at which we take our places. For some minutes he stands looking on in an attitude, and with an expression, of attention, and of readiness to fetch anything more that might be required. In his own thought he was sure that everything was of the best; that everything would go off well; that nothing had been forgotten; but he would stay for a few minutes to be assured of this by his visitors from that higher and better world. The assurance was given him; and he left the room, as if loath to go, but with his whole face beaming with the light that will suffuse the faces of those, who have heard the blessed words that have opened for them the gates of Paradise.

In all this, as we found the next morning, there was nothing assumed. It was his natural manner and disposition; only schnapps have the power of bringing out, and of making predominant over everything else, a man's natural temper and disposition. Schnapps reveal the true character. Through them the bad-tempered are made more bad-tempered, and nothing but bad-tempered, and the good-tempered more good-tempered, and nothing but good-tempered. And so on this day, they made our host all over, body and soul, a host, and nothing but a host. Everything else, if there had been anything else, was obliterated. From the bottom of his heart to the tip of his tongue, and the tip of his fingers, he was a host. If there was ever at other times a mask on him, it was now torn off, and what was the essence of his being—the host—remained unrepressed, unclouded, unqualified.

The guests' bedchamber contained three beds. Their scantling was so much beyond what is common in this part of the world, that one was almost brought to think that they had been intended to accommodate each of them two persons. This, however, is an uncertain inference, for of course they were the work of a native carpenter, and his ideas may have been enlarged by finding that in this room his handiwork would not be so much cramped for space as is usual hereabouts. Or perhaps the increase in the size of the beds might have been, and probably was, a result of this not being Grison ground; for we were now in Italy, and in Italy beds are generally as remarkable for amplitude, as in the Grisons for exiguity, of dimensions. As I had invited Christian to take his meals with me while we might remain here, I now extended the invitation to the offer of one of the three beds. The price I had to pay for this was, that I was obliged to sleep with the window closed. The good man had so unfeigned a horror of night air, that is to say of admitting fresh air from without, into the room in which he was sleeping, in consequence of some supposed ill-effects it would have on the eyes, that there was nothing for it but to comply with his prejudice.

We were now in Italy, and had been since we descended the Stretta. Our dinner, therefore, on the banks of the Spöl had been eaten in Italy, and this had somewhat heightened the flavour of the enjoyment so many other pleasant adjuncts had contributed to impart to it. Neither there, however, nor here, nor elsewhere on the way, had we seen anything of a custom-house, or of a custom-house official. We might, to the prejudice of the holders of the bonds of the Italian tobacco loan, have brought with us to Livigno, without let or hindrance of any kind, any amount of cigars that we could have carried. I take it, therefore, that the dwellers in these valleys on this part of the frontier, do not burn so many cents when consuming the fragrant leaf as other Italians, and so do not contribute much to the payment of the interest of that loan.

August 13.—At 6.30 A.M. I came down to see how things were going on. Snow was still falling. The hillsides down to the valley bottom were white, but the valley bottom was still green. It was a fête day, the greatest, I believe, of the year in these valleys. There was a stream of people passing the door on their way to the church, about half-a-mile off, just below the north end of the village. Men and women were all in their holiday attire. The get-up of the men was very like what was common some years ago, and may still be, in Ireland. Those who were in the fashion, perhaps who retained the old fashion, wore the swallow-tailed coat, of a frieze-like material, but of a dark colour, adorned with brass buttons, and the knee-breeches with dark gray stockings, I have already mentioned. Those who were of a less conservative turn of mind, wore a kind of shooting coat, and long trousers, but of the same dark material as the others; probably it was homespun. I saw no overcoats, which appear to be quite unknown in this part of the world, where people dress the same in fine weather and in foul, in summer and in winter. They give a reason for this practice; they say that what in this climate they have most to dread is checked *transpiration*; and that they dress the same at all times in order that they may not increase *transpiration* by additional clothing, or run the risk of having it checked by the removal of an overcoat: that to dress the same at all times is safest in their climate.

Several of the passers by at this early hour, and throughout the day, walked up to the table in the hall, on which stood the black bottles and small glasses. It would fortify them against the raw wet day. The shooting jackets which, perhaps, represented young Livigno and modern ideas, were more open to conviction on this point, than the swallow-tails. One brought with him a sturdy little fellow of about eleven years of age who took his schnapps with the same gravity and silence as his broad-shouldered parent. They walked together up to the table, did not ask for the glasses to be filled, emptied them when filled, and retired without a word, and without moving a muscle of the face any more than of the vocal mechanism.

At 7 o'clock a young man came into the kitchen to make a mess of polenta. When the milk had been raised to the full boiling-point, he added about an equal quantity of meal, perhaps a little more than as much, and stirred it continuously for about a quarter of an hour, with a strong crooked stick, to mix it equally and to prevent its burning. When the meal had absorbed all the milk, and had become very stiff, it was prepared. It required much strength to stir it. He and two companions now sat down at the kitchen table with the mess before them. One ate it with cheese; one with milk, and the other with butter. The old gentleman at the same time descended from his high stool in the chimney-corner, which he had in vain attempted to persuade me to occupy, and sat down at the same table for his breakfast, which his daughter-in-law had prepared for him. It was a large basin of soup, or more correctly, of a kind of vegetable broth. This he ate with black rye-bread. The maker of the polenta offered me some on a plate. As long as it is warm it is not a bad kind of food, though far from as good as the hot maize cakes you get in the United States, or as the same polenta would have been if in West Indian fashion it had been allowed to get cold, and then been cut into slices, and fried, or toasted. Its merit is that it is quickly prepared, and requires no apparatus but a pot and stick.

At 8.30 our turn came. Fish again, and everything we had had at supper last night. The anxious ministering of the good man was very impressive, though of course not in quite so high a degree as on the previous evening. It was too early in the day for that, though he was already on the road that would bring him to the same point. At 9.30 he announced that he must go to church, and that he should be absent for an hour and a half. I told him that I would accompany him. A gleam of satisfaction, felt in his heart, irradiated his face. 'Well! well!' was his reply. He disappeared for a few minutes, and returned in his festa dress; his face brightened with soap and with satisfaction. His attire was that of the innovating party. The function, at which we were to assist, was to commence at 10. All the world was on the road, and every face was towards the church. He conducted me into a detached chapel, a few yards from the church; it was already full. There were about sixty men in it—all men. No priest was present. All were employed in chanting a Latin Litany to the Holy Virgin. The harshness of their voices was great, and so was the dissonance, for hardly any attempt was made to keep together. When the Litany was concluded, we all left the chapel, and entered the church. Here mass was to be celebrated. We, that is to say the men, occupied the right side of the building; the women, who far outnumbered us, occupying the left side, and the whole of what might have been the west end. The service commenced by seven or eight women walking up the main aisle to the priest, and, as it appeared, making an offering, and then returning again down the aisle to their seats. The large proportion of men in the congregation, and the demeanour of all indicated that the controversies of the day had not reached Livigno. Here the sense of the Unseen, which, under whatever form it may show itself, is Religion, was quick and strong, and prepotent in shaping the thought and lives of all. In them debates about forms had not weakened the effect of the substance.

As we returned from the church the snow had at last begun to lie in the valley bottom. The grass was now buried, and everything on which the eye rested was white, with the exception of the roofs of the *châlets*, and the paved roadway, which, however, was slushy with half-melted snow. The contrast with the bright sun of yesterday at the same hour was complete. Twenty-four hours had transported us from Italy to Lapland. Probably in Lapland the aspect of things was at the moment more summer-like. There was no prospect now of doing anything to-day, for even if it were to clear speedily, it would be too late to cross the mountains. Dinner, therefore, began to assume in one's thoughts a disproportionate importance; and we were not long in broaching the subject to the good man. What could he give us? We should be glad of the best he had. Had he any meat? He had. What was it? Was it dried beef? Well! it was a day for dried beef. That would be one thing. 'No,' he replied with sorrowful firmness. 'That I cannot let you have.' Why not? We can eat it; we have already become acquainted with it, and you see it has done us no harm. 'No,' again, but with the sorrowfulness and firmness more accentuated. 'I can let you have eggs, and fat cheese, and butter, and soup, and fish, but not the dried beef.'

'My good man, we shall be glad to have it. Why not let us have it?'

'Because your souls are due to heaven as well as my own.'

It was, then, because it was the festa. 'But,' quoth the visitor, 'that is just the reason why we should have it. To-day is not a fast, but a festa.'

'No! no! It is impossible.' Such subtleties were ensnaring. They came from the enemy of souls. The fact was that schnapps had quickened the good man's religiosity, while they had obscured his understanding. It would have been unfeeling, and perhaps unavailing, to have argued the point, or pressed the request further in any way. And so with thanks for having reminded us of the road we must both travel to reach heaven, he was told that his guests would be content to-day with what elements of meat there might be in the eggs, and fat cheese, and soup, and fish, and would dispense with the thing itself in its ordinary Livigno form of dried beef. Who would not have abstained from a few shreds of the hock of a mummied ox for the sake of witnessing the satisfaction this announcement gave the good man? The momentary cloud passed away from his face, and he instantly became again, and, as the afternoon advanced, in a still higher degree than he had been yesterday, the man of one thought—the host, and nothing else. At dinner his ministerings were bliss; at supper they became devotion.

But dinner, though made the most of, was at last over; and supper, the next event, was a long way off. The roadway, and the roofs of the *châlets* had at last succumbed to the ceaseless snow, and everything was now unbroken white. The question was, therefore, forced upon us of What was to be done? How was the afternoon to be got through? The cold in the house was getting down to the bone, notwithstanding the dinner, and frequent visits to the kitchen fire, for the outer hall door, and all other doors were constantly kept open for the sake of the light, and the kitchen fire was a mere pretence, except when some cooking was going on. The card-players had again returned, notwithstanding the festa, or perhaps because of the festa, for 'on festas the church before midday, and the tavern after midday' is a saying here. What, then, can be done? Rather for the sake of saying something than from the hope of hearing any useful suggestion, I put my despair in the form of a question to the good man.

'The best thing you can do,' he replied with a readiness and decision which indicated that what he was announcing was the familiar practice of Livigno, the outcome of the experience of life in the place, 'the best thing you can do is to go to bed till supper time.'

The novelty of the idea precluded an immediate answer. The time, however, required for fully taking it in, was also sufficient for enabling one to see that there was reason in it. Really there was nothing else that could be done; and so half an hour's more looking out at the door, and walking up and down the hall, overcame the repugnance I had at first felt to the suggestion. Do at Livigno as the Livignese do worked in the same direction. And so at 3 P.M. we went up stairs, lay down upon our beds, drew our coverlets over us, and were soon lost, and continued lost for three hours, to all sense of the incongruity of a day that would have been wretched in the middle of January coming upon us suddenly in the middle of August.

CHAPTER XI.

M. DELLA NEVE—VAL DI DENTRO—BORMIO—VAL DI BRAULIO—SANTA MARIA—THE STELVIO—TRAFOI—THE ORTLER.

>Where nature seems to sit alone
>Majestic on her craggy throne.—WARTON.

August 16.—Last night when we returned to our beds the snow was still falling: but we took it for granted that it could not continue into a third day, and, therefore, ordered breakfast for 4.40 this morning. True to time were we, and so was the breakfast. Nor were we disappointed in our anticipation of the weather. It had arranged itself favourably. Snow must have ceased to fall for some hours, for it was beginning to disappear from the valley bottom; nor was the cloud canopy either low down, or quite unbroken. With the expectation, then, that the day would be equal to our wishes, at 5 A.M. we were off. As to that indispensable part of the ceremony of taking leave—the bill—on so promising a morning I was not sorry, perhaps I was rather pleased, that the good man should find in it a reason for looking back with satisfaction to our visit, and with hope that it might be repeated. In respect of his bill the most attentive of Grison landlords, even one who on fête-days has his thoughts turned towards Paradise, and is desirous of helping others to take the right road to it, is likely to prove only a Grison man, or simply only a man. Francs here are very precious, and the opportunities for making them are very limited: we will, therefore, condone our friend's inability to withhold himself from turning his opportunity to the best account. As we were leaving the house, good nature, or, perhaps, conscience, prompted him to follow us into the road with a black bottle and two little glasses from the table on the left side of the hall. The morning was cold, and we ought to take something to fortify us against the cold. We declined on the ground that we had just breakfasted. Would we then fill our flasks? We should feel the want of something strong in crossing the mountain. This offer Christian in part accepted; and having again shaken hands, we went straight across the sloppy meadow, and began the ascent of the eastern mountain.

The first stage up to the forest was almost as sloppy as the valley bottom. The path through the forest was better. Above the forest the snow was dry. At 6 o'clock we had reached Trepalle, a scattered hamlet with a church. Nobody was stirring. Immediately beyond Trepalle is a little valley, but as it is very much higher than that of Livigno, it was completely buried in snow. So was every mountain side, and top within our range of vision all round. It was a polar scene. It gave us also a good idea of what these valleys and mountains must be in winter to the eye. What strikes one who comes on such a scene in summer is that the distinctions of colour are gone : the bright green prairie, the sunburnt houses, the dark green forest, the foamy silver stream, the brown green alpine pastures, the gray, or still darker crags, are now all alike. There is a grandeur in this, but a diminution of interest. You soon tire of it ; but of the colour-varied scene you never tire. A little further on we came on a large flock of Bergamesque, Roman-nosed sheep, attended by a tall, shaggy-headed shepherd in a sheepskin cloak. Months it seemed must have passed since he last washed his face, or combed his hair, or beard. His flock were bleating piteously, being pinched by the cold and their empty stomachs, for since the ground had been buried, which up here must have been at an early hour yesterday, they could have had nothing to eat. He seemed to have some difficulty in preventing them from straying ; his object being to keep them on the side of the hill on which the sun would first melt the snow. Some way beyond the shepherd and his flock, as we were nearing the top of the second range, where the new snow was in places two or three feet deep, we lost our buried path, and were some little time before we recovered it : but this was a matter of no consequence as we could not miss the right direction. Just on the top of this ridge we came on a black lake, with a black shaly margin; all the blacker because everything else was white.

From this point it was all down hill to the valley that would take us to Bormio. As soon as we could command the valley a strange sight opened on our view. The main valley, its ramifications, and the spurs of mountains protruded into it, were, at the distance from which we saw them, and with at the time no sunshine to light them up, of a dark, almost black aspect, for green hardly showed at all in their colouring. This blackness was in the valley bottoms, and about half-way up the mountain sides. At that height the snow began; and it began at an uniform height on all the mountains bounding the valley, and projecting into it. The snow line was as true, as if it had been set out by human hand. The upper part of the mountains, down to about half their height, was with perfect regularity uniformly white; the lower half as uniformly black. The division between the two colours had been made quite fairly, and the line had been drawn quite truly. We soon reached Foscagno, from which the Pass takes its name. Foscagno was just on the line where to-day the snow ceased. Semogo came next, still on the mountain side. Isolaccia was the first town in the valley. Then Pedenosso. After that Torripiano and Premadio. The number and size of the churches might alone have shown us that we were in Italy. By the time we had reached the valley the sun was shining brightly, and down in the bottom, though it is wide and airy, we felt midsummer heat. At Premadio we saw just the tip of the Ortler, peering over the intervening ranges, and looking like a snow *châlet* perched on the summit of the highest of them. At 11 o'clock, not having had any delays or halts, we reached the hotel of the New Baths of Bormio.

The altitude of the house is 4,580 feet. This, as it faces to the south, ought to admit of its having a pretty good summer climate, though I suppose considerable deductions must be made, particularly in the first part of the summer, for the contiguity of the vast snowfields of the Ortler, and for the other snowy eminences behind it. Its immediate *entourage* has a bleak, starved, naked aspect, the ground being poor, and only partially clothed with vegetation. This might at first be wearisome, and then repulsive, to one who was obliged to remain a week or more at the place, though it is just what gives it its character, and makes it interesting to the passing pedestrian, who only sees what can be seen in coming and going, and whose stay is limited to the time that is requisite for his dinner within doors, and his cigar on the terrace outside. He notes only with satisfaction the poverty of the immediate neighbourhood, the grand contiguous mountain masses, and the rich colouring of the long valley below open to the midday sun; and, before this source of satisfaction has been exhausted, is on his way to other scenes, full of pleasant anticipations for himself, seasoned perhaps a little with the commiseration he feels for those he leaves in quarantine, at all events at anchor, at Bormio. If you are to stay at a place, I almost think it preferable to be low down (of course not quite in the valley bottom) than to be high up. In the latter case you have a feeling that you have already seen everything. At all events you have no desire to go down into the valley: that is what, as a matter of fact and practice, no one does. But if your station is low down, you always feel an impulse on you to climb up some mountain, or to go somewhere or other to get a view, or to see something more of the country. We must except from this remark those cases where the height and the view are just what one has come for.

At 1 P.M., that is to say after a stay of two hours, which is about the right time for a midday halt, which is to include one's dinner, and which, too, seemed time enough for Bormio, we began the ascent to the Stelvio. As soon as you face up towards the Pass its distinctive character begins to display itself. The first mile brings you to the old Baths, constructed on a lofty cliff-niche, like an eagle's nest, high above the gloomy gorge of the Adda. As you pass the waste overflow of the hot spring, you feel that the air by its side has received some of its warmth. But this hardly withdraws your attention for a moment from the gray ravine, and the gray mountain, below steep

and deep, and above steep and high. Beyond this
the road, still carried high up on the right hand mountain flank, becomes more impressive. On the left,
beyond the point at which the Adda enters the Pass
from the Val Fraele, the road bends somewhat to the
right, and you enter a still more impressive stage of
the Pass. You are now in the gorge of the Braulio.
The mighty Braulio is on your left, and the south-
western buttresses of the still mightier Monte Cristallo are on your right. The Braulio has here, and
for some miles on, been cut down in mountain-high
perpendicular precipices of a yellowish-brown, for the
rock is dolomitic. On that side no road could have
been constructed; but so much the better, for it is
very grand as looked at from the road on the opposite side. On your side, the road side, the mountains
are not mountain walls, but mountain scarps. The
scarps, however, are so steep, and so seamed with
couloirs, that there was the utmost difficulty in making
the road, as there still is, and ever will continue to be
in maintaining it. As you look up the mountain
side from the road, you see, above, masses of detached
rock, as big as barns, temporarily arrested in their
descent, and ready on the slightest provocation to
crash down on the road. Sooner or later they all
must come. At the *couloirs* is the great danger and the
great difficulty. In them there is no solid foundation
for the road that must be carried across them. Its
foundation, therefore, had to be formed of masonry.

And when it had thus been carried across them, it was always exposed to be swept away at any time by a storm, which for the nonce makes the *couloir* the channel of a raging torrent of commingled water and rocks. It, therefore, became necessary first to put the road in a masonry tunnel, and then to fill the *couloir* immediately above it with solid masonry, in order that the commingled torrent of water and rocks might not dash upon it, but rush down over it. And, again, in places where there was not a *couloir*, but still, where rocks in bad weather might fall upon the road, or avalanches in spring, similar precautions became necessary: in such places the road must be either an excavated tunnel, or a constructed culvert. These precautions are indispensable both for the maintenance of the road, and for the protection of travellers in bad weather. And however strongly the work may be done, it has frequently to be renewed, for it is frequently broken in, or swept away. In several places we saw men at work repairing the damages of this kind of last spring. In some places the rocks that had fallen on the roof of the tunnels and galleries had done them more or less injury; in others it was the torrents that had dilapidated the masonry. Everything here is impressive: the deep gorge with the angry stream far below the road; the iron-faced mountain precipices opposite to you; the steep mountain side above you, which you see is only waiting for a storm to mobilize it; and which storm, as you look up at the great rocks caught on the loose *débris*, you think can hardly be needed for bringing them down ; because, indeed, for anything you can see, there is nothing to keep them from falling upon you while you are observing their massiveness and position. If you look down into the gorge your flesh creeps ; if you look across it, your mind is solemnized by a sense of the grandeur of those sheer mountain-high precipices ; if you look up at the rocks ready to fall upon you, your mind is awed by a sense of the inexorableness of nature.

Beyond this stage, which had been, pretty generally, for some miles, more or less on a level along the mountain flank, the scene changes. You now by a steep ascent cut off several zigzags, and reach a higher level, at the further end of which, some three miles on, is the fourth *cantoniera*, that of Santa Maria, where your day's work will end, and you will take up your quarters for the night. On this higher level we again encountered the snow. The day had been bright, and the snow-plough had not been used here, and so for the last three *kilometres* of this distance we had to walk through sloppy snow slush. In three hours and a half from the new Baths of Bormio, that is to say at 4.30 P.M., we reached our destination. It is a large building, for it contains a barrack, a custom-house, an inn, and lodgings for the people who keep the road open and in repair. It is well situated in a sheltered bend of the mountain basin, which lies below, and on the south side of, the summit of the Pass.

We found half-a-dozen Germans in the house: some of them had come up that morning from the Munsterthal. A little later, a dozen more arrived from the Tyrol side, in a light omnibus-like diligence, and its supplement. Of the whole number only three slept here : all the rest went down to Bormio. I was the only Englishman in the house, and in the visitors' book the proportion of English names was small; which, however, implies not so much that few English parties cross the Pass, as that few stay here for the night, or have any reason for entering their names in the book. Scarcely a French name was to be found in it. The sun was still bright, and as it was full on the verandah, it was pleasant to sit in and feel its warmth, while everything around on which the eye could rest was buried in snow.

I reminded Christian of how varied, and full of interest, our day had been. In the early morning Livigno, and the broad snowy ridges of M. della Neve, where nothing but snow had been seen, then the long green Val di Dentro with its meadows, corn-fields, towns, and churches, then Bormio, then the awe-inspiring Braulio, and now a return to the snow world as complete as what we had crossed in the early morning. 'Yes,' he said, for I knew that I was talking to a man who had a sense of the elements of interest in mountain scenery, 'yes, but we have not done wisely. We should have stopped at Bormio for the night. We might in some way or other have found this too much, and then the pleasure of the rest of our walk might have been much diminished.' I had myself not been without this thought, and, therefore, as he had to carry the load, I had at Bormio left it to him to decide whether we should go on from that point or not. But being a good and true man, because he knew what was my wish, and because it was left to him to decide, he had raised no objection to going further. Now, however, when the work was done, and there could be no suspicion of a wish to shirk, he could say what he really thought. I could only reply that the imprudence was all my fault: and that, as it was I who had nothing to carry, I ought not to have thrown the decision on him.

When those who were to pass the night at Bormio or elsewhere than at Santa Maria, had cleared out, and the sun was setting, the buxom and rather boisterous damsel, who had charge of the guests, brought in a large basketful of wood, and announced her intention of giving us a fire, which she forthwith kindled in a smaller room off the *salle-à-manger*, where there was an open fire-place. As the wood was cembra, in five minutes we had a blazing fire, and together with the three Germans, who were full of good-nature and talk, we spent a pleasant evening at an elevation of 8,317 feet in the highest house, the books say, in Europe, with, though it was the 16th of

August, a sharp frost outside, which had lost no time in reasserting its dominion so soon as the sun retired from the scene.

The buxom boisterous damsel assigned to me for the night a large room with three beds. One of these I invited Christian to occupy. He had spent the evening with us, and as we sat round the blazing cembra fire had taken part in the conversation, for he had in youth, as is the custom with so many of his countrymen, gone abroad, where he had learnt French and German. This bedroom had double windows, which appeared to be never opened: and this probably is the case from fear of letting in the cold. If so the room can only be aired, or rather dried, on the occasions when the stove is heated. The bedding, and everything in the room appeared damp. This I was told was a result of the snow being continuous throughout almost all the year, which keeps the roof and walls permanently chilled through. One cannot but suppose that dampness, as well as cold, must be a consequence of such conditions: at all events I could not but believe that my hempen sheets, three heavy blankets, and heavy coverlet, owed some of their weight, I might almost say of their adhesiveness, to this cause. In the morning, however, we found that whatever had been the hygrometric state of the beds, and of the room, in which we had slept, we were ourselves none the worse. I believe that when you are taking a great deal of exercise you can resist the bad effects of a damp bed far more effectually than you can when your manner of life is sedentary. Your system is acting more vigorously, and giving off a greater amount of animal heat, which enables you to repel the damp, and saves you from becoming its victim. In fact, you do yourself air your bed before it can do you any harm. Be the cause, however, what it may, we suffered not from cold or damp that night, while sleeping high above all the other sleepers of Europe.

August 17.—As we were to have an easy day—only to Trafoi at the foot of Ortler—we were not off till 6 A.M. The sun was not yet on our path, and the morning was arctic. If there were such things as summer mornings at the pole, such might a fine one be there. Everything was hard bound in frost, and everything was deep buried in snow, except the black streak along the centre of the road, from which the snow from Santa Maria to the summit had been cleared off by the snow-plough. Of course overcoats, gloves, and scarfs are unknown on these excursions, so on first emerging from the hotel I felt as if I were thinly clad, and my ungloved hands were soon pocketed. But as our way was at first all up hill, and the air quite still, the chill of the first contact with the frost was soon lost, which, however, had indeed not been much more than the chilliness of the interior of the house in the early morning without a fire. By the time we had reached the summit (somewhat under an hour) we were ready to blunder through the knee-deep new snow up to a little eminence on the left of the road, from which there is a commanding view. The path to it leaves the road just alongside of the roadmender's quarters on the summit of the Pass, at the point of junction of the Austrian and Italian frontiers. It is ascended in twenty minutes; or if there be less snow than there was to-day, then in a little less time. To the north-east, in which direction you can see furthest, the view is very extensive. To the west it is grandly intercepted by the contiguous mighty masses of Umbrail and Braulio. Of these the former is in Switzerland, the latter in Italy. To the south are the still mightier masses of Monte Cristallo, and of the dome-topped Ortler, which send down towards you two mighty and strangely contrasted glaciers; that on the right is long and broad, has a gentle descent, and had on this day a surface that was white and smooth from the lately fallen snow; its neighbour to the left, and which is only separated from it by a narrow rocky ridge, is most unlike it in every one of the above respects. As seen from our point of observation it appeared of no great length; it was not spread out into a large field, but jammed into a narrow ravine between two mountains. It was not in the form of a stream, but of a cataract, of ice; its surface, too, was much rent and fissured; and to complete the contrast, for some reason which did not appear, the lately fallen snow had not rested upon it. As to the general effect of this extensive view, it seemed to me to be more than half lost by the covering of snow that had been laid over everything. If form is the first element of interest in a wide mountain scene, colour undoubtedly is the second; for colour it is that gives distinctiveness, and the suggestion of life, to the forms you are looking at. It not only enables you to distinguish more readily between the forms, but also to make out the peculiarities, and interpret the character of each. Meadows, cornfields, forests, villages, rocks, Alpine pastures, lakes, glaciers, as well as the snowfields, are all signalized and understood by their colour. But when colour is obliterated, and every object made white, the power of distinguishing mere form, even that of great masses, is greatly diminished, while all minor objects become pretty generally effaced. All nature has then but one aspect. The scene before us supplied us with a proof of this value of colour. The only exception to the universal white were two enormous black holes by the side of Mount Umbrail. These were points at which we could look down into the Munsterthal to somewhat below the line up to which the snow had been melted. As the sun was not yet touching these depths, they looked almost completely black by the side of the otherwise universal white. Of course the eye went back to them again and again, for they were more suggestive, and so more interesting, than anything else that could be seen. These two, as they appeared, black bottomless pits were just the two places in the world around us where the deep valley opened out most, and the sun had most power. They were, then, the most favoured spots; and we could translate their blackness into scenes of industry and village life. If the snow had been suddenly removed from the whole scene, with the exception of those summits it, on account of their height, legitimately occupies, then they would have been distinguishable from their lesser brethren. We should have known that they were the highest tops, however far off in the view they might have been, and so we should have regarded them with the respect that was their due. And in like manner with all the rest of the scene: every object, having been interpreted by its colour, would have become interesting. We should have been given to understand what it was, and should have known what to think of it. While as things were, the whole scene, because deprived of colour, was dumb. Nothing could give us any account of itself except the glaciers. Vegetation, which is the garb of nature, and which to so large an extent puts nature into relation to man, was lost to sight. Another proof of the value of colour is that, when it has been effaced by snow from an extensive view, the eye soon wearies of the view, and to such a degree as to refuse to attend to it any longer.

The descent was now commenced. As is usual in

Alpine Passes, there was no resemblance between the two sides. That by which we had ascended to the top was long, and had been formed by nature into several distinct stages, each possessing features and a character of its own. This presented nothing that at all corresponded to the upper crateriform stage on the other side, nor anything at all like the awe-inspiring V. di Braulio. The descent was very rapid, by an innumerable series of zigzags, constructed on so steep a face, that it was a long time, at all events now that the mountain side was covered with snow, before a cut-off could be made. The road continued steep, though the gradient was being eased all the way down to Trafoi, in reaching which we diminished our altitude by 4,000 feet. We could not but observe that the Austrian side was not so well cared for as the Italian. Here, for instance, the snow-plough had not been used at all. We had, therefore, as the sun was now well up, to walk through some miles of sloppy snow. On this side, too, there were no refuges. Probably, however, this omission arose from the fact that the whole of the first two or three miles is equally exposed to snow avalanches; there was, therefore, no more reason for protecting one part than another, and it would have cost too much to have protected the whole. We saw to-day evidence of this general exposure, for even the late midsummer fall of snow had yielded some half dozen avalanches; some small, but others of sufficient mass to have blocked the road;

these, therefore, it had been necessary to remove, in order to make a way for the traffic: they would, probably, have upset a carriage had they fallen upon it.

The contour of a mountain results from the nature of the rock of which it is formed. Here it is of talcose slate. This is readily broken up by frost. The consequence is that in the course of ages enough of the mountain has been disintegrated to form an incline from top to bottom, just at the angle at which it is possible for such rubble to rest. Such mountains will, therefore, be without precipices; their *pente*, however, will be very considerable. It was in the steep rubbly incline of this mountain that the zigzags had to be made. It will be also seen that in such a formation there can be no flat spaces, or protruding rocks. On such a face, therefore, snow will, as a general rule, begin to slide before it has accumulated to any great amount. There being nothing from the first to hold it up, as soon as it begins to gather weight, down it must come. Here therefore the avalanches will be very frequent, but not very serious.

When we were about half way down to Trafoi the snow ceased, as I have so frequently had on this excursion to observe of summer snow, at just about the line where the forest commenced. We were now descending along the north-western roots of the group of the Ortler, of which, and of its glaciers, we had frequent glimpses. As we approached Trafoi, we had a magnificent view down the Trafoier valley, in consequence of a bend in the road having opened the distance to us: a world of far-off summits, some topped with white, were in a moment brought into the field of the eye. One stood pre-eminent above all the rest. I was told that its name was Weisstobel. It was of purest white, in form resembling the black mountain superimposed on a mountain I had noticed at Livigno. It was as symmetrically shaped as if it had been the long, lofty nave of a cathedral, with a slanting roof, but without towers or pinnacles. It must be the king of the mountains of that district.

We reached Trafoi at 10 A.M. An Austrian custom-house officer was standing at the door of the inn. We asked him if it was there that he would inspect the little we had with us. He seemed to take it rather amiss, almost to be disposed to be offended, that we should have imagined him capable of so mean an action, one that might seem to imply some distrust. We found that he was staying at the inn, and was, as might be inferred from his forbearance, a goodnatured, convivial variety of the species.

Again what a contrast! Three hours ago I had been standing on the little rocky eminence above the Pass. Everything was buried deep in snow, and bound hard in frost. In the level rays of the early sun, the hard frozen particles on the surface of the deep snow around us gleamed like so much diamond dust. Around to the distant horizon the landscape was only arctic. Now the climate had been changed as well as the scene, for I was seated on the spacious verandah of the Trafoi inn, with the scattered village, its little church, and garden plots around me, not dazzled, nor scorched, but only so quickened by the flood of light and warmth the sun was pouring down on the spot, as to feel that they were life to myself, as I saw that they were to all organized nature around me.

The view from this verandah is food, and, too, very pleasant food, for the eye. The point of central attraction is the Ortler, with its smooth, massive, dome-shaped cap of snow. It seems quite close to you. To the right of it, standing well to the front of the snow-field, and very near to you, is the mighty black pyramid of the Madatsch. On this day it was profusely reticulated with veins of the new snow that had lodged in its crannies. The Ortler and the back of the Madatsch are, as viewed from this point, apparently joined together, on the furthest horizon, high up against the sky, by a long mountain wall of purest white. Between them, projecting toward you from this distant horizon of the snow wall, is Trafoier Spitze, a ridge of black, or of white, precipices, as each happens to be of naked rock, or to be faced with snow. On each side of this ridge of the Trafoier Spitze is a great glacier, one descending from the Ortler, the other from the Madatsch. The lower part of the Madatsch is cut diagonally by an ascending ridge which is clothed with a thick forest of dark green pine. All this is on your right, as you sit on the verandah with your back to the house, and just at the best distance for taking in all the features of the scene, the dark forest that rises athwart the lower part of the Madatsch being quite close to you. In front of you, beginning at the Ortler, beyond the green meadows and the Trafoier Bach, which are below you, is a range of slaty coloured mountains, so near that you can make out every object upon them, the detached rocks, the cattle, and the decaying trunks of fallen pines. The first of this range runs athwart the roots of the Ortler, its gray summit being overtopped by the Ortler's snowy dome. This range is steep, barren at its summit, and shagged with cliffs, some gray, and some stained black with lichens. Its flanks are seamed with slaty coloured *couloirs*, between which are breadths of Alpine pasture above, and below the more or less scattered pines of an open forest, in contrast with the close forest that rises against the black Madatsch. Then on your left, as you look down the Trafoier valley are many distant summits of the Tyrol: supreme among these is the snowy cathedral nave, gleaming in the bright midday sun.

This view was my most distant point; and it seemed a worthy conclusion of my outward course. It was a grand and varied scene: mountains black, and mountains gray, and mountains white; snow-fields and glaciers, cliffs and *couloirs*; forests of closely set, and forests of scattered, pines; emerald meadows in the valley, and sombre pastures on the heights. Within hearing the appropriate music of the Trafoier Bach. Above all the luminous field of unfathomable blue, sparingly chequered with a few streaks and flecks of white cloud, just as on the earth beneath the intermingled shade varied the bright sunlight that was being shed over the forests, and the mountain sides, and the cliffs of the ridges. Close by, somewhat to the left, was a small cluster of humble shingled *châlets*, the village of Trafoi, to suggest the hopes and fears, the joys and sorrows of the peasant's life; just in front, was the last and chief structure of the little village, the little church with its humble shingled spire, to suggest the villager's anticipations of a life beyond the present scene. At 4 P.M. clouds began to form on the highest summits. . First, the distant snow-wall, that seemed to connect the further side of the Ortler and of the Madatsch, became lost to sight; then the Ortler and the Madatsch themselves put on their cloud-woven *bonnets de nuit.* The bottom line of this cloud-mass was now ruled straight. It just reached down to the glaciers. All above and beyond them was utterly lost to sight. The level, gray cloud-mass was to the eye a solid stratum, which originated the glaciers, and out of which they streamed down into our valley.

In the evening we walked through the meadows and pine woods, and across the Trafoier Bach, to the foot of the glaciers.

CHAPTER XII.

TAUFFERS—VAL AVIGNA—CRUSCHETTA—SCARLTHAL—TARASP.

So for yourselves ye bear not fleece, ye sheep;
So for yourselves ye store not sweets, ye bees;
So for yourselves ye drag not ploughs, ye steers;
So for yourselves ye build not nests, ye birds.—VIRGIL.

August 18.—Down at 5 A.M.; but as the people of the house are not yet accustomed to such hours, did not get away till six. A good deal of linen that was in the washerwoman's hands had been left out during the night on the roadside rails in front of the inn. Here it is taken for granted that every peasant, and that every one, too, who passes along the road, and it is one of the most frequented roads of the country, is an honest man. Of course they are honest, because almost every one has property, or expects to have it, and has been brought up among those who have it. The instincts, therefore, which property engenders have become universal. These instincts, where the properties are small, are industry, frugality, forethought, and honesty. Some years ago, while travelling in the East, I had collected for my friends at home a bundle of walking-sticks, made from the mid-rib of the palm leaf, the olive wood of Jerusalem, and the balsam of the Jordan. Wherever I had gone I had left the bundle about unheeded, knowing that no one would meddle with it. Where a woman may go unmolested through lonely ways, with several gold coins conspicuously displayed on her head, there cannot be much disposition to pilfer. It was dark, when on my return to England, I landed at Southampton. My luggage had to be taken by the dock servants from the quay of the dock to the custom-house, only a few yards. In those first few yards on English soil, half-a-dozen of the best sticks were stolen. In the custom-house I called the attention of the dock people to this inferiority in our English civilization; and with some emphasis dwelt on the words stolen and thief. I was informed that my language was actionable; and that it would be taken down in writing, if only I would be so good as to repeat it. This I had no objection to do, if only the writer would head his notes with the *dicta*, that the man who endeavours to screen a thief is as bad as the thief; and that if the property stolen has been entrusted to the safe keeping of the thief, and he, and those whose servant he is, are paid for protecting it, the theft is of an aggravated kind. Of course no more was said about taking down in writing my estimate of the occurrence. The sight this morning of the linen which had been left out all night by the roadside brought that little matter back to my recollection, and led me to infer that there must be some condition in the arrangements of society at Trafoi, as there had been in the East, which worked effectively in favour of honesty, while there must have been something at Southampton that worked in the opposite direction.

The walk down the Stelvio below Trafoi was not altogether lacking in distinctiveness of feature, as must be the case with every mountain-bounded valley, and indeed with every object in nature. What most arrests attention here is some little peculiarity in the manner in which the mountain summits have been weathered away, and the decay of the rock brought down to form the lower slopes now occupied by forests, and by the bottom lands which man has reclaimed for grass. About Trafoi, and for some way below it, you are able to look into the forests on the flank of the mountain on the opposite side of the stream. You see there that many decaying trunks of pines strew the ground. They were thrown down by storms, or fell through age, and no one thought it worth his while to remove them, and bring them across the stream. The people, then, are few, and the pines are plentiful. This led us to discuss the question, whether it was on the cards that Trafoi should become another Pontresina. I was disposed to hold that it would. We can see no reason why the stream of tourists that has now reached Pontresina should not flow further. Trafoi comes next. What brought it to Pontresina is present here to bring it on to Trafoi. Here is a great snowfield, and a grand view of it: mighty summits, more or less difficult of access and ascent; and a better climate, for it admits of the growth of potatoes, and even of cabbages; and the Tyrol is open to you by the Vintschgau in much the same way as the eastern Grisons are from Pontresina by the Engadin. Its turn then, I think, will come, unless some better point of view can be found in the circumference of the Ortler group, and which shall be at the same time easily accessible. Indeed, even now all that is wanted is the construction of a carriage road over the Stretta and Foscagno Passes to save the long round by Tirano on the south, or by Martinsbruck on the north. I am, therefore, disposed to think that the purchase of land at Trafoi would prove a good investment. I saw that the line for a road over the Foscagno was already staked out. The special advantages of Pontresina are the sense of space about it, which you have not here at Trafoi, and that it is not only accessible itself but that also much is accessible from it. Should the stream, however, reach Trafoi, we may be sure that charges will not remain at the moderate level at which I found them, both there and at Santa Maria.

At last our valley of Trafoi, which had been trending north, debouched into the valley of the Adige, the direction of which at this point is from west to east. Had we descended it on the right, it would have brought us to Meran and Botzen. But as I now had to begin to set my face homewards we took the road to the left up the valley. Our destination was Tauffers. The day was very warm, and there was little air; we now, therefore, began to regret the hour that had been lost at starting. Between the point at which we left the Stelvio road and Glurns are two villages. We stopped at the inn of the first of the two for a glass of Austrian beer. I do not know whether the Austrian excise, plus the cost of carriage, would justify the price asked, or whether the lady of the house was demoralized by the unwonted apparition of an Englishman, it being supposed popularly, that every Englishman has a gold mine in his pocket; she did, however, demand, and received, one franc and forty cents for two glasses, each of which contained not much more than half a pint. Glurns, which is walled and fortified in the old style, is the chief town hereabouts. A little beyond it you come to a scene which has a curious effect. You are turning round the foot of the mountain on your left; but if you will look up the valley of the Adige beyond Glurns, you will see a perfectly smooth, broad grass expanse, descending gradually towards you. It may be somewhat less than a mile wide, and two miles or more long. It is impossible for you to see it without thinking of a glacier; indeed it is very like the one we saw yesterday, flowing down from Monte Cristallo towards the summit of the Stelvio. If it were buried in snow you would probably take it for a glacier. Of course the site of this grand breadth of prairie was in old time formed by glacier action: but it is strange that the glacier should have formed it so precisely after its own image. Another peculiarity of this prairie is that it is totally unbacked by either near or distant mountains. All along its further side the sky line is the grass line. I never saw this before in Alpine scenery. Everywhere else whether you look up, or down, an expanse of grass land, mountains close the view, and supply the sky line.

Some two miles from Tauffers we passed through a short-turfed cow-pasture, with thinly scattered small larch, and thickly scattered small fragments of rock. It was several hundred acres in extent. Its whole surface was blue with the flower spikes of a small species of Veronica. Christian, who is somewhat observant of plants, was unacquainted with it. This shows that the climate is here very different from what it is in the neighbourhood of Pontresina, of course in the direction of being warmer and drier. This field of blue supported an observation I had previously made that I know of no country—we were now again close to the Swiss frontier—in which there are so many flowers as in Switzerland of this colour, both as regards the number of species and of individuals. The preponderance of blue is certainly not the rule on the limestone hills that stand round about Jerusalem, and which are remarkable in spring for abundance of flowers, nor is it in any other mountain region with which I am acquainted.

Our road was now again on the ascent; the sun was hot; the air was still; and perhaps the Austrian beer aggravated the effects of the ascent and of the heat. Tauffers, contrary to what we had expected, was not yet in sight; and so our then state of body and mind suggested to us the thought that the Teufel had taken away Tauffers. At last, however, it came in sight, and this expression of our discomfort was no longer tenable. Still the ascent continued, and the heat became more aggravating; and though we plodded on we got no nearer to it. It was clear now that Tauffers was the Teufel. Even the sight of its three churches did not dissipate this supposition; for we were disposed to be cynical, and so they only reminded us of the saying, of course the result of the experience of mankind, that 'the nearer the church the farther from heaven.' The village, therefore, which has the greatest number must be the farthest off of all. Our suppositions and cynicism were not abandoned when we had entered Tauffers, and on applying at the White Cross, which the Austrian Preventive official at Trafoi had strongly recommended to us, had found that their only bedroom was engaged for the night. These are small jests, but they were at the time enough to laugh at, and lightened the way.

There was, however, another inn in the place, the Lamb, and that, fortunately, was both a better house and had all its accommodation at our disposal. We were shown upstairs to the reception-room. It was evident that it had not been used for some days, for the table and benches were covered with a thick stratum of long undisturbed dust. This, as the windows were closed, and are seldom opened, their purpose being to admit light, and not also air, must have required a long time for its deposition. The woman of the house, with an infant in her arms, and radiant with good-nature, and the desire to do all she could for her guests, swept off the dust with her apron. The first question was of course the old standing question of all wayfarers. What could be had for dinner? We did not care whether it was *bifteck*, or *côtelettes de mouton*. The radiancy was extinguished. It was as if a rosy dawn had been suddenly overcast by dark clouds. These viands were unknown in Tauffers. Having failed in this *reconnaissance*, we fell back on what we deemed must always be in this part of the world a secure position : she could, then, let us have some dried beef. In Tauffers that also was unknown. Things began to look serious. There was nothing to fall back upon ; and so we must now take our chance, from which, however, we could not see exactly what was to be expected. We, therefore, gave the good woman a *carte blanche:* let us have whatever could be had for keeping body and soul together in Tauffers. This seemed to reassure her. She began to enumerate the best resources, the luxuries, of the place. We might have macaroni soup. Very well! We might have a salad with eggs. Excellent! A pause. Could we have bread and butter? We might have the bread but not the butter. There was no butter in Tauffers. None? None: but she would send off a despatch to the alpe, and perhaps might get us some for supper. At all events she could let us have some cheese? She could: but it would be only meagre cheese. There was no fat cheese in the place. Well, then, let us have for dinner the macaroni soup, the salad and eggs, the bread and the meagre cheese; and let us have all these viands as soon as possible. Yes, yes. We should have them all in half an hour.

More than an hour having passed, and there being no symptoms even that the table would ever be prepared for receiving the dinner, we again summoned the good woman to ask the cause of the delay. Had she to wait till the macaroni was made, or till her hens had laid the eggs? No! no! She had lost the key of the linen chest, and had been an hour looking for it: but now she would break the lock. This we peremptorily forbade. To-morrow it would be all the same to us that we had dined to-day, as we had dined often before, and might often again in the future, without a table-cloth and napkins. But the loss of the lock would to the good woman be an abiding loss: for such places have no locksmiths; and the franc, or so, a new lock would cost, is in Tauffers something considerable. Like the good man of Livigno, she regarded our reasoning as sophistical. It was the voice of the Tempter, endeavouring to persuade her to do what her conscience told her was wrong. The sacrifice must be made. And so it was: for a few minutes afterwards she re-entered the room with the indispensable linen, and began to lay the cloth, smoothing it down with a touch and air that implied that she knew its value, and how much it had just cost her.

The dinner soon followed. First the soup. After one has been out for six and a half hours in a hot sun, and has withal begun to feel a little fagged, any warm liquid, that can be swallowed without offence to the palate, seems comfortable. Fatigue makes one shrink from anything cold, from an instinct of the system that it would rather not make the effort to bring the cold draught up to the temperature of the body. We were, therefore, not rigid critics of the gastronomic merits, or demerits, of this macaroni soup. It was enough that it was comforting; as it certainly was to the good woman to find that we had so far approved of it, as to have emptied the basin. Like the soup at Peist, it would probably on analysis have yielded no evidence that meat of any kind had in any way entered into its composition. Of what, then, had it been made? I believe of the same ingredients; that is to say, it was a broth of herbs, enriched with spices, among which mace predominated, and thickened with vermicelli and flat macaroni. And now the *pièce de résistance,* the salad, was placed on the table, supported with twelve hard-boiled eggs. The lettuce was crisp and good, and the oil with which it was profusely dressed, was not rancid. I managed to dispose of three of the eggs. I could go no further. Christian placed himself outside the remaining nine. For this, though he had been encouraged to complete the achievement, he thought some apologies necessary. Guides, he remarked deprecatingly, always had good appetites. Apologies, I told him, were quite unnecessary, for his dinner had to sustain the porter as well as the guide. And this justification of his appetite I made him understand was not invented for the occasion, but was the result of the long and hard experience of a poor woman, who having had to provide daily bread for eight small children, had explained to me that, though there were only eight mouths to feed, yet in fact, as each child had two natures, his growing nature, and his natural nature, she had to feed daily sixteen natures. This put Christian quite at his ease. It did even more, for it made him feel how superior his bachelor condition was to that of the poor sixteen-natures-weighted woman. As to the meagre cheese, it tasted like nothing in particular: not even much like cheese. The bread was white, and not yet sufficiently old to have become a petrifaction.

So ended our dinner to the satisfaction of all concerned; perhaps to that of the good woman most of all, who, seeing how her soup, and salad, and eggs had been dealt with, could not refrain from an announcement of her hope of being able to get the butter by supper time. As soon as we had taken possession of the room, I had opened the window. I now leaned out of it to see what from this point could be seen of Tauffers. Our inn was on what might be called the *place* of Tauffers. Opposite to it was the public fountain ; and beyond that a large house. It was now four in the afternoon. The village is far from small, and must contain about 500 inhabitants. Several ploughs, drawn by cows, or bullocks, of a diminutive breed, were returning from their daily tasks. For the human toilers, however, the day's work was far from done, for a continued succession of little carts, full of manure, each containing at most what might have been put into four or five wheelbarrows, was going out to the fields. Every now and then a woman would pass with an enormous bundle of hay in a hempen sheet on her head, or shoulders. The woman of the large house opposite was in the road, cutting the trunks of some long cembras with a cross-cut saw into klafter lengths (six feet), aided by a sturdy little boy as her mate. When the cutting was completed, the pieces were carried by the two, and piled up against the outer wall of the house, facing the street. This is done universally, for though the fuel is thus left in the street, there are no dishonest people to pilfer it. This woman's house was a large one, and would require here an establishment of two or three servants, and an income of 300*l*. or 400*l*. a year. But I was told that the family that occupied it had no servants; indeed, that there was not a domestic servant in the place; that every family in Tauffers did its own work; and that the family in the big house had not 60*l*. a year to spend.

Behind the big house, and just above the town, for as things go in these parts it is more than a village, is a strange-looking mountain. It is of an equally sharp incline from top to bottom, smooth on the surface, without rocks or trees, and only half clothed with a very threadbare vegetation; this half clothing being as even as the underlying soil which shows through it. The vegetation, then, being poor, and the soil pale, the general colouring is not grass green, but a kind of celadine. In the evening I went some way up it to see of what its soil and vegetation consisted. The soil was of a much disintegrated gritty kind of rock; but as the disintegration hardly proceeded beyond the point of grit, no turf could be formed upon it, for the rainwater that did not run down its steep incline, ran through it, as through a sieve. And that, of course, that ran down over such a surface would take with it any mould that there might have been an incipient attempt to accumulate. This decided the character of the vegetation. No plant could maintain itself on such a station, unless it had good roots for holding on, was able also to do with very little moisture, and to live all the while on a diet as simple and meagre as that which was supporting the inhabitants of the neighbouring town. The species were mostly veronicas, pinks, sedums, and saxifrages. The majority of them, therefore, were such as are on a close inspection conspicuous for their flowers. Almost the only grass was an agrostis which affects poor and dry stations. These plants were nowhere continuous. Each seemed to require, or had at all events received from the grace of circumstances, some elbowroom. The vegetation, then, of the mountain belonged to the class of things that improve on a near acquaintance, for when you were upon it you found that it was decked with a great variety of very bright, though humble, flowers. I was sorry to see that an attempt had been made to plant a part of the mountain with cembras. The little plants had been set each in a little hole, and were only a few inches high. One can hardly believe that in a century they will be many more feet. But should they ever rise above the ground, which as yet they show no disposition to do, their presence will destroy the singular character of the mountain.

The first stage of the ascent brings you to a church : I suppose the pilgrimage church of Tauffers, for it is very common in this part of the world to find a church on an eminence, at a little distance off, to climb up to which, and attend its services on certain days, and at certain seasons, or for certain classes, or for certain objects, is a meritorious act, which will secure some special favour from some local saint, or some saint that respects the locality, or whom the locality respects. On reaching this church, I found that it stood on a little excavated and levelled platform, a kind of niche, on the shoulder of the mountain. On this little stage the water could hang longer than on the declivity, and there was besides the water that came off the roof of the building. This had encouraged the grass immediately around it, and up to its walls, to grow vigorously. While walking round it, to get a view of a ruined castle beyond it, I came suddenly on a little girl upon her knees, intently employed in chopping the long grass with a sickle-shaped knife, and depositing the handfuls in an old cloth. Not another soul was in sight, or within hailing. She appeared to be about 9 years of age. It was evening. The sun was low, and the valley was in shade; but, here was this little body, not playing with her fellows at the end of the day, not looking out for her father's return from his labours, but labouring hard herself, far from home, and all alone. The evening, which brings rest to all, and the mother to her child, had not brought rest to this little premature grass-cutter, and had separated her from her mother. As I came down the mountain, half an hour later, when the remains of light were fast retiring before the brown shades of approaching night, I overtook on the path the little body, with her burden, as big as herself, on her head. This bundle of coarse grass was to be made into hay, and added to the store of winter provender for the goats and cows of the family.

Such is the training of life for all in Tauffers. Nature intended it to be hard, but not so hard as the crimes and follies of man have made it. Half of this little body's evening task, and half of the daily and yearly toil of every man, woman, and child in Tauffers is lost to them. They have to task themselves with the toil; and then half the fruits of the toil is snatched from the hands of the toilers, and sent to Vienna to support 1,000,000 men in arms, for which a second tax in flesh and blood is levied on poor Tauffers, and to pay the bondholders of a debt incurred through the profitless, and futile attempts of Austria to maintain a hateful dominion in Italy, and a shadowy and impossible hegemony in northern Germany.

On the mountain above the church you get a good view of this broad interesting valley—up and down. You see how much land there is available for cultivation, and how carefully it is cultivated, and what a large population it is supporting. Several villages are in sight, and you will be able to count a hundred houses in Tauffers, which lies at your feet. The view is more diversified than one coming from the Grisons will have lately seen. It has much land in corn as well as in grass. The expanse is sufficiently broad to give you the idea of its being a substantial component part of the scene, and not merely a little strip reclaimed from the foot of the mountains. It is in itself something considerable, and in the general effects of the view can hold its own against them. The mountains, too, right and left, and before you, are grand; the latter ending against the sky in the snowy summits about the Stelvio. At this point also you are not far from the three old ruined castles of Tauffers. As I looked at them, I thought that if we could recover the details of their day, we should find that the civilized exactions of a modern empire are not greater—perhaps they may be more all-pervading, though we will not be positive even on that point— than were the rude exactions of mediæval local oppressors. The old Baron, like the modern Kaiser, appealed to the sense of glory, but whoever it might have been that was glorified, it was no more then, than it is now, the poor peasant. And there was then, as now, a claim for personal loyalty, in return for protection; but then, as now, it was a protection that was very costly to those who were supposed to be protected. So wags the world. One unsatisfactory condition is exchanged for another that does not give satisfaction. But, throughout, men are dreaming of, and hoping and striving for, something better. And dreams, and hopes, and efforts have hitherto been the salt of life.

As I re-entered the village I passed a *châlet* surrounded by grass. On the grass, in front of the house, were spread out to bleach three pieces of coarse hempen linen, the winter labours of, I suppose,

S

three families. They were of varying lengths. I paced them, as I passed, and found that the longest measured about fifty yards. The differences in length indicated, perhaps, not so much differences in industry, for here all are industrious to the best of their ability, as differences in the opportunities for this kind of work, and in the number of hands, in the families to which the pieces respectively belonged. Considering how slowly the shuttle advances in the hand-loom, I wondered that any human being could have the patience to weave these fifty yards of linen, and hoped that the time would come when the rewards of labour would in these valleys be such as to enable these poor women to withdraw from this old-world monotonous form of labour; and when among them, as among all people claiming to be civilized, all the coarser kinds of labour, which task not the intelligence, but only the hands and muscles, of men, and still more if of women, will be delegated to iron and steam.

And now we had returned to the hotel; for, as it was getting late, Christian had gone out to the mountain to fetch me in for supper. The good woman set before us the coffee, the milk, the cheese, the bread, and last of all another platter, with 'Behold the butter!' She was duly thanked; and afterwards assured that the world could show none better, and that the merits of the coffee and of the milk were equally indisputable. While we were at supper three German pedestrians came in. They were on their way to Bormio by the Umbrail Pass. They took the other end of the long table, and in time their supper was served. They had no coffee, but instead of it, the same kind of soup we had had at dinner. The salad and eggs were not reproduced. Our dinner, possibly, had caused a dearth of the latter. Instead of the white wheaten bread, with which we had been served, they had black rye-bread.

August 19.—Left Tauffers at 5 A.M. Our destination for the day was Tarasp in the Engadin; the way was up the Val Avigna over the Cruschetta, the Pass of the Scarljöchl, and then by the Scarlthal. The morning was bright and frosty with the air from the north. After ascending for two hours, all the way through forest, to my surprise we came on an irrigated meadow of about four acres. It could belong only to Tauffers, for there had been no gaps in the mountains all the way up. So far then, had these industrious people gone, and up so rough a way, to level and irrigate this little bit of land. Every stone had been cleared from it. It was as smooth as a lawn. The channel, too, for bringing the water to it, though not long, had not been easy to construct. I imagined them toiling up to their work, and then bringing down the hay along the rocky pathway they had made for this purpose, and for bringing down timber; and then in imagination I saw the Austrian tax-collector seize upon, and carry off, half the produce of their labour.

It would have been a cruel misfortune, if, after they had had all the trouble of making their meadow and road, an earthquake had swallowed up, or a slip from the mountain had buried, just half of their meadow. But in that case the first loss would have been all. There would have been no more labour expended on the swallowed up, or buried half. That would have been bad; but what the government does is worse. It obliges them, year after year, to keep up, to irrigate, and to make the hay upon, this half, and to bring it down to Tauffers; and then it takes it all away from them. And this is to go on for ever.

We had now got beyond the forest, and, therefore, looked back for the Ortler: and there was its perfectly-shaped dome, rising above the mountains that form the eastern boundary of the Munsterthal, not to any great height above them, but still a conspicuous and noble object—a symmetrical dome of purest snow. Of course the higher up we advanced, the loftier to us the dome would become. Forty minutes further on, just below the last rise to the summit of the Pass, we came upon another surprise in the form of a second prairie. We were now nearly three hours from Tauffers, and as the forest had ended with the first prairie, the road had been continued up to this point exclusively for the sake of the second: this last part of it, however, had not been difficult to make for it was over Alpine pasture, and only required the removal of rocks and stones in the lines the rullies would take in going to and fro. The moral of the sight was that when people work upon their own land and in that sense for themselves, they work with a will, which will take no denial, and which will not even be discouraged by the claims of a government to go shares with them in the fruit of their labours. This prairie was larger than the one lower down. Like that it had been carefully levelled and irrigated; though, of course, as the elevation was much greater, the hay was not so good: it was, in fact, not so grassy, being largely compounded of non-gramineous plants. From the same cause its growth was shorter, and it came later to maturity. This was August 19, and the last load was, as we passed by, being laid on the little rully on which it was to be taken down to Tauffers. The man who was loading it, was working alone. He was a spare weather-beaten veteran.

Beyond this last upland prairie was the summer *châlet* for the alpe around, on the mountain flanks. At the back of the *châlet* was the natural rock staircase up to and over the Pass. When we got near the top the path lay over a stream of clean loose rock, with unfilled interstices, and beneath these, quite out of sight but well within hearing, was rushing along the stream of water, collected from the heights right and left. On the summit we stood for some minutes feeding our eyes with a farewell look at the noble Ortler. Its snowy dome now stood high above the black ridge of the Munsterthal mountains, which, as a base, with the two long ranges of the Val Avigna for its equal side-lines, formed at this point a long acute-angled triangle. At its apex on the Cruschetta we were standing.

The way was now down hill for four hours to Tarasp: at first over high Alpine pastures. Here we passed the ashes of a fire that had been kept up last night to scare away from the cattle a bear, which was supposed to be in the neighbourhood. After a time the pastures thinned out, and the path entered on a narrow gorge between precipitous fawn-coloured mountains. It then passed over a reach of pebbly *débris*, which the stream of the Clemgia had in times of flood washed clean. It was a scene of much desolation. 'You see,' said Christian, 'how much more destructive in this country water is than fire can be. Fire may be arrested; and at the worst destroys only what can be replaced. But water cannot be arrested, and it destroys not only moveables and houses, but also the precious land itself, the source of all our wealth.' As we passed through this scene of its destructive action, walking over the rocks, and rocky rubble it had brought down, and across the deep seams it had cut in these deposits, I felt that if one must be caught in a bad storm, there would be few places that would not be preferable for the encounter to such a gorge as this, where one would have about as much chance of escaping as a minnow has from the throat of a pike. As the gorge became still narrower the path was now obliged to leave the level of the torrent, and mount some way up the flank of the right hand mountain. This soon brought us into the forest; and, as the sun was bright, the air was incensed with the fragrant exhalations of the Scotch fir, which hereabouts was abundant. We were now about four miles from Tarasp. In front of us to the north-west, beyond the Engadin, many snowy summits were in sight. On the topmost point of each the sun had raised into the otherwise unbroken blue a cloud-banner. These cloud-banners were of very different forms, each appearing to retain its own form persistently. One was a cap of liberty; another a wide-spread oak; another an inverted pyramid attached to its mountain-top by its apex. At last after about four miles of the forest, its trees having now become larch, we got down to the level of the Engadin. Schuls was on the opposite bank; but instead of crossing the Inn to Schuls, we turned to the left, and having crossed the Clemgia, not far from its junction with the Inn, took up our quarters at, I believe, the Belvidere, the most southern of the numerous hotels of Vulpera, a hamlet of hotels, about half a mile from the Curhaus of Tarasp, which is an enormous establishment on the left bank of the Inn. It was 12.30 P.M. and we had been out seven and half hours without a halt.

As we had now got back to the Engadin Christian Grass's engagement had terminated. He was to receive 15 francs a day, returning being paid for at the same rate as service. This is the regular market price at Pontresina for long engagements. It would not be so high were there more guides, or fewer tourists. You may sometimes hear those who have paid lower prices elsewhere speak of Pontresina guides as extortionate. This is a mistake. The higher and the lower prices are alike the market prices: only here the market is in favour of the guide, while in such a population as that of Meiringen it is in favour of the tourist. I was sorry to part with Christian, but my plans would not for the next three or four days require a porter; and as the wind was now northerly, and the weather seemed to have arranged itself for a period of 'settled fine,' he appeared to wish to get back to Pontresina for the chance of some twenty-five franc days on the glaciers. After dinner, then, having entrusted my belongings to the Post, which would now for a few days be my porter, I accompanied him, for he would forthwith commence his return home, as far as Tarasp. As I returned up hill to my hotel at Vulpera, a feeling came over me as though I had undergone a sudden transformation from a well enough contented tourist into a lone wanderer far from home. For the moment neither the thought of home, nor of wandering far from home, pleased. Life seemed a pilgrimage without an object. Of what use could it be to see the world? What pleasure was there in being where I was? Nor could I say to myself that

I wished to be anywhere else. 'Vanity of vanities, all is vanity and vexation of spirit.' Such was the effect this evening of suddenly finding one's self alone.

As I re-entered the hotel, some two hours later, its sixty German inmates were sitting down to a solid supper. At one o'clock I had seen them acquitting themselves like Germans in quelling the sacred rage of appetite: but now at six o'clock it had to be quelled again. No wonder that they were disposed to give the Tarasp waters a trial. The only thing to wonder at would have been that they had been made any the better by drinking them. I stood quite alone in being content, instead of the solid supper, with 'a complete coffee.' Probably some of the sixty thought me too far gone, or too poor a creature, for the waters to benefit.

Of course the Engadin is everywhere good. Here at Vulpera the mountains are bold and varied. One of the nearest—it is the one just before you as you stand at the door of the Belvidere—has a grand summit of massive jagged rock. Equal merit cannot be predicated of its climate at all times, or at any time for long together. In its three months of cold, the annual supplement to its nine months of winter, the south wind brings rain and snow, and the north wind brings frosty mornings, and disagreeably chilly evenings. So had it been this morning; and so was it now this evening: there was no sitting, or loitering about out of doors.

CHAPTER XIII.

THE LOWER ENGADIN—SÜS—THE FLUELA—DAVOS DÖRFLI—THE PRÄTIGÄU—SCHIERSCH—GRÜSCH.

> Oh! this life
> Is nobler than attending for a check,
> Richer than doing nothing for a bauble,
> Prouder than rustling in unpaid for silk.—SHAKESPEARE.

August 20.—My plan for to-day was to walk over the Fluela Pass from Süs in the Engadin to Davos Dörfli, a little place at the head of the Davosthal, just below the summit of the ridge, which in nature separates the Davosthal from, though by road it connects it with, the Prätigäu. I had to turn out at 4 A.M., that I might have time to get breakfast, and to walk to Tarasp for the 5.10 diligence from Schuls, which was to take me to Süs. Süs I reached at 7.40. Several villages, some of them almost little towns, were passed by the way. The combinations of mountains, woods, villages, reclaimed land, a good road often constructed in difficult places, and all the time by your side a full stream, worthy of being one of the main head waters of the Danube, were enough to maintain the interest of a drive of two hours and a half.

Now that, having left Süs, I was on the road absolutely alone—for that could not have been said of my position yesterday evening with sixty Teutons under the same roof, to dine and sup with at the same table—and alone, too, for the whole day, but, however, with something to see and to do, I was no longer disposed to feel like a lone wanderer far from home. The world seemed a home, and a glorious home, full of objects in every direction that had plenty to say, and were very good company. For the first two hours the valley is narrow, not quite of the ravine kind, but still generally with very little grass, and sometimes with none at all. When at this distance from Süs you are just getting clear of the forest, the dreariness and desolateness of the scene begin to be felt. You are high above the brawling stream; you see its foamy line, but cannot make out its movement, nor hear its brawling. Summits scarred with dark cliffs are right and left of you. Before you, and, if you look back, behind you also, are summits capped with snow. The snowy summits before you are those of Piz Vadred, from which you see descending the great Grialetsch glacier. Between that and you is a singularly dead looking grayish valley. You think that there is no indication of man's presence here, except the road on which you are walking. A few steps, however, further on bring into sight a *châlet* in the bottom. The singularly dead-looking grayish valley does, then, maintain for two or three months in the year a herd of cows. You had been thinking that its produce could not go much beyond lichens and mosses. You go a little further, and come upon another *châlet*, that of the alpe of the next higher level, which carries you up to the summit of the Pass. But the cows and herdsmen are this day out of sight. You see nothing moving. Rocks and snow alone attract your attention. You pass a forbidding looking stream ; dark, chilly, gruff. It is snarling at you, and telling you to be gone. As you get to the further end of the long lozenge-shaped amphitheatre, which conducts you to the summit of the Pass, with the Fluela Weisshorn on your right, and the Schwarzhorn on your left, the snow-patches begin to cross the road. On the actual summit the road is on a level, with a small lake on either hand. The raised viaduct separates, and their respective colours distinguish, the two. That on your left being fed by water coming direct from the near glaciers is a lake of milk. That on your right is so crystal-clear that you might take it for mountain air liquefied.

Just beyond these two contrasted lakes was a small hotel. I felt, however, no inclination to exchange the glorious day and scene outside for the interior of a small room ; and so with a salute to the landlord, who was standing at his door to offer me the hospitality of his house—under such circumstances the salute seemed almost a kind of mockery—I continued my way on. The scene, as is usual on reaching the top of a Pass, was now totally different from what I had lately been noting. The immediate *entourage* was of a darker rock, and the mountain tops were green and rounded. The road for the first mile, or so, seemed to be along the arc of the segment of a circle. In a spirit of speculation I took to the scattered rocks along the chord of the segment. Among the rocks were many pools of water of marvellous transparency. Every stain and scratch on the rocks at the bottom of the water was as distinct as if there had been no water at all, indeed they might have been more distinct, for as seen under the water they had the appearance of having been brought out by varnish. This water, too, was so pure and fresh for drinking, that a draught of it made me think that I had never drank water before, and could not hope ever to drink it again. As I regained the road I was overtaken by the diligence, which I had left at Süs, preparing to start, three hours previously.

One welcomes the return of the first trees. It is good to be in the zone above the trees. It is good also to find yourself returning to the zone of trees. The first you come upon tell you they have a hard time of it. You interpret their stunted form and irregular growth, and their crooked, broken branches as so many accusations brought against the cold long winters, and the cruel storms, and the summer frosts, whose assaults they have had to sustain. They are maimed, and scarred veterans who from their youth up have lived in the midst of war's alarms and injuries, but who will not yet be driven from the field. Their reappearance, too, reminds you that, in respect of the effects of the landscape, they stand in the same relation to the grassy turf that the mountains do to the plains. They feed the eye of man, and furnish his mind with ideas and images. Without them vegetation would have no more interest than the earth's surface would have without the mountains. Each, too, has its place in the working arrangements of the general scheme; the mountains in those of the world-organism, and the trees in those of organized life.

With these thoughts I passed the little inn of Tschuggen, five miles below the summit. About a mile and a quarter below Tschuggen, and a little above the inn of the Alpen Rose, I called my midday halt. I took my position among some clean slabs and fragments of a slaty-coloured glistening rock, a few paces above the road, and on the right side of it. I was here sheltered by a wood of larch from the north wind, which was cold at midday. As I looked towards Tschuggen, up the way I had been descending, a snow-topped pyramid, perhaps the Schwarzhorn, bounded the view. Then looking across, instead of up, the road, the mountain of the opposite side rose near and steeply. It was a big mountain, but not of the naked rocky order, for its flank, full in view before me, was pretty well covered with a vestment of vegetation. In this, the predominant element was a sedum now profusely in flower, which made yellow the predominant colour of the vestment. Just below me, on the other side of the road, and somewhat below the road, was a *châlet*, surrounded by little grass patches, wherever the land could be levelled, from the road down to the valley bottom, out of which rose, immediately beyond the little stream of the valley, the yellow-vested mountain. The family, that lived in the *châlet*, were alertly at work spreading, or carrying, their little parcels of hay. Old and young, all appeared to be together in the field. As I watched the labours of this busily employed family I thought their position not unlike that of the first trees I had just seen some miles above. Like them, and from the same causes, they had to sustain the struggle for life against great difficulties. In the contemplation, however, of their industry there was something to suggest the thought that their hard days were not rendered additionally hard by the discontent and the vice, which are seen and felt wherever life is maintained on easier conditions.

From this halt an hour and a half of pleasant walking brought me to Davos Dörfli, a well situated village in a broad expanse of grass land at the foot of the Davoser see. It is only a mile and a half from Davos am Platz, at which I had dined on my descent from the Strela seventeen days back. My way then lay to the south. I had since made a round I was disposed to think worth the time. To-morrow I was to set my face north for the Prätigäu.

When you are walking, and the more so if you are alone, you are disposed to note the changing aspects of the weather. Here, then, are the observations that were made on this day. At 4 A.M. at Tarasp there was an unbroken canopy of cloud: but it was not low down the mountain sides. At 6 the summits that were lofty enough for snow were standing clear; but the lesser summits were still shrouded with clouds. At 8 most of these had disappeared. From 9 till 12 only thin streaks and flecks of cloud high above all the summits. The definition of every mountain ridge and pinnacle against the deep blue was now very remarkable. At 12 clouds began to form on the tops of the mountains, and spreading widely to a considerable extent obscured the blue. At 4 these formed solid masses, and the sky was much more obscured. At 6 the clouds sunk low down on the mountain sides, so as to shut out the view. The wind was northerly all day. In the early morning it had been so cold from Tarasp to Süs as to make the *banquette* of the diligence not altogether pleasant. Near Süs I saw potato-patches by the road side that had been blackened at the extremities of the haulm by frost. Throughout the day, even when for some hours I was walking up hill with the sun on the road, the air was fresh and crisp. I have already mentioned that on the previous evening at Tarasp it had been disagreeably cold. This evening at Davos Dörfli I again saw potato haulm that had been injured by frost.

Not, then, taking this day as a sample of the climate, for its merits were too much above the average for that, but taking it as a sample of a fine day, almost the best kind of day the climate has to show, we may say that in summer on some days, for some hours, the climate is pleasant. The mornings and evenings, when the weather is fine, that is to say when the wind is from the north, are too cold. In the fine hours of the fine days the sense of enjoyment from a sense of penetrating freshness, and of penetrating warmth, is very delightful.

August 21.—Had been assured last night that coffee would be ready at 5 this morning. This promise was a case of deception prepense, for there had been no intention of letting me have it till half an hour later, when eight or ten Germans, who were to leave at 6, would have their breakfast served. On these occasions it is of no manner of use to complain, or to give yourself the trouble of showing in any way your dissatisfaction; or rather it is better not to allow yourself to feel any dissatisfaction at all. The master of the hotel is master of the situation. And in a place like Davos Dörfli, where there is only one moderately good hotel, the rule of its master is a despotism, untempered by any effectual competition. Here again, as at Tarasp, I found the hotel full of Germans, and of German-speaking Swiss; and, as a consequence, the table well supplied, and the charges moderate.

T

At both of these places I had been reminded of three portions of cold meat I had ordered at Pontresina. To give the particulars—they consisted of six circular pieces, each of them of the diameter of a florin, and no thicker than a well-worn three-penny. For this the charge was about equal to the weight of the pieces in francs. Such doings would be impossible at Tarasp, or at the Dörfli of Davos, or at the Platz of that ilk.

At 5.45, then, I got under weigh. My road for the Prätigäu lay at first along the level shore of the Davoser see for about a mile, and then for about a mile or so more up a gentle rise of some hundred or two feet in all to the Davoser Kulm, which from this side seems rather to connect than to separate the two valleys. Though, indeed, you afterwards find that the one you are bound for is a considerable way down on the opposite side. About a mile below the summit I descended into a cloud, and walked in it for about five miles, that is down to Klosters. I heard a stream at times, but did not see it; and the books say that I passed a lake, but I know no more of it than what is said in the books. All that I saw was the road, and the mist-shrouded trees by the roadside, from which abundant drops were falling. Not a breath was stirring, and it was very chilly. The altitudes were from 5,300 feet on the Kulm to 4,000 at Klosters. I might as well have been on a November morning in the Essex marshes, or in the Lincolnshire fens. Just above Klosters, without any intimation of the coming change, I stepped out of the cloud. There before me, a little below, were the four villages that form the commune. Many of their houses were goodly structures of stone. Around the villages was a large expanse of good land. This first glimpse of the Prätigäu was worthy of its reputation of being one of the best cultivated valleys in Switzerland, which, arising out of, and taken in connexion with, their system of land tenure, is what accounts for its large population of 10,000 souls. It was for the sake of the contrasts its high cultivation and its populousness would offer to what I had seen in the valleys I had lately been wandering through, that I was here to-day. The altitude and climate of most of them restricted the industry of the inhabitants to the cultivation of grass; and this in its turn was a great restriction on the number of the inhabitants.

From the first to the second village the road re-ascended a little. This brought me again almost to the level of the cloud, and here the position of the road placed a long reach of the valley before me. The effect was strange, and such as I do not recollect ever to have seen elsewhere. The stratum of cloud just roofed the valley. To the eye it was a flat roof, both on the upper, and on the lower, sides. As I looked forward the eye traversed the valley, below the roof, just as it might a long gallery. The cloud-roof was at an uniform level, resting on the mountains right and left, but of course the valley below it fell away as it advanced in its descent. I cannot say how many miles I saw down the valley under this roof. Though from my point of view it appeared perfectly continuous, and without holes or fissures, such could not have been the case, as was evident from there being several patches of sunlight in the valley. These patches of sunlight were poured in through fissures or holes in the cloud-roof, that is to say through skylights in it, and they not only gave a strange and unwonted effect of light and shade in the valley—the unlighted, which was the greater part, showing of a dark gloomy green, and the lighted patches of a bright golden green—but also enabled one to see under the roof to a great distance.

On turning round to look back in the direction by which I had reached Klosters, I saw another curious effect of cloud. The valley all about Klosters was clear and bright. Somewhat above this visible, sun-lit, lower expanse began the masses of cloud I had passed through in descending. As I was just below these clouds, and looking up at them through the opening over the neighbourhood of Klosters, in the area of which opening I was standing, they hid from me the whole mighty mass of Piz Buin—it is 10,700 feet high—except just the snowy summit. None of the supports of the summit were seen or suggested. While I looked at it, it disappeared and reappeared, again and again, as the vast stratum of cloud moved on, or rose, or sunk a little. Of course the head of

Piz Buin was very far above my stratum of cloud, but as I was close to it, and looking up at it, it was enough to intercept all but the summit, which every now and then it did intercept. As the snowy summit appeared and disappeared, it seemed as if it was not the cloud but the summit that was moving; for was it not at one moment peering down into the valley, and the next moment withdrawing itself? The effect was most unnatural. The unsubstantial fleeting cloud became the solid and fixed, and the top of the mountain which stands fast for ever the floating, object.

A further acquaintance with the Prätigäu confirmed the first impression. I have nowhere seen a richer green, or more of it, or a more pleasing, I might almost say a more wonderful, combination of woodland, grass, corn, and fruit trees, or more numerous villages, or so many scattered *châlets*. Of course there is not much of this kind in the grassy elevated valleys I had lately been traversing; indeed, I had seen nothing of the kind since I had left Coire on the third of the month; and what you see here is far in advance of what you can see in the neighbourhood of Coire, with the exception of the vineyards. The bottom of the valley is well cultivated. As you ascend to a higher zone the fruit trees are gradually replaced by forest trees, and the garden ground by grass, the *châlets*, however, still continuing. When the amount of population is recalled all this can be imagined almost without its being seen. The amount of cultivable land, almost all of it made land, is of course the first condition. The next is the altitude of the valley which ranges from about 2,000 feet at Grüsch to about 4,000 at Klosters; and then its direction, which is such as to give it protection from the northerly winds, and to expose one side to the midday sun, while its length is raked both by the morning and evening sun. These physical conditions, however, would not count for much were they not accompanied by certain human conditions. Every man of these 10,000 souls, in proportion to his ability, turns to the best possible account every square foot of his land, and every ray of sunshine that falls upon it, because he and his family will get the whole benefit of his thought and labour. They clear the ground, and dig it deep, and enrich it all they can, because it is their own ground. They plant, and they tend what they plant carefully, because they, and not others, will get the fruit of what they plant and tend. Herein lies the motive of their industry.

Neither, however, this motive, nor the *terrain* nature and the course of events have placed at their disposal, would be of any avail were it not for the presence of another condition, which has been entirely overlooked by those who advocate in the press, and on the platform, the system of peasant proprietorship. This other condition is knowledge—the knowledge of all that is required for supporting a family throughout the whole of the twelve months, the knowledge of how all these things are to be produced from two or three acres of land, and the knowledge of how each article is to be kept in store, and when used to be used most advantageously. These are the particulars of what is very far from being a simple problem. It is, in fact, the most complicated form in which the problem of how life is to be sustained is submitted to any portion of the human family. In comparison with it the form in which the same problem is submitted to our agricultural labourer is simplicity itself. He has nothing to do but to take from his employer's hand on Saturday evening the regulation wages of the neighbourhood, and to transfer them to the hand of the village shopkeeper for all that he will want during the next seven days. Add to this that the law has established for his behoof a national benefit society, which will provide for him in sickness, and in old age, and which will not forsake him even when he has shuffled off this mortal coil, for it will supply the coffin in which he will be carried to his grave;[1] and then we shall be able not quite to see, but to get a glimpse of, how completely his life is a school for the non-attainment of this knowledge. In precisely the same fashion, and to precisely the same result, domestic service will have acted on the mind of his wife. They have both been thoroughly and most efficiently trained not to have the knowledge,

---

[1] See note at the end of the volume.

and the habits of mind, a peasant proprietor must have, if he is to live as a peasant proprietor. I think it may be safely asserted that out of our agricultural labourers not one in 10,000 has this knowledge, and that not one out of 1,000 is, as things now are with that class, of the mental stuff which would enable him to attain to this knowledge; for it is a kind of knowledge which is the result of the accumulated experience and training of many generations. It is not the knowledge of how to live as a market-gardener, or as a small farmer: they live by selling and buying: but the knowledge of how to produce from a little bit of land what will directly, and without the intervention of much buying and selling, support a family. The main support of the family is to be the produce of their own labour applied to their own land. This is a most special kind of knowledge. It involves a multiplicity of calculations and considerations. It is as special as, and far more complicated than, that required for enabling an Esquimaux family to live within the arctic circle. To be carried out successfully it requires the hearty single-minded devotion to the work in hand of every day of the life of every member of the family, that work varying much from day to day. If an acre or two, or two or three acres, of land were given to an English agricultural labourer, it would never occur to him to turn it to this account. He would only think of making it a petty farm, or a market-garden. This is what, whenever he chances to get hold of a bit of land, he invariably does. He has not the kind of knowledge which is requisite for enabling him to entertain the idea of peasant proprietorship, that is of maintaining his family by the direct produce of the two or three acres. That would require an amount of forethought, forbearance, hard work, helpfulness, and above all of varied knowledge, of which he is quite incapable of so much as forming any adequate conception.

Now turn your attention for a few moments to the Prätigäu peasant proprietor. He has no wages to receive. Wages in this connexion mean in one word all that is requisite for supporting life. They include everything. Nothing is omitted from them. He has to find all these requisites by another road, and in another fashion. He has no village shop to procure for him, and to keep in store for him, all the articles that he will want. Pretty nearly everything that he and his family will require for the twelve months he has to procure from his small plot of land. This will require all the ingenuity, forethought, and industry a man is capable of. Consider what it implies. He will have to produce every article himself, to keep it in store himself, and to make it go as far as contrivance and frugality can. His house, too, is his own, and he has to take the same care of it as of everything else. There is no one but himself to repair it. The same remark applies to his fuel, every stick of which represents so much of his own labour, and to his clothes, which represent so much of the labour of the family. The wife, too, must be as great an adept in this kind of knowledge as the husband. They were both brought up in its traditions, and were trained to it from their earliest years. Every day of their lives they have under the pressure of a quite inexorable necessity been perfecting themselves in its practice. All their neighbours are employed in the same way. There is nothing going on among them that diverts attention to anything else.

If these Prätigäu peasants were transferred to this country, they could do in England what they do in the Prätigäu. If 10,000 of our peasantry were transferred to the Prätigäu, and put in possession of the existing houses, and of the land, and of every appliance needed for cultivating it, the only result would be universal starvation. Simply because they would not have the knowledge, and habits of mind, requisite for enabling each family to live from its little plot of land. The land would be the same ; the motives for turning it to account would be the same ; but the moral and intellectual conditions would be wanting. These conditions, then, must not be omitted in answering the question of what it is that has made this valley a garden that is maintaining its 10,000 gardeners.

In old times it may have been held by some half dozen mailed lords. The ruins of the castles of several of these old oppressors may still be seen in the valley. Of one we are told that the peasants took it with clubs and stakes; the wall with which the lord of another barred the lower ravine is still standing. One object of this wall was that it might enable him to levy imposts on the necessaries of life, in order that his own life might be more affluent at the cost of the poor. Such a state of things may have its picturesque side; but who would not very much prefer to see the valley as it is, the garden of 10,000 gardeners? Or in these days we can imagine its becoming a Chamois preserve. But again, I suppose most people would prefer to see it remain as it is, the garden of 10,000 gardeners. We know of nothing better in this world than men and women; and when the men and women are intelligent, industrious, honest, and can, under very difficult conditions, steer their course clear of the rocks and quicksands of pauperism, then, although they may be deficient in the refinements which culture may confer on those who have wealth and leisure, still they are in many valuable and attractive qualities far above large classes that we in this country wot of. But be this as it may, the average human heart is more pleasingly touched by the picture of their hard and humble labours than by that of the mailed Baron and his dependents, or of the Chamois preserver, and his Chamois. Probably they have as brave hearts as the Baron and his dependents had: at all events their fathers drove them off with sticks and stones, and even the women of Schiersch in 1622 showed such heroism in assisting their husbands to repel their Austrian invaders, that the men of Schiersch have since that day conceded to the women of Schiersch the honour of receiving the sacrament first. And, too, probably they are as much disposed to respect humanity, and to help those that need, and to do to others as they would that others should do to them, as the imaginary Chamois preserver would be.

A little above Kublis on the pebbly borders of a torrent, down the flank of a mountain, where it was impossible to retain soil enough for cultivation of any kind, for the occasional rushes of storm water would sweep from the surface anything soluble or tender, I found the coarse shingle dotted with hazel, and briar roses, and barberry, and much of this open thicket almost smothered with the wild clematis then in flower. This vegetation again reminded me of how completely I had this morning changed the climate. Where I had been of late nothing of this could have been seen. A few hours ago, in leaving Davos Dörfli, I had passed frost-blackened potato haulm; and for three weeks I had not had much to look upon, in the way of vegetation, besides pine woods and grass. What I now saw prepared me for the advent on the scene of the broad glazed leaf and feathery arrow of the maize.

A mile or so below Kublis the green valley is suddenly contracted into a rock-bound and wooded ravine, which has in the bottom no more space than is sufficient for the blustering Lanquart and the road. Whatever good land is hereabouts must be high above you on the top of the ravine. This ravine ends at Frederis Au, a kind of watering-place, some little way off from the road. Here you again come on good bottom land, some of it under maize. A little further on, the stream is again compressed between high rocky banks.

At Schiersch, having now done twenty-five miles, I stopped for dinner. It is a place of some size, and has many goodly stone houses; but what attracts you most is the story of the still-honoured heroism of its women. The books told me that the Lion was the chief hotel of the place. Accordingly I entered the Lion, and was shown up to the first floor. It was evident that the room into which I was shown, like the sword of Achilles which could either hack a baron of beef, or carve a Trojan, was used for two purposes. The long table and benches on one side of it showed that it was intended for travellers' accommodation. The sofa, however, and chairs, a little work-table on the other side, together with the presence of Madame herself and four children, one asleep on the sofa, one suffering from whooping-cough, the third waiting on the invalid, and the fourth in the mother's arms, indicated that it was also the Lady's sitting-room, and the nursery. The guests who came and went while I was in the house were waited upon by the husband only. My successive inquiries for mutton, beef, butter, eggs, fruit, cognac, extracted from him only negative replies. What, then, did the good people of Schiersch live upon? He could let me have cheese and dried beef. I had been expecting mutton *côtelettes*, with a dessert of figs and peaches. In my disappointment I felt disposed to go on further. I could hardly fare worse by doing so. But after I had entered the house I felt a disinclination, by leaving it, to balk the expectations of the good people, and perhaps my own too. And so I spent half an hour at the Lion. As to the dried beef, I had ceased to think it actively bad. The wine was rather sour. Against the cheese nothing could be said.

Together with the above viands there was presented to me this problem. If this is all that Schiersch can set before its guests, what is the usual fare of the Schierschers themselves? Few of us as we pass through a smiling Swiss valley think, or know, how hard its inhabitants live. They, poor souls, or rather their hard-worked bodies, have neither the dried beef, nor the half sour wine, nor yet such cheese as I had. Meagre cheese, the curd that rises, on the second heating, after the first curd for the cheese has been removed, black rye-bread, polenta, and potatoes constitute, with coffee for their chief beverage, the normal fare of the inhabitants of most of these valleys. The greater part of the butter, and of the fresh meat that they produce is sent off to places, where there are hotels with many travellers to be provided for. All the fat of the land of the Prätigäu is in this way forwarded to Davos am Platz, Ragatz, and Coire. Having disposed of this question not quite satisfactorily, for I had rather that its settlement had been more in favour of the good people of Schiersch—the brave women of Schiersch at all events deserve something better; and having, too, disposed of the comestibles which had suggested it, I said my adieux to the members of the family of the Lion, and proceeded on my way, caring little, and not knowing much more, where I was going, except that there was a place two miles further on called Grüsch.

The first mile was through low wet meadows. Beyond these the torrent of the Lanquart had in times of flood, carried away all the soil, leaving behind nothing but rubbly stones. These covered a wide expanse, rather more than a mile in length. The peasants of the locality, like a community of bees, or ants, whose nest, or hive, has been disturbed, had taken in hand the repair of the whole of this damage. They had carried a dozen, or more, dikes across the valley, and crossed these again at right angles by another series of dikes. This had divided the whole of the desolated space into a considerable number of square compartments. Their plan was to fill these in succession with the muddy water of the Lanquart, hoping that the deposit from this, would in time bury the stones, and give them a surface of alluvium, capable of supporting grass. Some of the compartments were already supporting beds of reeds. If, therefore, the dikes should not be washed away by some unusually heavy flood, the time must come when soil enough will be accumulated for grass. May this precious grass one day crown and reward their labours!

At Grüsch I was well repaid for having preferred the ills I knew not of to those of which I had had experience at Schiersch. I found it in many respects an interesting little place. First it is well situated. There are points of view in the village, from which the mountains seem to stand round about it grandly, quite to come down into it. On the north side a bold ravine has been rent from some height up in the mountain just down to the level of the road. Some of the houses are old and large, and were once the residences of local grandees, of the days when Grüsch had grandees. In one of these I found my supper and bed—a supper of veal cutlets, coffee, butter, cheese, and raspberry *compote*. I give the particulars not only from a sense of what is due to Grüsch, but also for the sake of encouraging Schiersch to greater efforts. As to my berth for the night; I was at first shown up a stone staircase to a spacious room containing three beds. From its ornamented panelling and ceiling it must originally have been intended for a sitting-room. I was more than satisfied with it. When, however, there was no further prospect of the arrival of a family, or party, of distinction, I was informed that there was a better bedroom in the house, that it was at my disposal, and that the few things I had brought with me had been removed to it. Even after this announcement I was quite unprepared for its magnificence. It was a kind of state apartment. It was gorgeously papered. It had muslin window-curtains. The stove cased with white china, and bound with hoops of polished brass, had an imposing effect. The pillows and coverlet were edged with cotton lace. All this was overpowering, coming so close on Schiersch. And, then, the manageress was so good-natured and obliging, so anxious to know what might be wanted, and seemed to have so much pleasure in doing it—almost as much as the good man at Livigno had had, whose regard for his guests had extended even beyond this world. But the crowning grace has still to come. After breakfast to-morrow morning, I shall have to pay for this substantial fare, the splendour of my bedroom, and so much pleasing attention, only 3 francs, 30 cents: the same sum, except the 30 cents, I had paid at Schiersch for the refection of dried beef and sour wine. This will compare, too, very favourably with the bill at Livigno. That had been 30 francs, 60 cents. But then our friend at Livigno had catered for both worlds, for soul as well as for body. At parting I could not but shake

U

hands with the young woman who had waited on me and her satisfaction at finding that her attentions and ministerings had been appreciated was alone quite worth the 3 francs, 30 cents. All this was a great deal to get for so little in this hard world.

CHAPTER XIV.

THE RHEINTHAL—PFÄFFERS—RAGATZ—COIRE—DISSENTIS— VAL MEDELS—PERDATSCH.

> He durst upon a truth give doom
> He knew no more of than the Pope of Rome.—HUDIBRAS.

August 22.—Was off at 5 A.M. Just below Grüsch the road passed by a scene of recent devastation, very similar to what I had seen yesterday evening just above the town. A late flood of the Lanquart had swept over some three or four acres of garden ground, from which it had washed out every particle of soil, leaving behind only a bed of clean pebbles. Some corners and shreds of potato and corn patches alone remained to show the passer-by what the poor peasants had lost. One saw proofs of the efforts they had made to save not only their crops, but that which was of far more value than the crops of a single season—the precious land, their only means of living. In the hope of turning the flood back again into its channel they had constructed a kind of long *chevaux-de-frise*, first by fastening pieces of timber together at right angles to each other, each piece being about ten feet long, and then lashing several of these cross-tied bars, at intervals of about three feet, to a long pine trunk. These contrivances they had fixed at points they wished to protect. Faggots had then been laid athwart the three-feet interstices, in order that the pebbles and rubbish the flood would bring down might be piled against them. Of course these fortifications had not been set at right angles to the line of the flood, but slightly inclined down it, so that when it impinged upon them, the line of least resistance to the impinging flood would be in the direction that would take it back to the main channel. I suppose the plan had been to some extent successful, for the land behind the second line had been mostly saved. I was reminded of Christian Grass's remark on a similar scene in the Scarlthal, that for these poor people to see a torrent sweeping away their land is a far more dreadful spectacle than to see the flames devouring their houses.

Just beyond this scene of devastation was the stock of pine trunks, that had last winter been cut in, and brought down from, the forest above by the men of Grüsch, for their supply, during the coming winter, of fuel and of timber for house repairs. The size of the trunks is, if age be taken into account, an indication of the nature of the soil and of the climate. These gave good evidence in favour of the soil and climate of the Prätigäu. I measured the butt end of the largest of them. It was nearly four feet in diameter without the bark. This must have been a stately tree. I counted, too, the rings of its annual growth. It had been one of the patriarchs of the forest, for one hundred and forty had been the number of its years. Four generations of Grüschers had withheld their hands from converting it into fuel or money, and a fifth generation were now to have the benefit of their educated forbearance.

The exit from the Prätigäu is through a grand portal. The precipices are high and sheer; the Lanquart is rapid, dashing, and dinning; the road is tortuous. At the last turn of the road, where the precipices are highest and sheerest, and the Lanquart most rapid, dashing, and dinning, you suddenly step out on the long and broad expanse, here two miles wide, of the Rhine valley. The spirit of the scene is changed. Some of this broad flat is so poor, all vegetable mould having ages ago been washed out of it, that it will grow only stunted trees, and some so low and wet that it will grow only reeds and rushes. Should you be making for Ragatz, as I was, two roads will be before you; one along the foot of the right-hand mountain range by Malans and Maienfeld, the other straight across the valley and the Rhine, which is here on its further side, and then along the foot of the left-hand range. For a moment I looked on the scene before me, and then went straight on. The two miles of dead level would be something new, and would give me some idea of what the Rhine valley is here. The two next miles beyond the bridge over the Rhine, and on to Ragatz, with the morning sun full on the road, and against the side of the overhanging mountain, were memorably warm.

Ragatz commences on this side with a monster hotel. Between a large orchard, which you reach first, and this hotel is a road which brings you in three or four hundred yards to the road from the town to the gorge of Pfäffers, at the very mouth of which Ragatz stands on the beginning of the level ground. It was still early, and so, without stopping at Ragatz, I went straight up the gorge. From Ragatz to the old baths is a distance of two and a half miles, and an ascent of somewhat more than five hundred feet. The road is good, though it must have been very costly to construct, and must be so to maintain. The side on which it is excavated and built is not so precipitous as the other, which is generally sheer cliff from five to eight hundred feet high. All the way along, the Tamina is rushing by and tumbling down before you. You see that it is wearing away its rocky bed; and you can see no evidence, nor imagine any reason, why you should not suppose that it was the same stream that in the same manner cut out the whole of the ravine. If sufficient time be given, it is as easy to cut out eight hundred feet as eight. The perpendicular face of the cliff which looks to the east does not at all stand in the way of this conclusion. Of course the rapidly descending water was disposed to take a straight line, and even, if diverted from the straight line, to work back to it as soon as possible. And then it would naturally cut down its channel perpendicularly, because, as it would be flowing rapidly, it would keep its cutting tools, the bits of rock and the sand it was carrying along, at work in the middle of the stream. If you throw anything into a confined mill-race, you will see that it does not grate along the sides, but, as it sinks, is forced into the middle, and swept along the middle, of the stream, there being a pressure on it from both sides. The natural tendency, therefore, is that the erosion of a rapid stream would be both straight and perpendicular. You see this in all the gorges where the water is now, or has at former times been, flowing rapidly. Only one point remains, Why is the face of the gorge which looks to the west less perpendicular than that face which looks to the east? This also may be explained. The afternoon sun shines with sufficient force on the western-looking cliff to melt the snow on its summit, and some little way down. As soon as the sun is withdrawn the water from the melted snow may be recongealed. These alternations of thawing and freezing are a cause that is at work every spring to disintegrate the rock on the side that faces west. This cause is not at work on the side that faces east; that, therefore, remains perpendicular. The other side, however, which is acted on by this cause, has receded a little, and become somewhat inclined. Had there been no frosts, there would have been no weathering of this side, which would then have remained throughout, with the exception of the few places where little lateral streams enter the gorge from this side, as perpendicular as the other side. The rain also being generally on the west-looking side, helps to bring down the disintegrated rubble, and dislodged rocks, to the bottom of the gorge, where the Tamina immediately, if it cannot sweep them away, begins to wear them away.

As to the Baths of Pfäffers, those I mean near the head of the gorge : while at a second breakfast there at 9.30 I thought the appearance of the servants did not say much for the salubrity of the place. They looked fleshless, bloodless, nerveless. But this was no more than you might expect to see in people who had been living for two or three months in so damp and deep a hole. The owner of the establishment ought to change his servants every Saturday night, otherwise they will, or at all events they ought to, scare away his visitors ; their pale and emaciated faces are so many finger-posts, on which is written the word dangerous. No breath of air can reach the house. If the stagnation of the air is what in ordinary valleys produces *goîtres*, what must its stagnation in this wet gorge be capable of producing? If the exterior of the house were not frequently rewhitewashed it would, I suppose, be covered with the lichens and moss, and such like damp growths as you may see on the wall by its side. It may, however, be argued that the actual baths must be a prophylactic against rheumatism, because many of those who have been here a week are still able to walk away.

I spent four hours at Ragatz. It is a loosely put together place, consisting very much of large hotels in the style of Interlaken. The interstices, as it is rapidly increasing in population, will probably soon be filled up. The water of Pfäffers is brought down to the town in a wooden pipe two and a half miles long. This water and the gorge are the sources of the prosperity of Ragatz. As to Pfäffers, it is worth seeing. As to the water it may possibly do no harm to drink it. It issues from the rock at a temperature of about a hundred degrees. This appears to be its only peculiarity; at all events it smells and tastes, we are told, like any other water. No one seemed to know what, if any, therapeutic ingredients it possesses, or what are the maladies in the treatment of which it may be held to be efficacious. These, however, are not the only ways in which it may be regarded. If it can give any sufferer an excuse for hope, so far well, unless it should prevent his having recourse at the same time to some other rational treatment of his ailment. Or if it give an excuse to some for leaving too fast, or too slow, a home, and to others for withdrawing themselves from overwork, for a time, that also may be set down to the credit side of the account.

In the evening I went by rail to Coire. As I passed along the broad valley of the Rhine, I saw several mountains cut down almost as perpendicularly as the gorge at Pfäffers. To the thought, though of course not to the unthinking eye, the valley is more impressive than the gorge. Here mountains have been planed down by old world glaciers, and cut through by still existing streams, to such an extent as to form a valley in places two miles wide. The face of many of the mountains is still a precipice. In many the precipice at the top has been slanted back by the weather, and the chips falling to the bottom have continued the incline in the form of a long *talus*, which still remains only because in all the centuries that have passed since the chips began to accumulate, the stream has never been working on that side. These are grander operations, and they contain more elements of interest to the thought, than the narrow ravine of Pfäffers.

August 23.—At Coire I had got back to a point already passed in my outward course. Among the guests of the hotel, who were taking an early breakfast to be in time for the early diligence, was a German of the Hercynian forest type. There was an item in his bill of which he did not approve. At the sight of this entry his wrath kindled in a moment. He was not satisfied with assailing the waiters, he must have the manager before him. The manager came.

The grievance was detailed with much emphasis. Its enormity was dwelt upon. But the manager was not taken by surprise. He was as firm as a rock, and with a surface as incapable of being ruffled. Again the Teuton returned to the assault. Again the manager received it unmoved. How the conflict ended cannot be recorded, for at this point I left the room.

This German was not more irascible than two of our young compatriots, their ages might have been between twenty-five and thirty, whom I had lately met, were impassive. I sat opposite to them at supper. To each other they had hardly a word to say. Observing this I addressed to them an occasional remark or two. Their replies, however, were seldom more than monosyllabic. They were as indisposed to talk to a stranger as to each other. The next day I sat for several hours in the diligence with them. During the whole of that time, the least taciturn of the two only twice uttered a word. Looking at his watch, which was ostensibly his chief employment, he announced to his companion that it was nine o'clock. Some time later, while we were changing horses, he looked out of the window, and announced in tones expressive of interest suddenly awakened, that a *supplément* was being got ready. I heard the sound of his more taciturn companion's voice but once. A Swiss gentleman, who was seated opposite to him, endeavoured to direct his attention to a very celebrated mountain which happened at the moment to be in sight. 'Oh!' was his reply, but it was addressed not so much to the gentleman who had just spoken to him as to vacancy, 'oh! we have had enough of walking.' Of course exhibitions of this kind are no evidence of a national inferiority in natural gifts. They do, however, suggest a suspicion of the inadequacy of our eight-parts-of-speech system of education. To these two young gentlemen nature may have been not less bountiful in her gifts, or, if the German observation that nature has given to Germans industry, but to Englishmen genius, be true, may have been even more bountiful, than to most men; and if so, then the fault may not have been so much in them, as in the system to which they had presumably been sacrificed: possibly they had not been fairly dealt with. The improbability of any other conclusion arises from this, that if their state of mind was not natural, and we can hardly regard it as natural, it must have been produced artificially.

At Dissentis, too, which I reached this day at 1 P.M., I was still on old ground. My object in stopping here was to get a porter for a walk by the Lukmanier road, the Uomo Pass, Altanca, and Val Bedretto to the Gries glacier, with the descent from which into the Rhone Valley at Ulrichen my excursion would end. As soon as I had reached Dissentis I requested the manager of the hotel to get me the best guide in the place, asking him so to interpret best as to give intelligence a prominent place in his estimate: because what I wanted was not merely a two-legged pack-horse, but a man with whom it would also be pleasant to carry on a conversation of four days' duration. He knew, he said, exactly what I wanted, and a man who would completely meet my requirements—a man in every respect good, but in respect of intelligence exceptionally good. This was promising; so the possessor of these good qualities was summoned forthwith, and it was agreed that we should, at 3 P.M., start for Perdatsch, ten and a half miles on the way to the Lukmanier, which would be enough for an evening walk. The man's get-up was elaborate for a guide; and there was a jauntiness in his manner, and, as it struck me, an expression of wiliness in his eye, which suggested to me the thought that it would be as well to put the agreement between us into black and white; and this I accordingly did. He returned half an hour later than the time fixed for starting. We had not got clear of the village before he had informed me that he regarded priests as *canaille* of the first class. Such was his form of the superlative of that already vigorous superlative of contempt. Why, I asked, did he give them this pre-eminent position? Because, he replied, they did no work at all, and lived better than he did. The fact was that he did not recognize, because he could not understand, that there was any kind of work in the world, except manual labour. He then passed on to the landlords of hotels, the only well-to-do class he was acquainted with in his own neighbourhood, and included them in the same category: they too were *canaille*. In their case, however, he did not add his superlative suffix. The real reason of his dislike to them appeared to be that they had more capital than himself; for he had only enough to keep a small shop, while they had enough to keep hotels. Of course I could only infer that, as I was unfortunately, or rather heinously, able to pay him for accompanying me, he was regarding me at that moment in the same light, and referring me to the same class. All this was soon explained. He had lately returned from Paris, where he had been at the time of the siege and of the commune; and if he was not an actually affiliated member of the *Internationale*, he was at all events in opinions and sympathy a communist of the first class. This was not quite the kind of man I should have myself chosen; but still there he was by my side, and must remain there for some days. There was, therefore, nothing to be done now but to make the best of a bad bargain. I had at all events an opportunity for studying at leisure the kind of stuff of which not of course all communists must be, but of which it is not unlikely that some are, made.

For the first six miles, that is as far as Platta, our way was along the new road, which is being made from Dissentis by the Lukmanier to Olivone. It is a grand piece of mountain road-making, as may be understood from there being eleven tunnels in the first four miles. This will also indicate the nature of the ravine, which necessitates such work for the road that traverses it. The stream below the road is the Mittel Rhein, which at Dissentis joins the Vorder Rhein—the main headwater of the Rhine. These new roads, of which so many are being constructed in Switzerland, are, I was told, made at the cost partly of the respective cantons, and partly of the Confederation. This is as it should be, for they are not of local advantage only, but are also indispensable for the general prosperity of the country. Of course there can be no internal or external exchange of commodities, and no human circulation either of natives or of foreigners without roads; and exactly in proportion as roads are multiplied and improved, are these advantages extended. No people see this more clearly than the Swiss. These are questions which their practical lives and practical education enable them to understand readily and thoroughly. They are, therefore, always adding to, and improving their means of communication. And, as far as I know, there is not in the country a road for the use of which a toll is charged: for to their apprehension a toll would be a contradiction of the very purpose for which the road was made. It was made to facilitate communication; and the toll by making communication dearer, has the same effect in discouraging it that needlessly severe gradients, or unnecessary circuits of many miles, or a shockingly bad condition of the roadway itself would have. For this reason, that is to say, because they see distinctly what is the object of having roads, they make them as well as they can be made, keep them in as good repair as possible, and make the use of them perfectly free to all.

The scenery is interesting at first in the ravine, and not the less so afterwards, when you have emerged from the ravine, and have entered on something more valley-like, with the mountains standing somewhat back, and with openings in them to allow you some glimpses of snowy summits. These, however, were matters about which the communist felt no interest. All that he would here talk about was the profligacy of the government in making the roads. The local and the general government were equally culpable, for each raised its funds by taxation. It was the people who paid for it all. Roads and everything else, were only excuses for extracting money from them. It was vain to argue that the roads were made for the people, and were for them a necessity; that they increased their resources; enabled many to live well who had lived miserably before; and increased the opportunities and comforts of all. Probably it was just in this that the sting of the road lay: because for those who had land it raised the value of their property, and enlarged the opportunities of innkeepers and such like folk. The wound this inflicted on the feelings could not be salved by the fact, that while the road did hurt to no one, it must in their proportion have benefited even the smallest tradesmen, for it created a demand for what they had to sell by bringing buyers, while it also enabled them to get from a distance, and more cheaply than before, the commodities in which they dealt. Through such helps and facilities many petty tradesmen had become far more flourishing than they were formerly. Of course there would have been no objection to this last effect. Had it stood by itself it would have been approved of. But, then, the movement had not stopped at this point, but had also benefited innkeepers, and some other such Tritons; indeed, had made them Tritons, and that was intolerable.

It was a pleasant walk to Perdatsch. The new road has not yet got beyond Platta. But there was nothing to regret in this. The new road was good; but so also was the old paved horseway. This also one was glad to see: it was rudely constructed of blocks and slabs of gneiss, long since worn smooth by many centuries of local traffic, and the passage over them, too, of many armies, which in old times, as we are told, went and returned this way, during the long period when the Lukmanier, because it was the easiest, was the most frequented, of all Alpine Passes. It had been 3.30 when we left Dissentis, and as my companion had stopped at Platta for twenty minutes for a *chopine* of wine, the last gleams of daylight were dying away as we reached Perdatsch. To be still on the tramp at the close of evening gave rise almost to a new sensation, which, too, was not altogether a pleasant one; for you seemed to be still at work when all nature was either going to rest, or counselling rest. The peasants had returned home, and so had the goats and cows. Those belonging to the little inn had come down from the mountain, and, having now been milked, were taking up their berths for the night on the lee side of the *châlet*, and contiguous rocks. It was the hour, not for walking, but for talking, at your ease, over what had been seen during the day that was past, and for forming plans for the day that was coming.

The inn of Perdatsch is well situated. You have lately been passing several little villages, which had, successively, been becoming smaller, as the height had increased, and so the means for supporting life had decreased. And now at the point where the stream from the Val Cristallina meets that of the Medelser Rhein, and at the foot of M. Garviel, which rises up before you to divide the V. Cristallina from the Val Medels, stands the little wood-built structure. Your memory of what is behind, and the sight of what is in front, suggest to you that you have now reached the verge of inhabitable altitude. As you approach Perdatsch, you see that the stream, in the leap it there takes of a hundred feet, is of considerable volume; and you find it putting in a claim to be a Rhine, the Mittel, or Medelser, Rhein; on the

Splügen you had met a second Rhine, the Hinter Rhein; on the Julier, a third, the Oberhalbstein Rhein; in Aversthal a fourth, the Averser Rhein; and you have seen all these joining a fifth, the Vorder Rhein. Each of the five by assuming the famous name seems to insist on your remembering that it bears an important part in the origination of the great river, or at least is among its first contributories. I believe, however, that the word in its original signification was not so much the proper name as the appellative of a stream, or river. The Rhine may have meant the river, the flowing water. Etymologists will say whether it has any blood relationship with *rivus*, river, and Rhone, and possibly Eridanus, which appears to have been the name of a river that emptied itself into the Baltic, as well as an alias of the Po. But to propound conjectures without an adequate knowledge of the subject, in etymology as in other matters, is easy, and in both senses of the word endless.

This inn was about the smallest *châlet* I ever entered. The following were its internal arrangements. The entrance door was at the south-east corner. From the door were two little passages. The one facing the door led to the room occupied by the landlord and his wife. This room might have been nine feet wide and a dozen in length. The second passage turned to the right of the door along the wall. It was about four feet wide. In this passage came first the cooking stove; the passage was in fact the kitchen; and then beyond the cooking stove the door of the reception room. This was about eleven feet square, and so low that a tall man could not stand erect in it. Opposite the door of the landlord's own room, and rising over the door of the house, was a ladder, by which one ascended to a passage corresponding to that which formed the kitchen. At the further end of this upper passage was a miniature bed, which my guide will occupy to-night. Close to his crib was the door which opened into the guests' bedroom. This was the largest room in the house. It contained three beds. Its extent, however, was only in area, for it was so low that it required some manœuvring to get into bed, and I could not have attempted to sit up in bed without knocking my head against the ceiling. This was the whole structure, which to-night will shelter thirteen mortals. *Absit omen!*

On my arrival I found a solitary Frenchman—the only Frenchman I met during this expedition—in possession of the little parlour. He had left Dissentis an hour earlier than I; I had, however, seen him there, and as we were in the same hotel, and bound for the same place, I had addressed a few words to him; but he had then appeared to be indisposed to engage in conversation. I now found him full of conversation, and a pleasant man to talk with. He told me that he was a member of the French Alpine Club; that its members had made so few ascents that he was desirous of doing something, and so that he had come out to get into training for an ascent of Mount Blanc; but that he did not contemplate making the attempt till next year. He was a stout and sturdy but rather short man of about thirty-four years of age. He carried his knapsack himself.

The usual question now arose, What could we have for supper? In so small a house, so far from the world, we did not expect to find much. We, therefore, summoned the landlord, and asked him to give us a list of everything in the way of eatables and drinkables his house contained. He had dried beef, and also dried mutton : the latter was quite a novelty to both of us. His wife could make soup. She could also fry eggs in butter. He had, too, Piora cheese, not of course actual Piora, but equally of course quite as good, wine, white bread, and coffee. He was congratulated on having so many good things, and such a wife; and requested to place every one of the good things on the table as soon as his wife could prepare them. The cembra fire was kindled, and its cooking power got up, as soon as the match was put to it; and so in about half an hour, there being hardly room on the little table for all the viands, supper was served. We found there was no reason why we should desert our old acquaintance, the dried beef, for our new acquaintance, the dried mutton. The soup was an instance of the deceptiveness of words. It had no more resemblance to the Tauffers mess of herbs, spice, and macaroni than chicken broth has to the ambrosia of terrapin or turtle. It had but two ingredients, and those were rice and milk; enough of the latter to float the former. It was an undecided question whether the eggs would not have been better without the butter. The plain butter and the Pioresque cheese were good. The white bread was an old world petrifaction. The wine was acid, if not sour. The coffee was good, as was the milk that accompanied it. On the whole we were content. Things were far better than we might have anticipated. We loitered over them; and it was 10 o'clock —a late hour for such places, and for such work as we were engaged in—before we went up the ladder, and crept into our cribs.

I had not been long in the house before eight peasants arrived for the night. They walked into the reception room. We, however, were already in possession. There was hardly standing space for them all; and it was evident that there was no space for another table, and benches, for so many. The landlord and his wife were equal to the occasion; and the peasants being reasonable people at once recognized the necessities of the situation, and accepted the alternative the host offered them till we might retire to bed. They had, too, come to make a night of it, and would not be disappointed. Besides there was nowhere else to go. The alternative was that they might have for the present our host's and his wife's bedroom. To this, then, they withdrew, and forthwith commenced playing at cards and drinking, transferring themselves to the reception room when we left it. There they remained till 3 o'clock in the morning; at which hour they quitted the house, to proceed further up the mountains to make hay. They were Platta men, and the foreman of the party was the Platta schoolmaster, a tall wiry man, with a black bushy beard. At times during the night we were woke by their shouts and laughter, as the fortunes of their game varied. The stakes they were playing for was the wine they were drinking, for which the losers had to pay. When disturbed by their merriment, I cannot say that I was lulled again to sleep—the effect was rather in the opposite direction—by the rude bluster of the stream, which was tumbling down its rocky channel not many yards from my head—still I had no wish that either the merrymakers or the stream were further off.

CHAPTER XV.

VAL MEDELS—THE UOMO PASS—VAL PIORA—RITOM—ALTANCA.

> With the imagination be content,
> Not wishing more; repining not to tread
> The little sinuous path of earthly care,
> By flowers embellished, and by springs refreshed.
> WORDSWORTH.

August 24.—Last night I had proposed that we should start this morning at 5—my usual hour for getting under weigh. But as my proposal appeared to be objectionable to the communist I withdrew it, and told him that we would breakfast at 5.45, and be off at 6. At 5.45, as I left my room, I saw that he was still asleep in his crib in the upper passage. While sitting down to breakfast I requested the landlord to make him get up. After breakfast I asked for the bill. The landlord left the room to make it out with the aid of his wife. As the room was very small, and they were only just beyond the open door, I could not but hear what passed. They agreed between them that the charge should be 4 francs. I then found that my man had descended the ladder, for I heard him suggest that they should write 5 francs. A little after 6 we got under weigh. Having crossed the stream of the Val Cristallina, and rounded the foot of M. Garviel, over large blocks of gneiss, we entered the long upper stage of the Val Medels. It is a grand valley about 6 miles in length. The only buildings it contains are the three small refuges of St. Gion, St. Gall, and Santa Maria. The ascent is gradual, for in the 6 miles you only rise about 1,000 feet—from 5,036 at Perdatsch to 6,243 at Santa Maria. There is no bottom land in it capable of being mown for hay. This results from the rocks, with which it is thickly strewn, being so large that they could not be removed for levelling the ground. Its lofty ranges stand some way back from each other. The concavity of the valley is grandly simple. The long lines of descent sweep down from the summits of the two ridges to meet in the stream of the Mittel Rhein. At first, and high up, the descent of these lines is steep, but all the way down the steepness is lessening, at an even rate of diminution, till they almost come to a level in the bottom at their point of contact. In this long open valley there are no trees, though we are told that the name Lukmanier (*Lucus magnus*) implies that there were once many. If ever it were so, their place has now been taken by tufts of dwarf alder, and of dwarf juniper, which rise only a foot or two from the ground, and at the lower part of the valley thickly stud the hillsides. The alder dies out after a time, but the juniper continues, though in ever lessening amount, to the further end. As this long valley is throughout pretty well turfed, it must be capable of maintaining during the few months it is free from snow, a great amount of stock. I saw in it some large flocks and herds.

My companion appeared to take no interest in the scene, or in the people; and this morning I was not disposed to take much interest in him, and so I left him very much to himself. At last he began of his own suggestion to talk about our fellow-traveller of last night, his thoughts still running on Paris. He wished to know whether I had discovered who our fellow-traveller was, or whether he had himself told me. Yes, I replied, he had told me that he was a Frenchman. 'A Frenchman!' he exclaimed; 'he was an accursed Prussian spy. You could see it in his face. You could see it in his maps. You could see it in his being alone. He had been sent from Berlin to map the country, that the Prussians might know beforehand to what account the Lukmanier might be turned, should the Pass ever in any way be needed in any coming war. A Frenchman! What Frenchman ever could speak both German and English? But many Germans could speak both English and French. He was an accursed Prussian spy. The French it was who had gained all the glory of the late war. They had shown that they were the braver of the two people. They had not employed spies, nor had they trusted to gold.' This was meant for England. 'In the next war they would crush the accursed Prussians.'

And so we reached Santa Maria—a hospice which is much cleaner and more commodious inside than you would expect from the outside. I should not have entered it had not my miso-Prussian companion thought that his two hours' walk had earned him a half hour's halt and a *chopine* of wine. It was as fine a morning as nature could put together at this elevation. No ingredient required for the composition had been stinted. The sun was shining brightly. The air was fresh, and crisp; for its current, as is the rule on quiet mornings till about 9 o'clock, was down from the snowy tops around. When the valley after 9 A.M. begins to get heated, the current is reversed, and continues upward till about 4 or 5 P.M. In the sunshine the warmth felt like a kind of subtle ether, which permeated one's whole system, for the moment you were out of it, you felt the want of it; and the moment you returned to it, you felt again, throughout your whole frame, the influence of the all-pervading fluid. I sat on a rock on the sunny side of the cheese-house, in front of the hospice. Immediately behind the hospice was the long flank of a greenish brown, and the snowy summit, of the Scopi, nearly 1,450 feet above me. Straight before me, twenty minutes off, was the summit of the Lukmanier Pass, only 250 feet higher than my seat. To the right, at the distance of an hour and a half, and 1,200 feet higher, was the Uomo Pass. It was a grand and impressive mountain scene. There was at the time in sight a party of Italians bringing bags of salt on their asses down the Lukmanier, and showing in the distance no bigger than mice. The salt was for distribution among the cheese-makers of this, and of the contiguous valleys. For how many centuries had salt travelled that way! What a large part had its traffic played in the early communications of mankind! How surely does what is wanted wear for itself a way. This commodity is bulky, and but little is to be gained by bringing it, and yet the supply has never failed. But here the days of the traffic in its present form are now numbered, for the new road is all staked out; and when it shall be made, these asses laden with salt will no longer come down the Lukmanier, accompanied by their shaggy owners. Salt, however, will be cheaper in V. Medels, and V. Cristallina, and the other valleys of this group of mountains. Some figures that now add a suggestion to the scene, will have disappeared from it; but human life will have become a little easier and better supplied, and that not in salt only, but in many other things besides.

Half an hour having passed with some discontent, though on the balance of the whole without much reason for it, we began the ascent of the Uomo. It would be worth walking up it were it only to see in some of the little rock basins of its stream, when you are about two-thirds of the way up, how wonderfully transparent water can become, or rather is before it has become charged in one way or another with extraneous matters. On reaching the summit you there find that the water cannot readily get away on account of the number of little depressions spread over the surface. Here, therefore, it is rather swampy. These depressions have, perhaps, been caused by the concussion of falling avalanches. Where the momentum of such masses in motion is arrested, some soil must be thrown out, and a depression formed, which same soil perhaps is again thrown back by the subsequent fall of other avalanches to the right or left. By action of this kind the whole surface may be kept in a swampy state. This swampy summit is a common watershed both for the Rhine and for the Po, so that you are uncertain whether the little pool before you will send its overflow to the North sea, or to the Adriatic, or divide it between the two.

On leaving the summit you turn to the right, your path at first being on the mid flank of the mountain which forms the northern range of the Val Piora, on which you now enter. Hitherto Piora has been known only for its cheese; but I am disposed to think that the day is coming, when it will have a place in the memories of the eye as well as of the palate. As you take your first glance down the valley, you see beyond it the grand group of the St. Gothard, standing up well before you, gray-sided, many-peaked, precipitous, and snowy, looking down on the lesser heights of the Val Canaria. As you descend the valley, you ask why its cheese should have become so famous? You find the answer beneath your feet. Its wholesome-looking turf is rooted in disintegrated limestone. If, then, it be true that good horses cannot be bred except on limestone pastures, and that even the human organism is the better for having, as we may say, been bred at second, or third hand upon them, through its vegetable and animal food, then we can understand how it comes about that the cheese of Piora takes high rank in the order of merit. I recollect having heard more than thirty years ago the Sir George Crewe of those days affirm, that when he left home he generally missed in the vegetables served at his dinner the flavour, which a dressing of lime imparted to the same sorts, when grown in his own garden at Calke Abbey. People then thought this fanciful; it was, however, an anticipation of what we are now told is demonstrable. He at all events would not have overlooked its limestone pastures in endeavouring to account for the merits of Piora cheese.

At what, till you reach it, appears to be the lower end of the valley, you find a small lake, with a village on its further shore. To the left of the lake, and somewhat above it, is one of the chief cheese-stores of Piora. It is a roomy stone structure, partially sunk in the ground, with the view of keeping its temperature equable. I cannot say how many cheeses I saw in it; but there were a great many, and they weighed about fifty pounds each, and their wholesale price was eighty cents a pound. From this point, bearing to the left, and descending to a lower level, you reach a second lake of a blue-green colour, about a mile in length. Its name is Ritom. You pass along its right-hand shore, at the bottom of a steep range, from which you see that rocks must frequently be detached in spring. At about the middle of the path along the lake is a second store for Piora cheese. The cheeses are made on the Alps, and are brought to these store-houses to mature. Here we again stopped. At both of these storehouses we found two men in charge. Our object now was to make inquiries about Altanca, a village on the northern ridge of the Val Leventina, where I proposed to spend the afternoon, and to stop for the night. I had been told at Dissentis, by a horse-dealer who frequented these valleys in the way of his business, that at Altanca the only person who undertook to provide accommodation for travellers was the Curé. As we were now drawing near to the place I thought that I might here get some definite information on this point. The head cheese-maker, to whom I addressed myself, might have sat for the model of a Hercules. I never saw a man who, I could have supposed, would in the days of clubs and spears have had a better chance in encounters with hundred-headed hydras, gigantic boars, and man-eating lions. His features, which were garnished by a thick, curly, black beard, though large, were not at all coarse, but only in fair proportion to his massive frame. To my inquiries about the capabilities of the Curé's establishment, he replied that the Curé himself was old, and deaf, and that he had three sisters of about his own age residing with him. I noticed the indirectness of his reply, which left it to me to draw for myself from the particulars he had given whatever inferences I pleased, and thought that there was rather more of diplomacy in this than I should have expected in a mountain cow-herd. Taking it, however, to imply that an evening spent with the deaf old Curé and his three equæval sisters would not be a lively one, I asked him if he could put me in the way of finding something more promising. 'I can commend to you,' he replied, 'a *Parisienne*.' It was clear from his look, as well as from his confining himself to that single word, that he knew very well what were the ideas it called up in people's minds—vivacity, as much as could be maintained at Altanca, good cookery, as far as the materials of Altanca admitted, and some mementos of a more embellished mode of life than was native to Altanca. Of course I was obliged to him, and would entrust myself to the *Parisienne*. On my offering him a glass of Scotch whisky, of which I had a flask with me, he saw that I was a Britisher, and replied in English. His story was that he had gone out to California as a digger, and there it was that he had picked up his modicum of French and English, and his knowledge of the world. After some years of digging, he had found that gold was no compensation for absence from his native mountains. Hercules in the garden of the Hesperides was pining for houseless and treeless Piora; and so he had returned, and become a cowherd once more on the borders of the blue lake, and at the foot of the craggy mountain. As I left him, I thought how much more tender his heart was than his hand, which I felt could have crushed mine almost as easily as it could an egg-shell.

At the foot of the lake I came upon an hotel in construction. It was nearly completed. There were at work upon it forty-six Italian masons and carpenters. The architect, and the future landlord, were present superintending and expediting the work. The old Curé, too, who had come up from Altanca, was seated on a rock close by, alone, watching its progress. Perhaps he was thinking that a new order of things was about to commence; that Altanca was about to be introduced to the world, and the world to Altanca; that the quietude of centuries was about to end; that troublous times might be coming: but if so that it would be his successor that would have to deal with them. Perhaps also the Curé of Altanca may have wondered where the fifty guests, who it is hoped will fill the fifty beds of this hotel, are to come from. Those, however, who are aware that there will be no difficulty in finding many fifties who are ready to come, will be rather disposed to ask how they are to get to the hotel? People hereabouts say, that when the road over the Lukmanier shall be completed, there will be taken in hand a branch from it over the Uomo, down the Piora, and by Altanca to Val Leventina. This is probable enough, for one improvement generally suggests, and leads on to others, which in fact it renders possible. The road, however, from this hotel by Altanca to Val Leventina will be a very difficult piece of engineering, for it will be down an unusually steep descent of 2,500 feet.

The existing horse-track from the hotel at the foot of the lake down to Altanca covers about half of these 2,500 feet. Though steep it is for the most part paved, and must have been a great undertaking for so small a community, for it comprises only twenty-five families; and all this was done to enable these poor villagers to send their cows up to the mountain pastures, and to bring down their produce. It was one more instance, and, though you have instances of it everywhere in Switzerland, a very striking one, of how much people will do, when they are working for themselves. The road was to be made, if it ever could be made, to enable them to send their own cows to their own pastures, and therefore it was that the arduous work was taken in hand, and carried through. In places the road is along the edge of a grand ravine, at the bottom of which is the stream that drains the lake into the Ticino. It has two very fine cascades. One of the mountains that rises above it is Hadrian's tomb expanded into a mountain.

And now we are at Altanca. Just above it are some little prairies and small pine woods. Wherever there was a chance that a tree might be able to hold on, one had been persuaded to make the attempt; and wherever there was a chance that a little soil might be able to hold on, an attempt had been made to form a prairie. The village itself is on a ledge of rock. About fifty feet below it is a little area of some dozen acres, sufficiently level for spade husbandry. Here the twenty-five families grow their little patches of rye, cabbages, and potatoes. It was now towards the end of August, and so their busiest time. The rye harvest, and the hay harvest, were both being brought home; and this glorious day would perhaps be the busiest of their brief summer. We found all the houses closed. In the village no one was to be seen. Everyone was in the field. Almost the first house we passed was the Curé's: surely one of the three sisters would be at home, though, indeed, I had some disinclination to tapping at the door, for conscience told me that I was deserting the recognised host of the place for selfish reasons, that it would hurt the feelings of the sisterhood to find that I was in search of entertainment elsewhere, and that there would be something cruel in selecting them of all people for such inquiries. It was, therefore, a relief to find that they, too, were in the field. On such a day to have remained within doors at Altanca would have been a reproach. I might have guessed that they were not at home, for a large bundle of hay in a hempen sheet had been deposited on the door-step. Some fifty yards below this house was a row of twenty-barred *kraschners*, the kind of gigantic clothes-horses on which at these altitudes corn is stacked and dried in sheaf. About a dozen of the dames and maidens of Altanca were clambering up the bars of these *kraschners*, with loads of sheaves on their shoulders, and packing them away between the bars. They do not work from top to bottom, but from end to end, beginning at the bottom. A few sheaves are put in over the bottom bar. Of these only the heads are passed through the opening between the two bars. The sheaves are then bent on the bar so that their long butt-ends hang down. In each row all the head ends are on one side, and all the butt-ends on the other. The heads and butt-ends of the alternate rows being reversed, the long butt-ends of each row, as you ascend from bottom to top, completely protect from wet the short head ends of the row below it. Of course when the whole is full, no head ends are seen on either side, all being covered, as it were thatched, by the rows of butt-ends. The topmost row is protected either by a wooden ridge, or by a little straw. Our appearance on the scene, as might have been expected, caused an instantaneous suspension of work.

Those who were going aloft with loads on their backs, and those who were thrusting into their places the sheaves that had been brought to them, came to a standstill as they were made aware from below of the unwonted intrusion. Everyone seemed to know the *Parisienne*, and so the interruption did not last many moments.

This busy quarter of Altanca was at its extreme east. The *Parisienne's* mansion was at the west end. We soon reached it, for here distances are not great. The front door opened on the kitchen and store-room. You passed through this and entered the 'keeping' room, a large and tidy room for a *châlet*. It did, however, also contain a bed in an obscure corner. No one was at home. But the master of the house was soon summoned. He had spent his days of foreign sojourn at Paris, where he had made the money which he had spent on his house, and where he had also found his wife, and learnt to speak French. He immediately produced a bottle of wholesome wine, some mummy beef, and petrified white bread. I asked for fresh rye-bread and Piora cheese. He assured us that his wife would be at home early in the evening, and would do all she could for us. He had a new bedroom which he would place at my disposal. Fortunately it had but one bed. He would, therefore, procure a bed for the communist in a neighbouring *châlet*. He was a tall handsome man, as almost all the men are in these valleys. He despatched a messenger for his nephew to spend the evening with me, for he was one who had seen much of the world; he could, too, speak English.

At last evening came, and with it the nephew, and the long expected *Parisienne*. Her first thought was to offer me a pair of slippers, and to ask me to take off my boots. As is the case with so many of her countrywomen in middle-age she had lost her figure, but had retained her vivacity. She was full of lively talk, and, to be Irish, equally so of good nature. She would do all she could, but, as an aside, Altanca was not Paris. During my stay in this house I had this aside in many forms, and *àpropos* to many matters. But though, as she impressed on me, Altanca was not Paris, she did what she could to show that it had not extinguished her recollections of Paris. It was pleasant in such a place, and under such circumstances, to hear what in some degree reminded one of French *esprit*, and of the neatness of French expression. As was natural, too, in a Frenchwoman, she was proud of her *potage*. I thought it rather salt. The stock probably had been made of dried salt beef. 'Excuse me, monsieur, the French kitchen is even more *salée* than the Swiss.'

'Madame, you are right. The *potage* is excellent; and to-morrow at All' Acqua, and often in the future elsewhere, I shall have reason to recall its merits, which will ever be accompanied with pleasing recollections of its maker.'

If the cheesemaker of Ritom might have sat for a model of Hercules, the nephew of our host might have sat for a model of Apollo. He was tall, clean-built, and strong-limbed, without showing much muscular development. His features were regular, and finely-chiselled, and full of thought. His voice was clear and musical. And yet he was only a carpenter of Altanca, who had just returned to see his family, after having followed his trade for nine years in California. Below the window at which we were sitting were the few acres of the corn and garden ground of the twenty-five families of Altanca. As we looked out upon it, watching the people at work in the gloaming, I knew what thoughts were passing through his mind, and so, addressing myself to them, I said, ' That little bit of land would be but a neglected corner in a Californian farm.'

'Yes,' he replied; 'things are on a very small scale here. But that is not all. There is no liberty here.'

'How?' I asked. 'The people here manage their own affairs as completely as they do in California. Both are equally republican.'

'Yes,' he again replied, 'but it is so only in form. There is no liberty here.'

He meant liberty of opinion, and scope for action.

CHAPTER XVI.

AIROLO—VAL BEDRETTO—ALL' ACQUA—THE CRUINA ALPE—THE CORNO GLACIER—THE GRIES GLACIER—DOWN TO ULRICHEN—CONCLUSION.

> So build we up the being that we are:
> Thus deeply drinking in the soul of things,
> We shall be wise perforce.—WORDSWORTH.

August 25.—The *Parisienne's* estimate of the services that had been rendered to me was nine francs: a low estimate if compared with English charges; still for some even of it I was indebted to the communist, as I was also for my not being able to get away before six o'clock. Our destination was All' Acqua, at the head of the Val Bedretto. As we left Altanca I found that many of the goats and cows of the place were suffering from the foot and mouth disease, that has of late years been very troublesome here among our own herds. It was sad to find such a calamity lessening the resources—and their cows and goats are their chief resource—of these hardworking and scantily provided people. The view, as we began to descend to the valley of the Ticino, was very grand, as it had been from Lake Ritom down to

Altanca—far grander, indeed, than anything you can see from the valley itself. Between the village and the valley the path is all the way over very steep reclaimed grass land. To reclaim it had been the labour of many generations. The dusty road of the hot valley was a poor exchange for the Medelserthal, the Uomo, the Piora, the Ritom, and the Altanca of yesterday. We had not, however, much of it, for we were to leave it at Airolo. At Airolo, however, I was provokingly detained for half an hour by my thirsty and lazy attendant, who could not, after a walk of only an hour and a half in the early morning, pass a wine-shop without turning into it. The long main street of Airolo was up, just as if it had been Cheapside, in order that an iron water-main might be laid down in it, in anticipation of its coming wants, when the railway beneath the St. Gothard shall be opened.

A troop of artillery passed through the place. They had been out somewhere near Andermatt for their summer manœuvres. Yesterday at Piora we had heard the booming of their guns. I thought of them, and of the national force to which they belonged, in connection with the railway. Switzerland was strong when it was self-contained, and when a large part of the country was almost inaccessible. This was what enabled it to establish its independence. It could support itself, and its enemies could not get at it. Now, however, it is not self-contained, for it is very largely dependent on trade and travellers. It can no longer produce its own food, but must look to trade and travellers for the means of purchasing a large portion of its daily bread. If, then, the railways that bring these travellers, and the cotton, the wool, and the silk its factories work up, and carry to their markets the manufactured fabrics, and which, too, bring a considerable proportion of its daily bread, were held by an enemy, the country would be starved into submission. This might be done in two or three years without firing many guns, or much fighting. Nor if an enemy should desire to invade it, would any part of the country be inaccessible. Railways and roads have opened the whole of it. Either, then, it might be starved into submission by having its supplies cut off, or the enemy might take advantage of the means of communication it has already constructed, and to which it is still adding, to make himself master of its strongholds, and chief centres of population. Modern Switzerland, therefore, is now no stronger than any other part of Europe: indeed, not so strong as many of its more behindhand districts. All the grand appliances of modern science, wealth, and organization, such as railways, gas-works, water-works, large factories, extensive commerce, banking facilities, must in future wars be so many sources of weakness to the weaker powers, that is to those who are not strong enough to protect the costly material mechanism of modern civilization. The strength with which nature had endowed Switzerland under the old condition of things has under their existing condition been well-nigh completely cancelled. This may in proportion be applied generally to the whole Continent, with the single exception of its strongest nation, for the weaker are now in a degree and manner peculiar to these times at the mercy of the strongest. This suggests the question, what will be the eventual result of the developments of science and wealth having made the weaker nations almost powerless, and the strongest nation almost omnipotent?

It was pleasant on this sunny morning to get out of the stifling heat of Airolo. Before we could enter the Val Bedretto we had to cross the Ticino, close to the mouth of the railway tunnel. Here was presented to us a very busy scene, which showed how much work was doing, and would have to be done. No sooner had we entered the Val Bedretto than we were met by a current of crisply fresh air descending it. There is nothing to a cursory glance particularly striking in this valley. Still it has its own features; but if I were to attempt to put them into words the description would appear to be not unlike that of many another Alpine valley. This, however, would be an injustice; its pathway, its forests, its villages, its mountains, the rents in its mountains, some of them very deep, and from the colour of the rock almost of a pure white, the main valley itself, its laterals, and its broad pebbly stream, have each and all their own character, and quite enough to interest and satisfy the mind ; at least I have never found a Swiss valley, and certainly did not find the Val Bedretto, uninteresting ; even though, as it happened, I had to stop for a quarter of an hour at Fontana, and again for half an hour at Villa for those ever-craved, and never-satisfying *chopines* of wine. This annoyance, however, even if in some degree it amounted to that, was one of very small dimensions : it was not, for instance, to be compared in respect of any inconvenience that attended it, with a high wind, or a smart shower, or even an overclouded sky, or still less with a battered foot. At all events, all is well that ends well ; and so I thought, as early in the afternoon we reached our day's halting place at All' Acqua, though not at first knowing the good-fortune that was awaiting me there ; for I had now, without the least anticipation that it would be so, heard the last of those unconscionable *chopines* of wine.

Here, then, I am in my last little mountain inn. I have now had my last dinner of macaroni soup, and of crude beef, and am sitting outside in the bright sun, very pleasant at this height, and am noting the composition of the scene. The little house stands some hundreds of feet above the Ticino, on the left bank. The stream, though lost to sight, is still heard from down below. Beyond it, on the opposite side, are steep mountains, clothed on their lower flanks with more or less detached larch, tufts of dwarf alder, and patches of grass, to the upper limit of the tree line, and then up to the summit with open grass and rocks. On my side, around me, the foreground is open pasture strewn with rocks. It is studded with a few large venerable larch. A small stream threads its way down it to supply the house with water. This open, rock-strewn pasture rises into a near line of wooded mountains, with a few patches of grass. These constitute the middle distance, beyond the immediate foreground. They are backed by another quite distinct line of mountains, which are the background of this part of the panorama. The second range is in complete contrast to the first, for it is much loftier, and steeper, and absolutely naked. Its summits are in the forms of pyramids, peaks, and cliffs, and grandly dominate the interposed green range. It is against the sky line. Down the valley are the snow-patched finials of the St. Gothard group. Up the valley are dark scantily-turfed slopes, tipped with snow. In that direction will lie my path to-morrow.

I returned to the house with three Italians, who had come from Domo d'Ossola by the Falls of the Tosa. Their coloured scarfs, patent-leather buskins, and the rest to match, were more elaborate, and more designed for artistic effects, than would have been considered appropriate for mountain work by any people from the north of the Alps. But they were engaged in a great undertaking, and this get-up would magnify it in their friends', and, too, in their own, eyes. While they were at dinner the landlord came in to ask me, if I would give up to them my guide, who in that case would accompany them as their guide and porter in the afternoon back to Airolo, adding that he would himself, to-morrow, take my man's place with me. I was only too happy to hear the proposal. I declined, however, to have anything to do with the pecuniary part of the arrangement: that the two men must settle between themselves. I would pay my man the whole sum for which he had agreed to go with me across the Pass to Ulrichen, and he must pay the landlord for taking his place for the day. This would be a gain in more ways than one to him, for he would be paid by the Italians for returning with them this evening to Airolo, and I would give him two days' pay for returning, whereas he could return from Airolo to Dissentis in one day easily, having nothing but himself to carry. He would thus get home two days sooner, get all I had agreed to give him for the longer time, and what the Italians would give him for a day, having only, *per contra*, to pay his substitute for one day. At this proposal he burst into a storm of wrath, and demanded three days' pay for returning. This I told him would be contrary to the contract, even had he gone to Ulrichen. In his rage he denied that there had ever been any contract. I produced it. He then took his money; and much to my satisfaction, I saw no more of 'the most intelligent, and in every respect the best guide in Dissentis.'

The family of the inn comprised six little barefooted, bare-headed children. The eldest could hardly have been more than eight years old; the youngest was an infant in arms. Their confidence was readily won by a distribution of ten cent pieces. The infant clutched his piece as tenaciously, and appreciated it as highly, as the eldest. The good-natured signora was pleased to find that her little ones were regarded with some interest, and not as nuisances. I spent half an hour in the evening in the dairy to witness the economies of the butter, and of the cheese making. The good man had a sturdy female assistant, with broader shoulders than his own, who accompanied him to the alpe to milk the cows and to bring home the milk, which was immediately curded over the fire, and set for cheese of the Pioresque kind. The milk that had been set for cream, was now skimmed for butter. The sturdy assistant churned the cream, while the good man converted the skimmed milk into meagre cheese. The whey from both the fat and the meagre curd, was set to the fire a second time, for the production of the second curd. This is too soft and poor for cheese. In French Switzerland it is called serré; here it goes by a name which is pronounced muscarp, but written *mascarpa*. The thin watery whey expressed from this is given to the pigs, who stand outside, with their snouts thrust in at the door, to claim their rights. By the time the whey is ready for them it is almost dark, only just enough light remaining to enable you to see that, as they silently absorb gallon after gallon of the liquid, they are 'visibly swelling before your eyes.' The muscarp is then carried into the house in a wooden keeler, and the good man, his prolific wife, the sturdy female attendant, and the six children, the two eldest of whom had, to the extent of their capacities assisted at the butter and the cheese making, sit at the table round the tub, and with wooden spoons address themselves to its contents. I take a spoonful. I had not tasted curds and whey since I was a boy in the West Indies, where the mess goes by I suppose the Scotch name of bonnie clabber. To encourage the family party, for the junket does not quite equal my fancied recollections, I pronounce it to be good. 'But,' quoth the good man, 'you would not think so, if it were all your supper every evening.'

August 26.—At 5 A.M. was off with Clemente Forni. It was as fresh and bright as could be wished for one's last morning among the mountains. The way was over short rock-strewn turf, by the side of the infant Ticino, with near mountains right and left and before me. Clemente was of the kind of men you take to at once, and who give you afterwards no reason—I will suppose this of him—for changing your opinion. Everything around, and within, promised well for a pleasant day on the Gries glacier, which both last year, and the year before, I had looked at over the head of the Valais, from the top of the Grimsel, with a desire for a nearer acquaintance. From what I had seen of Clemente yesterday he seemed industrious, thoughtful, gentle, honest, one who had a head, a heart, and a conscience. Indeed, the stream of his discursive talk, fed from these fountains, never ran dry. This made him a man whom it was pleasant to walk and to talk with. His only scheming was how he might by his own hard labour bring up his six little folk, and as many more as might come. In about an hour and a half we reached the cheese *châlet* of the Cruina alpe, in a little mountain-locked bay, well sheltered from every wind. The sixty-four cows kept upon it had all been milked, and with but a few exceptions here and there, were all again lying down, knowing that they should not be taken for the day to pasture, till the four herdsmen had made the cheese, and had their own breakfast.

We entered the *châlet*. The milk of the sixty-four cows was being curded in a gigantic copper caldron, over a clear smokeless cembra fire. A man of about six-and-thirty, not tall, but broad and bony, of iron frame and massive muscles, was in charge of the caldron. At another fire was another of the party, preparing a pot of polenta made with cream. The other two were lying on thick gray blankets at the further end of the single room. The polenta was soon ready, and was carried, in the pot in which it had been made, outside the *châlet*—there was no room for the party within—and six one-legged stools set round it for the four herdsmen, my guide, and myself, and a round-bowled spoon brought out for each of us. We ranged ourselves on the one-legged stools around the pot. One who hails from the south of the Tweed will probably prefer polenta made with cream to oatmeal porridge. When they had finished the polenta, each dipped with a miniature wooden keeler, which does duty for dish, plate, and basin, out of a large wooden tub as much muscarp as he would require for supplementing his first course of polenta. A great deal of muscarp is made from sixty-four cows, and it is the work of one of the herdsmen to take this down daily to All' Acqua, from whence it is sent on upon another back to Bedretto. The man who takes it down to All' Acqua returns with a load of wood. On leaving the party I had some difficulty in persuading the broad-shouldered, brawny-muscled cheese-maker to accept a franc for his hospitality.

As we passed through the herd one of the cows that was on her legs came up to us, and rubbed her head against my guide. 'That,' he said, ' is my cow.' While she was thus expressing, in her dumb fashion, her satisfaction at seeing him—there was no hypocrisy in this recognition—two dun yearling heifers rose from the ground, and coming up to him, as the cow had done, began to lick his hand. These also, I needed not to have been told it, were his. Here was irrefragable evidence of the gentleness of the good man. What a pleasant sight to the cow was the familiar form and dress! How often had those yearling heifers eaten from that hand! They had never been cuffed, or kicked, or sworn at. The wife and children, too, then, had had, and would continue to have, done for them all that man could do at All' Acqua; and so would all who might come in the good man's way. Who could help liking and respecting one, for whom his beasts were showing such confiding regard, or could fail to be reminded of very different scenes he had witnessed elsewhere? When a horse shrinks from the man who has charge of it, you need not be told in words how he is in the habit of treating it. No further evidence is needed. On this occasion I, too, came in for some share of attention, for a goat that was kept with the herd ran up to me, and, rubbing her nose on my hand, begged for a pinch of salt. How gladly would I have complied with her request! Were I ever again to visit the alpe of Cruina I would not go without a pinch or two of salt.

We were now near the head of the Pass. The grass was beginning to thin out. The marmots were abroad for their morning feed. As we disturbed them, they wriggled home with a slow and awkward movement, for their bodies are long and their legs short; and when they had reached the door of their runs, so that they could feel somewhat secure, paused for a moment or two to make out the designs of the intruders. Just before us was the Corno glacier to which we were approaching, and on to which a few more steps would take us. We had ascended about 3,000 feet from All' Acqua, and were now at an elevation of 8,000 feet. 'The little sinuous paths of earthly care' were far below, and around us were some of 'the flowers that embellish' the pedestrian's way, and 'the springs that refresh' him at these heights. One of the former was a pale sky-blue gentian, a flower that still embellishes memory, as it did on that day my path, and from one of the latter I had a rare draught, at the spot where it welled out of the rock a little below the glacier. And now we are upon the Corno glacier, itself. It has some peculiarities. First it is in the form of a saddle, or the segment of a circle, with the glacier for the arc of the segment, the chord being underground. In a word it is convex. This double inclination is one peculiarity. Another is found in its *moraine*. As it has no lateral glaciers to cause medial *moraines*, you would suppose that it would have two lateral *moraines*, and nothing more. It has, however, nothing of the kind on either side, but, instead, one large, well compacted, wall-like *moraine* some considerable way from the margin. And now we are struck with another peculiarity. The glacier on the Gries side is depressed along the middle in the axis of its length. As, then, the *moraine* is not on the margin, we should have expected to find it following the line of greatest central depression, whereas it runs along the face of one of the inclines midway between the margin and the line of greatest depression. These, then, are the questions the sight suggests to us; Why are there not two *moraines*, one on each margin of the glacier? How comes it that the single *moraine*, which must have been formed from the mountains above, seeing that it is not on one of the margins, is not in the line of the central depression? How comes it to be so compactly and cleanly built along the middle of the descent of one side towards the central depression? And what has produced this central depression? Clemente from his knowledge of the locality was able to answer all these questions, I think, satisfactorily. In winter the glacier is buried in snow to a great depth. At that season, and in the spring, the snow-inclines from the two mountains meet not above the line of longitudinal greatest depression in summer, but exactly along the line of the *moraine*. Here in winter and spring is the line of greatest depression. Every rock, therefore, that falls from either mountain rolls down to this line, and is added to the *moraine*. As a general rule rocks only fall in winter and spring. This accounts for their being nowhere except along this line, that is to say for the strange position of the *moraine* along the flank of an incline of ice. In the early spring, when the snow is beginning to melt, and for some time longer, the *moraine* continues to be the line of greatest depression. At this time, therefore, all the surface melting flows along it through its open pile of stones: this accounts for their being washed clean and kept open. As the summer advances, and the sun becomes more vertical, the snow is melted away to some distance below the *moraine*, and the line of greatest depression is advanced considerably, along which, as long as there is any surface snow melting, there is a stream flowing, which, as long as it lasts, aids in deepening the central depression. This accounts for the summer line of depression along the middle of the glacier, far below the *moraine*. This glacier, then, as we said at first, is, when regarded as a whole, of a convex form; but a transverse section of it on the Gries side, and taken at a point alongside of the *moraine* would be concave. Its position explains its convexity. It descends on the summit of a gentle ridge, or if you prefer so to state it, is formed on the summit of a gentle ridge; it naturally, therefore, flows down each side of this ridge. I have given Clemente's explanation of the singular position of the *moraine*, and of the central concavity of the western limb of the glacier.

Having left the Corno we got upon the Gries by passing along the flank of the last spur of the mountain to the north of the Corno glacier. At its extremity, with the Corno on your left, you command a grand view of the broad expanse of the Gries. To this we now descended. It here presents a smooth surface, rising to the south-west. We passed the line of poles, each fixed in a counterpoise of rock to keep it erect, which mark the horse track across the glacier from the Upper Valais to Domo d'Ossola. We spent about an hour upon it, walking up it, in the direction of the lofty, massive, smooth-faced, umber-coloured mountain, which protrudes through it to the west of the track to Domo d'Ossola. We then recovered the path to Ulrichen.

One goes on a glacier, or goes to see anything, for the sake of the thoughts the sight will awaken. This is as much the case with the man who is unconscious, as with the man who is conscious, of thinking; as much with the clod as with the philosopher; with the man who sneers at thought, that is to say all thought but his own, as with the man who knows that thought is his life, and himself. Now one of the thoughts that interest the mind as you stand on this mighty mass of ice, and know that, as you stand upon it, you and it are being invisibly, imperceptibly, and regularly moved on together, is what moves it? That the movement of the Gries is for local reasons unusually slow, even for a glacier, heightens the interest of the question submitted to your thought. I had at that time a wound on one of my finger-nails, which had been caused by the bite of a dog two months back. It had originally been at the root of the nail. But now it had in the course of those two months advanced almost to the outer edge of the nail, that is to say it had with the utmost slowness, but also with the utmost regularity, travelled from the inner to the outer edge, a journey of an inch in two months. Now what had caused it to move in this way? It was evident that the whole nail, which appears to be firmly fixed to the finger, had moved on with it. Day and night the movement had been going on; but what was it that had been making it move? I suppose the pressure from behind caused by the growth of new matter. This growth of new matter at the root of the nail had caused continuous pressure from behind. This continuous pressure had been propagated throughout the whole extent of the nail, and so had obliged it to move on. Is not the growth of the upper snow-field, and the consequent pressure from it, exactly analogous? Is it not equally continuous? And is it not similarly propagated throughout the whole glacier? And, too, with the same result, that is to say is it not this pressure which obliges the whole mass to move on in the line of least resistance? The wounded point in the nail marked the rate of advance, just as a rock on the surface of the glacier might.

We may see an instance of what continuous pressure will do in the case of a tree growing near an iron fence. They at last come in contact, and the pressure being from the direction of the tree bends the iron. The comparatively soft bark is not cut into: it is the iron that gives way. If the pressure had been in the reverse direction, that is from the iron, the tree would have been cut into. So with the root of a tree in an old wall. The pressure being continuous from the root cracks the wall, though the root is soft and the wall hard. Some ilexes, which a few years back I saw growing on the ruins of the Palace of the Cæsars on the Palatine, supplied good instances of the effect of this continuous action of soft on hard substances. Their roots had rent and lifted large masses of what had previously been solid blocks of the firmest masonry, that had stood uninjured through so long a series of centuries, and, had it not been for these roots, would still have been solid and unmoved. So also with the expansion of water when freezing in the cranny of a rock, the expansion of the soft material burst the hard one. The propagation then of continuous pressure throughout the mass of the Gries glacier, although it is four miles long, and one mile broad, and no one can say how thick, may possibly be sufficient to account for its being moved on in the line of least resistance. And if the principle be correct may it not be applied to glaciers of twenty times the magnitude of the Gries? that is to say to all glaciers? In the instances referred to, the formation of new matter at the root of the nail, and of new wood upon the trunk and on the root of a tree, the pressure comes from what is soft, and is applied effectually to what is hard : so may it be with the action of the snow-field on the glacier.

We left the Gries by the same mountain by which we had reached it, with the difference that we now, instead of traversing its southern, had to descend its northern side. First, however, we had to ascend for a few hundred yards. When you have reached the highest point of the path, you look upon a large expanse of the Bernese Oberland. You may find among the Alps many views that are more extensive, and many that in some one feature, or other, are more striking than this. What, however, is before you from this point is in a very high degree impressive. It is a wondrous scene of Alpine architecture, simple in its elements, but grand in its simplicity. To your left is one of the exits of the Gries. The branch glacier in it terminates abruptly, not after a gentle declivity, such as that of the body of the glacier, but in the mid descent of a precipitous outfall. The previously smooth surface is here ruptured with many deep, yawning, transverse seams. Beyond the glacier—to you its further boundary—is a mountain so steep that you may suppose, and perhaps rightly, that no human foot could ascend it. This glacier gorge at your side is a lateral of the transverse valley below you, a valley of enormous depth, scantily clad with humble Alpine pasturage. You can just make out the herd that is grazing in it. On looking over the long steep-sided mountain which forms its opposite range, at the foot of which the cows are grazing, the south-eastern region of the Bernese Oberland is spread out before you. It is at that distance at which the field of vision may comprise many objects, but every object is still seen distinctly. In this wide, verdureless field, there is no suggestion of life. The midday sun, which is shining brightly upon it, brings out nothing but the gray of the summits of rock, which, when not in the shade, show of a pale ash colour, and the white of the summits of snow, which gleams and dazzles in its purity. This dark gray, pale ash, and gleamy white are the only colouring. The gray and pale ash predominate in an endless variety of forms—mountain walls, ridges, battlements, bastions, and escarpments. Every here and there above these is a dome, or a tower, or a pinnacle of gleaming white, just as the domes, and towers, and pinnacles of a great city rise above its other buildings. This is a city of the world's Builder in which every building is an Alp.

You continue your descent, and soon lose this grand view. But the mountain side, down which your way lies, is grander than usual, longer, and steeper. Your path takes you by intrusive dykes of gneiss and of a black basaltic-looking rock. We here overtook two professors, a botanist with his cases, and an entomologist with his net. They had been beaten by the ascent, and were retracing their steps, fagged, crestfallen, and disappointed. They had our sympathy for their pursuits, and our condolence for their disappointment. Poor fellows! they had just made the painful discovery—may it not have been made too late—that in their mode of life there had been too much desk work, and not enough field work. When human physiology shall be better understood these sad mistakes will not be so frequent. You have now got down into the valley. You look up at the mountain you have been descending. Its height, its steepness, its mass, its ruggedness, its hardness, its inexorableness are so overpowering that your eye shrinks from the effort to aid you in constructing an image of it. At the foot of that high, overhanging, cloud-cleaving upheaval of adamant, you feel very small, very feeble; to your present apprehension your bones are no more than straws, if so much. For a time you allow these impressions of the locality to run their course. Your way is then along the deep valley. As you advance down it you give more heed than usual to the hurrying dashing stream, and you note with more observance than usual the reappearance of the first trees, and of the first *châlets*, and even the form and size of the detached rocks, for the thought is in your mind that these sounds and sights are being presented to you, for this year at all events, now for the last time. And so about midday you reach the little flat of Ulrichen, and your Month is ended. Your walk will have taken you over between 300 and 400 miles, comprising more than a dozen Passes of one kind or another; and you will have seen much of nature and of man to awaken thought, and to interest you. Every day will have been worth living, and not least so the last. But whatever your capacity for being benefited, or interested, by what you may have seen, you will be but slightly, if at all, indebted for it to that eight-parts-of-speech lore, the study of which, though it formed the chief occupation of all the days of our blessed youth, did not issue in enabling all of us to know so much, or so little, as the names of those eight parts of speech.

NOTE TO CHAPTER XIII.

SOME REMARKS ON THE HISTORY AND EFFECTS OF OUR POOR LAW IN CONNEXION WITH PEASANT PROPRIETORSHIP.

I relegate this note to the end of the volume, because its introduction into the body of the work would have been too great an interruption of the continuity of the narrative.

A little comparative history may add to the interest of the picture which the Prätigäu presents. In that valley, as in many others in Switzerland, the peasants are ready to give so high a price for an acre of land that large properties have become impossible; that is to say, there cannot be, as the general rule, any proprietors in localities so circumstanced excepting peasants. In England, however, where an acre of agricultural land does not sell for more than, or for as much as, half of what an acre sells for in these valleys, there are no peasant proprietors. Here, notwithstanding the cheapness of land, it is the small properties that have become impossible, and the general rule is that there can be none but large proprietors. The difference is diametrical. Can it in any way be accounted for?

The question suggested to us is, How has it come about that, while the peasant proprietors have extinguished the large proprietors in the Prätigäu, the large proprietors have extinguished the peasant proprietors in England? As respects the case of the former there can be no difficulty in seeing that, if the peasant cultivators will give more for land than those who would buy for investment could afford to give, then those who would buy for investment must disappear from the market, and that already existing large properties will gradually melt away under the action of this solvent. As respects ourselves the answer usually given is that the land in this country is too dear for peasant proprietors. This supposition, however, as I have just noticed, is the very reverse of the fact. In Switzerland, France, Belgium, Holland, and in parts of Germany and of Italy peasant proprietors give a great deal more for land than it would cost them in England. It may, therefore, be true that in England the cheapness of land has been one of the conditions that has contributed to the formation of large estates; but it is quite impossible to maintain that in this country the dearness of agricultural land has extinguished the class of peasant proprietors, because here the price of land, so far from being an obstacle to the existence of the class, has presented, and at this moment presents, quite exceptionally favourable conditions for its maintenance and increase.

Can any other reason be alleged? In the Chapter to which this note is appended I have pointed out that the English agricultural labourer does not possess the knowledge and the habits of thought and life, which are indispensable in a peasant proprietor. They are indispensable in him, because they it is that enable him to live as a peasant proprietor. This, if it be true, must be a serious impediment to the re-establishment of the class amongst us, but cannot be regarded as the primary cause of its extinction, because Englishmen were as capable as other people of this knowledge and of these habits. What was really and primarily in fault was not the decay of this knowledge and of these habits, but that which engendered and brought about this decay amongst us alone of all people.

If, then, the cause is neither in the present price of land here, nor in any inherent incapacity in Englishmen, that is to say, if it be neither in the land, nor in the men, where else can we look for it? There remains no other direction in which we can look but law, and the interpretation of law. In the Middle Ages we had the peasant class of those times fully developed here. There were in this country, as was perhaps the case everywhere then, variations in the possessions and rights of the class, but still at that time peasant proprietors pretty generally, if not quite universally, formed the basis of the English village community. Why did they cease to do so? I think the answer is that in this country, from a combination of exceptional causes, legislation and the interpretation of law and custom became adverse to the maintenance of the class. The exceptional causes were, first, the strength of the governing class (locally represented by Lords of manors), which was a consequence of the Norman conquest; and the great rise in the money value of cheese, hides, and wool, especially the last, consequent on the influx of silver from the New World during the sixteenth century, while for the production of these articles the climate, and for their export the easily traversed surface of the country, nowhere far from the coast, and numerous excellent harbours offered pre-eminent advantages. There was, therefore, both a strong motive for the extinction of peasant properties, and power sufficient for effecting it. Peasant properties, which everywhere implied rights of appurtenant common pasturage, made the formation of large runs for numerous flocks of sheep, or for a large combination of cattle breeding with arable culture, impossible. They were, therefore, apparently in the interests of the community, gradually rendered valueless to their owners, absorbed, and extinguished. This process, though it commenced at an earlier date, was chiefly carried out in the reign of Elizabeth. Events in this matter only took the direction and course which might have been expected.

But it is clear that if the right of the peasant to maintain himself from the produce of a piece of land which he himself cultivates for the support of his family is abrogated, he must either cease to exist, and then the cultivation of the land would be impossible, or he must be maintained in some other way. For centuries wages, the alternative method, were not universally, or even generally, sufficient for this purpose. The operations of agriculture were not at that time as continuous as they are now; the demand for any amount of agricultural produce was not as unfailing as it is now; and the farmer had not access to such stores of capital as exist now. Under these circumstances the alternative was insufficient. What then was to be done? How was the existence of the peasant to be maintained? He could not be allowed the hide of plough land and the common pasturage rights of his forefathers, for these were obstacles to the formation of sheep farms, and to large culture; nor could wages be relied on continuously. The method hit upon showed the inventiveness of the English mind quite as much as any one of the many institutions and discoveries for which the world is indebted to the inhabitants of this island. It was to give to the dispossessed peasantry, who were henceforth to become agricultural labourers, a claim on the parishes, in which they resided and laboured, to the amount requisite for the support of themselves and of their families, when through failure of work or of wages, through sickness or age, they became incapable of supporting themselves.

Three centuries ago this was the *rationale* of the English poor law, and it is so at this day. It was a substitute for peasant proprietorship, and it aided in utterly extinguishing it. If a little bit of land is the only means of supporting the life of a family, the family will, however great the cost in labour, support itself by this means. But if you make wages, supplemented by a claim on the produce of the land, an alternative means; and at the same time bring into play causes which shall partly dispose, and partly drive, the peasantry to accept this alternative; they will accept it, and peasant proprietorship will cease. This I think is in a few words the explanation of the unique fact that in this country there is no class of peasant proprietors. Our legislation favoured the consolidation and accumulation of large estates. It did not favour the maintenance of peasant properties: with respect to them its action and pressure were in the opposite direction; while at the same time it gave the peasants an alternative means of support. The tendency of events, and the pressure of circumstances were irresistible; and the whole class either became disposed, or was driven, to accept the alternative; and so the class of peasant proprietors was utterly extinguished. Had circumstances, legislation, and the interpretation the law put on the rights of the class favoured its maintenance in this country, we should have had here a peasant class similar to that of Switzerland, France, Belgium, Germany, Italy, and other countries. The existence here of exceptional conditions had an exceptional issue.

The extinction of the class has been followed by many large and important consequences. Of these the most obvious is the difference between the class that has been introduced as the basis of our social system, that of agricultural labourers, and the class that was extinguished, that of peasant proprietors. No greater difference can exist between men. Peasant proprietors in their industry, tenacity, and stability have just the qualities which might have fitted them for constituting an useful element in the foundation of so artificial and ill-balanced a social fabric as that of England, for as to their narrowness of view, their chief defect of character, that in so rich a community would have been of little detriment in any way ; and besides, too, in this country we must compare what their narrowness would have been with the far greater narrowness of our agricultural labourers. On the other side agricultural labourers are a very poor foundation for the social fabric, and most especially in a commercial and manufacturing community, which already from these sources has a dangerously numerous *prolétariat*. As a class they are improvident, thriftless, shiftless, have no sense of self-dependence, and not much of self-respect, their self-acting effectual education having been that which results from the teaching of wages, supplemented by a poor law.

The question of peasant proprietorship, as now discussed among ourselves, is generally restricted to economical considerations. It is asked, as if this contained the whole question, whether the economical results of peasant culture are as satisfactory, acre for acre, as those of large farms? This, though an important part of the question, is not the whole of it : perhaps it is not the chief part of it. The character of the basis of our social fabric may be a matter of more consequence to the nation than even the amount of produce per acre. It will explain what is contained in this remark, if I say that I suppose that everybody would think that to admit to our parliamentary constituency a million voters, whose sentiments and ideas were in the main those of peasant proprietors, would be a less hazardous operation than to admit a million pauperized agricultural labourers, who, possibly, might endeavour to use the franchise for the purpose of securing a more liberal administration of the poor aw. And, practically, there would be some justification for such an attempt, if made by them, for the poor law may be regarded historically as the compensation given to their class for the extinction of commonable rights in the land,

and, together with those commonable rights, of peasant properties; for it is clear that if those common rights, and the associated peasant properties, had been retained, there would so far have been no occasion for a poor law.

It is obvious that the improvidence and misery of our agricultural labourers have for many generations given us a large supply of labour for building up our manufacturing and commercial establishments, and for peopling the New World, and our Australian and other colonies. The same cause may also have enabled us to maintain our military force by voluntary enlistment. But as the same amount of land in the hands of peasant proprietors maintains four or five times as large an agricultural population as it does when cultivated by hired labourers, it is quite possible that we might have received even a better supply from the alternative system. At all events, now, in consequence of a largely increased demand for men, contemporaneously with an actual decrease of our relatively small agricultural population, which under existing circumstances is our chief nursery for recruits for all purposes, we are beginning to be pressed hard for men. We are now suffering from a want of men, and would be glad if there were some element in our agrarian system which made that ingredient of our population far more considerable than it now is. Another evil consequence, then, of a mistake made three hundred years ago has begun to manifest itself.

The price of labour is closely connected with its supply, insomuch that it may be argued that if a system has hitherto produced an abundant supply it must also have lowered its cost. It is obvious, however, to remark that the value of labour depends not so much on the amount of wages that are paid, as on the amount and character of work that is done. This is so much the case that it has come to be regarded as a general rule that holds good all over the world, that labour is least productive where wages are lowest ; and there have been some who have thought that this might have been said in their proportion of our agricultural labourers. As a matter of fact, however, wages have been higher in this than in neighbouring countries. Nor, in estimating the cost of our labour, would it be allowable to leave out of our calculation the amount of our poor rate. That has for centuries been raised for the purpose of supplementing wages, and so is practically a part of the wages of the labouring class, levied on the owners of land and houses. By the way, we often hear this limitation of the incidence of the poor rate complained of; but if our account of the *rationale* of the origin and action of the poor law be correct, it may be questioned whether the incidence of the rate ought not, in rural districts, to have been restricted entirely to land, because the motive of the law was to enable large estates to be formed, and to be cultivated by a poorly paid class of labourers, who for many generations were by the law tied to the land they cultivated.

Another consequence of the obliteration of the class of peasant proprietors, which is well worthy of notice on account of its wide and deep effects, is that it has prevented the price of every acre of agricultural land in the country from rising beyond half the sum it would now have reached had this class continued to exist amongst us. In far poorer countries than England peasants will gladly give for such land twice as much as is its market price here. If we had this class here, its members would do the same here. But, as this class has been eliminated here, those, who in this country purchase land as an investment for capital, have it all their own way. The class who would bid twice as much for the land as the capitalist now gets it for does not exist amongst us. The consequence is that he buys his land cheap, very cheap indeed. This will be seen, if what he gets for his money is compared with what other people get for theirs when it is put into consols. The latter get a little more than 3 per cent. with some prospect of depreciation of the capital, and with a certainty in these days of depreciation in the purchasing power of the 3 per cent. interest. The capitalist, however, who invests in land gets for the present a little less than 3 per cent., but besides this immediate percentage he gets the safest of all investments, plus the most improving in the long run of all investments, plus the social and political status the possession of land confers, plus several minor advantages. Investors, therefore, in land in this country have no reason to complain of the price they give for their land, or of what they get for their money.

For this they are indebted to the extinction amongst us of the class of peasant proprietors. Just as the people who buy ships are the people who want ships for the business they understand and are engaged in, and the people who buy factories are those who want factories for the business they understand and are engaged in, and those who buy stock in trade of any kind are those who understand and are engaged in the trade for which the stock they purchase is necessary, so those who are most eager to buy land are those who understand how to get a living out of the land by the application to it of their own labour. They are the class, who may be regarded as, *par excellence*, the natural purchasers of land. This class, however, has in this country been extinguished. The market, therefore, has been completely cleared for those who would wish to purchase land as an investment, and they, under the present condition of things amongst us, are limited to those who are able to invest largely, or who buy with the view of adding their purchases to properties that are already large. They, therefore, in buying land have it all their own way; and this is the reason why they get their land at a price which yields an immediate return of something less than 3 per cent., plus many other valuable considerations. If the peasant proprietor class existed here to such an extent as to effectually compete with them, they would have to give a price that would not yield 1½ per cent. for agricultural land. They do, then, get their land very cheap, which is a result, perhaps one that was not originally foreseen, of the action during three centuries of our poor law. The extinction of the class of peasant proprietors has thus very effectively aided the practice of settling and charging estates in bringing about the large agglomerations of landed property, together with all the resultant peculiarities, which distinguish our agrarian system from that of any other country.

But if those who buy land get it at half its value, those who sell it get for it only half of what they otherwise would. This suggests the question whether it would be better for the country that the value of the agricultural land of the United Kingdom should be doubled? This may be answered by the question whether it is not better for us to have land at its present price of say 60*l.* an acre, than it would be to have it at 30*l.*? If 60*l.* is better than 30*l.*, then I suppose 120*l.* would be better than 60*l.*

The facts and considerations that have been now referred to may throw some light on a question of which a great deal has been heard lately—that of what is called tenant rights. It may, of course, be asked whether the progress of time has endowed tenants with any new rights? How can the tenants of to-day have rights of which the tenants of yesterday had no conception? Or, to speak broadly, can a tenant, as a tenant, have any right except that of entering into a contract with a landowner, and of invoking the law for the enforcement of the provisions of his contract? But if it were answered that time can give him no new rights, and that he can have no rights but those for which he contracts, still what is really meant by the question would not be settled.

By a process of legislation the land of the country having been formed into estates of such dimensions that their owners cannot possibly cultivate them, and small proprietors having been extinguished, the tenants are now presented to us as the only producers of food for the community. Under these circumstances the question arises whether it would not be for the advantage of the community that the position of the tenants should be so improved as to lead to their investing more money than they can at present with safety in the cultivation of the soil, that is to say to their producing a great deal more food for the community? This improvement in the tenants' position can be conceded only at the cost of the existing legal rights of the landowners, and can be refused only at the cost of the imprescriptible natural rights of the community; for of such a character is the right of the community to the greatest amount of food the soil of the country can be made to yield. This is in a sense the highest of all rights, for it is the right of a community to existence. It was in the name, and for the sake, of this right that under the conditions of past times the rights of individual proprietorship, which were not primeval, were first conceded. They had become necessary for the cultivation of the soil, and, therefore, were allowed to be established at the expense of the previously existing common rights. In this view tenant rights are not rights which the tenants can claim in law, but rights which it may be supposed belong to the community, and the concession of which to the tenants the community may demand for the general advantage, it may be even for the general safety. The two years' notice which the present Premier is said to regard with favour is precisely a concession of this kind. It is a curtailment of the rights of the landowners, to which the tenants can have no legal, or rightful, claim: it is, however, a concession which, presumably, would promote the advantage of the public, and which, therefore, public policy may require. If improvements of this kind in the position of the tenants would increase the produce of the country by one half, then that addition of a half to the produce of the country is exactly the weight of the argument in favour of the concession of tenant rights so called : to endow the tenants with these rights would add, every year, one hundred million pounds' worth of food to the produce of this country, that is to say to the subsistence of the community.

This list of the consequences of the working for three centuries of our English poor law might be greatly increased; for instance, the division of the people it has helped to bring about into a comparatively small class who are very rich and a very large class who have not, and never can have, any real property, accounts for the elsewhere unheard of demands that are made on the charity of the small class, and which demands are complied with because of their obvious necessity. Again also the great bulk of the agricultural land of the kingdom being held in large estates—a result in part of the working of the same law—the owners of these large estates can afford to spend no inconsiderable part of the rent of the whole kingdom in London, which to a very appreciable extent accounts for the vastness of London. The poorness, and almost meanness of life in our provincial towns are also to be accounted for by a reference to the same fact. The rent of the land around these towns is not spent in them, but in London or elsewhere : at all events the adjacent landowners rarely live in, or contribute anything towards the embellishment of the life of, these towns. Enough, however, has been said to show that the endowment and establishment of pauperism, as an integral part of the British constitution, as much so as the Crown, or the Peerage, has had very extensive effects. It could not have been otherwise, for it was the elimination from the constitution of society, as far as the mass of the people were concerned, of the old elements of self-dependence and property, and the substitution in their place of dependence and of public doles. These were new conditions to which all the arrangements of society in their endless ramifications had to accommodate and adjust themselves, and to which the future progress of society had to conform.

The course of events, then, taking the words in their widest sense, is what has given to the Prätigäu its ten thousand peasant proprietors, and it is what has extinguished the class amongst ourselves. If the course of events affecting each of us had been interchanged their condition might have been witnessed in this country, and our condition might have been theirs. Whether it be possible in these days, in the face of emigration, of high wages, of settled estates, of the demoralization of the agricultural labourer, and of a poor law, to recover the lost class may well be doubted. But however that may be, it cannot be good policy to maintain any artificial, that is to say any legislative, obstacles in the way of the reappearance amongst us of the class, if that be possible, any more than it can be to maintain any arrangements that might be having the effect of hindering capital from being employed on the largest scale, and to the greatest profitable amount per acre, in increasing the produce of the soil. Food-factories, of at least 1,000 acres each, appear to be a natural result of the combination of capital and science now possible. Let us, therefore, have a clear stage for these. That, however, is no reason why we should not at the same time have a clear stage for peasant proprietors also. Let nothing be done with the view of favouring and nursing either one or the other, but at the same time let nothing be maintained that is a hindrance to the existence of either. There appears to be no ground for supposing that our present land-system favours either; it may not, however, be equally beyond controversy that it is not a hindrance to both.

INDEX.

ACL

ACLETTA, 26
    All' Acqua, 333. Family of landlord at, 335
Altanca, 323
Alveneu, 59
Andeer, 94
Andermatt, 17
Animals, domestic, at Dissentis, 27
Atmospheric effects in the Upper Engadin, 157
Aversthal, 97–136

BARONS, the old, 66, 73, 257, 283
Blue flowers, abundance of, 246
Bormio, 223
Braulio, Val di, 225
Burial, an early, 59
Buying cheap and selling dear, 82

CAMPSUT, 103
    Capital, uses and effects of, 75. What it requires, 79
Carpenter, a, of Altanca, 327
Casaccia, 143
Castles, old feudal, 66
Caterpillars, a colony of, 11
Cembra, what destroys forests of, 107. The Livigno candle, 207
Châlet, the first, 271. The smallest, 307

ENG

Church-going in winter, 93
Circumnavigator, a' Grison, 37, 164
Clemente Forni, 336. Recognised by his cattle, 338. Accounts for the peculiarities of the Corno glacier, 341
Clemgia, 262
Cloud-effects, 275
Coire, 35, 298
Communism, historical, 73
Communist, a, 301. Parting with, 334
Corno glacier, peculiarities of, 341
Cresta, 104–125
Cristallo, M., 232
Cruina alpe, 337
Cruschetta, 262

DAVOS AM PLATZ, 53
    Davos Dörfli, 271
Dentro, V. di, 222
Dinner at Peist, 46. At Juf, 129. At Tauffers, 250. At Schiersch, 286
Dissentis, 25, 300

EARTH-PILLARS, 43
    Electric telegraph at Dissentis, 30
Engadin, Upper, 150. Lower, 266

Etruscan, the Septimer an—trade route, 139

FAUNA of the Grisons, 127
Ferrera, Inner, 99. Ausser, 100
Flies, correlation of—to properties, 202
Fluela, the, 268
Forcellina, the, 132
Fountain at Dissentis, 29
Frenchman, the only—met, 308

GADMENTHAL, 9
Gatherings of men of different epochs, 166
Geese, live—sent by post, 114
Geologic history, 89
Germans in Switzerland, 81, 110. Exceptional, 193. At Santa Maria, 228. At Tarasp, 265. At Coire, 298
Glacier motion, 343
Glaciers, the Stein, 14. Of Upper Engadin, 159. The Roseg, 173. La Pischa, 181. The Morterasch, 185. The Grialetsch, 267. The Corno, 341. The Gries, 343
Glurns, 245
Göschenen, 17
Grass-cutter, a—at Tauffers, 255
Gries glacier, 343
Grison fortune-seekers, 20, 152, 187
Grüsch, 288
Guest, welcome the coming, 65
Gunpowder, unforeseen uses of, 85

HAYMAKING in the mountains, 311
Hen proposed for supper, 49
High-level road, 42

Hohen Rhätien, 66
Honesty, connexion of—with property, 241
Hypsometry of the Grisons, 177

IMPASSIVITY, English, 299
Inference, a comfortable—from excess, 119
Instinct, an—with a human motive, 116
Italian influences at Casaccia, 144. Tourists, 333

JUF, 128

KIRCHET, the, 3
Klosters, 274
Kublis, 284

LAKES of the Upper Engadin, 159
Land, efforts to obtain, 5. Reclamation of, 259, 261. Loss of, 262, 291
Lapland in central Europe, 121
Leuthold, Henri, 13, 17
Life, correlation of vegetable—to human, 34
Livigno, 201–220. Inn at, 205. The host at, 207. Festa at, 211. Lapland at, 215
Lunghino, Monte, 161

MALOJA, 149
Marmots, 132, 197, 339
Meienthal, 16
Meiringen, 2
Milk, a tub of, 103
Morterasch, the—glacier, 185
Mummy beef, 47, 117, 216, 286, 309, 325, 332

NATURE, love of, 169
    Natures, sixteen—to feed, 251
Neve, M. della, 221
Nolla, the, 64

OBER ALPE, 21
    Ortler, 238, 260, 261

PARISIENNE, a, 326
    Passes, Susten, 15. Oberalp, 23. Strela, 52. Splügen, 98. Forcellina, 133. Septimer, 136. Maloja, 149. La Pischa, 181. Stretta, 199. Foscagno, 222. Stelvio, 232. Cruchetta, 262. Fluela, 268. Davos Kulm, 274. Lukmanier, 301. Uomo, 317. Gries, 346
Pasteur of Cresta, 105
Peasant, sentiment of a, 204. Proprietors, 278-284
Peat, 23
Peist, 45
Perdatsch, 305. Inn at, 307
Pfäffers, 294
Pigs at Cresta, 123
Pines, adaptation of form in, 86. A large, 292
Piora, 317
Pischa, La, 179
Piz Languard, 175
Polenta, 213, 338
Pontresina, 165. High prices at, 189
Poor Law, an alternative to peasant proprietorship, 351. Has substituted agricultural labourers for an independent peasantry, 355. Has affected the supply of labour, 357. Has kept down the price of agricultural land, 358. Has made our food-producers a tenantry, 361.

Other consequences, 362. Legalized hindrances bad, 363
Porter, a circumnavigator, 19
Post in Aversthal, 112
Prätigäu, 277
Prayer, labour is, 97
Property, connexion of—with honesty, 241
Providence, 11

RACE against time for life, 125
Ragatz, 297
Rheinthal, Vorder, 33. Across the, 293
Rhine, 24, 26, 307
Riches, the best, 13
Ritom, Lake of, 319. New hotel at, 321
Road, new—in Scanfiggthal, 41. In Davosthal, 58. Proposed in Aversthal, 112. Across the Foscagno, 244. Swiss roads, 305
Rock-eroding power of running water, 3, 88
Romansch, 33, 110
Roseg glacier, 173

SABBATH, a daily, 96
    Saints, the island of, 35
Salt-carriers, 316
Santa Maria on Stelvio, 227. On Lukmanier, 315
S. Moritz, 162
Scanfiggthal, 37-50
Schamsthal, 91
Schiersch, 285
Schools, 92. Of Oberland Aversthal, 110
Schyn, the, 61
Selection in human society, 79
Septimer, the, 136
Snow-way for timber, 62

SOU

Soup, 49, 250, 309, 326
Spöl, halt on the, 199
Spy, a Prussian, 314
Stein glacier, 14
Stelvio, 233
Strela, 51
Stretta, 199
Sun in summer life in winter, 95
Süs, 266
Susten, 9
Snow, summer, 109, 203, 233

TARASP, 263
Tarns, mountain, 198, 317
Taufers, 247-261
Telegraph at Dissentis, 31
Telegrams v. letters, 65
Thusis, 63
Tourists, future, 167
Trafoi, 237. Chances of, 243
Trees, the first, 269

ZIL

ULRICHEN, 348
Uomo Pass, 317
Urbach, the valley of, 7

VAL AVIGNA, 259. Bedretto, 331. Di Dentro, 222. Del Fain, 183, 198. Medels, 313. Piora, 317
Via Mala, 83
Vulpera, 263

WAR and material progress, 329
Wasen, 16
Watersheds, 161
Watersmeet, a mountain, 101
Weather, one day's, 272

ZILLIS, 92